STUDYING THE BRITISH CRIME FILM

STUDYING THE BRITISH CRIME FILM
BY
PAUL ELLIOTT

DEDICATION

To Dad.

ACKNOWLEDGMENTS

My sincere thanks go to all those who have helped in the writing of this book: to John Atkinson at Auteur, Roy Pierce-Jones and the University of Worcester for giving me the time to finish it.

Mostly however I would like to thank the students of 'Underworld UK', especially Ian, Andreea, Phil, Liam, Dan, Will, Sarah, Tiffany, Meg, Sian, Jay and Carl. Thanks for the illuminating comments and sorry for the depressing films.

First published in 2014 by
Auteur
24 Hartwell Crescent, Leighton Buzzard LU7 1NP
www.auteur.co.uk

Copyright © Auteur Publishing 2014

Designed and set by Nikki Hamlett at Cassels Design

Printed and bound by Printondemand-worldwide, Peterborough, UK

Cover: *Harry Brown* © Marv Films / UK Film Council

British Library Cataloguing-in-Publication Data
A catalogue record for this book is available from the British Library

ISBN: 978-1-906733-74-2
ISBN e-book: 978-0-9930717-7-5

JAN 2 2 2015

CONTENTS

INTRODUCTION: ROUNDING UP THE USUAL SUSPECTS

Ever since its beginnings, British cinema has been obsessed with crime and the criminal: one of the first narrative films to be produced in Britain, Cecil Hepworth's 1905 short *Rescued by Rover*, was a fast paced, fast edited tale of abduction and kidnap; the first British sound film, Alfred Hitchcock's *Blackmail* (1929), was concerned with murder and criminal guilt; and the first ever BAFTA for Best British film was awarded to Carol Reed's 1947 work *Odd Man Out*, a narrative surrounding a failed robbery and prison escape.

More recently old favourites like *Sherlock Holmes* (2009), *Brighton Rock* (2010) and *The Sweeney* (2012) have been remade and 'rebooted' for the new millennium, serving up a mixture of traditional narrative and re-invigorated visuals to eager audiences in what is a testimony not only to the longevity of the crime film but to Britain's importance to the field.

This last point is vital to remember because, as we shall discover time and time again in this book, the basic building blocks of the crime film, its foundational texts, tend to originate from film cultures outside of Britain. The gangster film, for example is quintessentially American; the heist film gained much of its early flavour from French cinema, and so too the prostitute film; the serial killer film arose out of Hollywood and American indie cinema; the delinquent film, the 1950s B-movie and so on. Many of the sub-genres of the crime film, although successfully employed in Britain, cannot be said to belong to it.

The British crime film, then, is always a hybrid, always a symbiosis of British sensibility and foreign (usually Hollywood) cinematic conventions. However, the relationship British cinema has to Hollywood, like other national cinemas, is based on dialogue rather than domination, as indigenous film-makers bring their own cultural tools to bear on narratives and characterisations that come from elsewhere. As Tom O'Regan states:

> Films circulate across national, language and community boundaries reaching deep into social space. Audiences, critics and film-makers appropriate, negotiate, and transform this international cinema in various ways. It is in cinema's nature to cross cultural borders within and between nations, to circulate across heterogeneous linguistic and social formations.[1]

Genre cinema is ideally placed to allow us to understand this process of cultural exchange due, in the main, to the perceived dominance of Hollywood forms. Unlike more self-consciously constructed anti-imperialist discourses like Third cinema or Neo-Realism, genre cinema presents a more obvious example of indigenisation, lending to the critic a snapshot of how cultural and national identity can be both negotiated and threatened through popular texts. As Marcia Landy outlines, it is a mistake to imagine that the specifics of genre are universal, as not only do different national cinemas inflect incoming generic structures with their own style and cultural lexicons, but films are inevitably influenced, constrained and otherwise shaped by the budgets, the environment and the mode of production endemic to that industry.[2] British crime cinema is allied to Hollywood but is endlessly coloured by other filmic histories, most obviously the long tradition of documentary and social realism in Britain, but also German Expressionism, the French New Wave and work from American independents.

British crime cinema is obviously heavily influenced by foreign cultures; however it is also inevitably shaped by indigenous histories and traditions. As Kirsten Moana Thompson states, the crime film *per se* can be traced back to a variety of literary sources including detective fiction, Gothic writing and gallows biographies like the Newgate calendar, eighteen century chronicles that detailed the crimes of those condemned to swing in Newgate prison.[3] The antecedents of the British crime film however can also be found in sources as varied as Henry Mayhew's *London Labour and the London Poor*, Dickens' *Oliver Twist*, the New Journalism of the late nineteenth century, Music Hall theatre and traditional folklore.[4] In recent times, this has extended into the impact of Brutalist architecture on the collective consciousness of the nation, the influence of political figures like Margaret Thatcher and Tony Blair on public morality, and the prevalence of media images of contemporary folk devils such as the 'hoodie' and the juvenile delinquent. None of these things may be specific to Britain but their combined character shapes and characterises its cultural outputs.

The history of the British crime film, then, is dispersed throughout a plurality of other histories and traditions and the same could be said for scholarly work concerned with it. Up until 2012 the only work dedicated solely to the British crime film was Steve Chibnall and Robert Murphy's collection published in 1999.[5] This anthology went someway to addressing the paucity of studies in this area however it is neither a history nor a considered statement on the genre. Work on the British crime film in particular can be found in texts such as Robert Murphy's *Realism and Tinsel* which looks at, amongst other films, *Brighton Rock* (1947) and *Cosh Boy* (1953); Andrew Spicer's *Typical Men* which contains analyses of *Violent Playground* (1958), *Lock, Stock and Two Smoking Barrels* (1998) and *The Criminal* (1960); Charlotte Brundson's *London in Cinema*; Aldgate and Richards' *Best of British* and Phillip Gillet's *The British Working Class in Postwar Film*.[6] There are also substantial monographs on specific films like *Get Carter* (1971), *Brighton Rock*, *Performance* (1970) and *The Italian Job* (1969).[7] Barry Forshaw's *British Crime Film: Subverting the Social Order*, published in 2012, was the first monograph specifically dedicated to this area and covers much of the preparatory ground for its study.[8] Forshaw's book has a self-consciously broad definition of the crime film including works such as *Sapphire* (1959), *Victim* (1961) and *The Small World of Sammy Lee* (1963) as well as more canonical texts. As its subtitle suggests, Forshaw's book seeks to trace the lines of fissures in British post-war society through its depiction of crime and legality, a mandate that the present book shares. Where the two approaches differ however is that *Studying the British Crime Film* assumes the best way to do this is through (relatively) close understanding of the texts themselves – what might be termed formal as well as historical analysis.

As can be evidenced from a brief glance at these titles, one of the main problems with studying British crime cinema is the proliferation of what we might think of as the usual suspects in terms of films. The iconic status of some British crime films has tended to obscure the variety and breadth of production for both audiences and critics as films such as *Get Carter*, *The Italian Job*, *Brighton Rock* and *Lock, Stock and Two Smoking Barrels* dominate what is a relatively under represented critical field. This book aims to broaden out the dragnet somewhat and to look further afield for its likely suspects. Whereas there *is* consideration of the more canonical texts, where possible these are discussed alongside less well-known and under-represented works and directors. The chapter on the gangster film, for example, not only considers *Get Carter* but also looks at Michael Tuchner's *Villain* (1971), a film that has had very little written about it; the chapter on the heist movie looks at *The Italian Job* but also deals with Basil Dearden's *The League of Gentlemen* (1960); the chapter on prostitution outlines work carried out on *Mona Lisa* (1986) but also considers the 1980 Tony Garnett film, *Prostitute*. This philosophy has provided the basis for all the chapters presented here; if the British crime film is to be taken seriously as a genre and as an expression of Britishness, it is vital that critics and audiences alike consider the full range of texts available.

The British crime film is both highly reflective *of* and highly responsive *to* the wider social zeitgeist and changes in the physical environment. Canonically the crime film is an urban genre and therefore it is the constantly evolving cityscape that we see most obviously depicted.[9] Films of the immediate post-war period like *Cosh Boy* and *Appointment with Crime* (1946) reveal a country still smarting from the scars of the Blitz, the urban environment is broken and the dilapidated streets are littered with rubble and bombed-out houses like the missing teeth of a post-fight smile. In the 1960s we see a noticeable change as new buildings and modernist architecture begin to emerge, by the 1970s with films like *Villain* and *The Offence* (1972) we can detect the rise of the New Towns that are dominated by concrete tower blocks and housing estates. The streets become narrower and more suburban and the narratives reflect this, as the post-war generation battles with the new world that emerged from the ashes of war. By the 1990s and 2000s the estate and the tower block become the backdrop for a host of different criminal activities from petty drug deals to urban gang warfare. The brutality of 1960s architecture, in films like *Tony: London Serial Killer* (2009) and *Sket* (2011), forms part of the internal textual debate of cinema and inextricably links it to the wider culture. The settings are more than mere narrative backdrop, they are characters in their own right; sometimes malevolent, often disturbing, they are reflections of the changing relation of the nation to itself. The rootedness of the film within its spatial environment is a characteristic of social realism and the British crime film has imbued this.

Another area that is inevitably traced by the crime film is public morality. Perhaps more than any other genre, the crime film reflects the debates that surround contemporary ethics, social mores and opinions on law and order. As Stuart Hall details, however, popular culture (which of course includes the crime film) can be viewed as a site of struggle between containment and resistance and between official ideology and counter-discourse.[10] Crime films, like the films of the British New Wave, promise political and social liberation but often fall back on a consoling conservatism where the dominance of the social order prevails and deviancy is punished. Within such generic conventions, however, are endless opportunities for subversion as characters that are outsiders by their nature challenge and question the dominant cultural norms encouraging audiences to do so as well. If, as Sarah Casey Benyahia suggests, 'criminals are frightening and repellent but also the most charismatic and appealing characters in the story' then the crime film can be seen to offer a counter-discourse to the dominant culture as well as, ultimately, providing a medium for its proliferation.[11]

As well as examining the films within their cultural context this book also discusses them alongside changes in legislation. For areas such as prostitution and juvenile delinquency this is especially useful as the law not only shapes and dictates what constitutes these crimes but also reflects public opinion on how such 'criminals' are treated within the legal system. The narrative resolution of many films often belies the wider political ideologies of the directors and the times that they work in. The 1950 Ealing drama *The Blue Lamp* for example famously enacted the post-war social consensus that was also being proliferated through governmental discourse; whereas in 1979's *The Long Good Friday*, we see a literal rendering of the dangers (not to mention the glamour) of Thatcherite socio-economic politics in the character of gangland boss Harold Shand who, symbolically, evokes the wrath of the 'old enemy' the IRA. In both examples we see how the crime film is ineluctably influenced by the wider social scene and how the surrounding political and legal position inflects the characters of the narrative.

This book, then, draws its research from four main textual areas: firstly, texts that deal primarily with crime cinema;[12] secondly, sources that deal with British cinema as it relates to pertinent thematic areas and cultural periods;[13] thirdly, legal statutes and reports; and lastly, texts emanating from criminology and sociology.[14] To add to this rather eclectic list of source material we might make mention of the various biographies and popular studies of crime and criminals.[15]

The varied textual base of this book not only mirrors the variety of films covered but also its methodological stance, one which is unashamedly wide-ranging in its approach. Where possible this book attempts to place the British crime film at the centre of a network of different discourses, from the popular and the folkloric, to the legal; from the socio-political to the purely aesthetic. In the main, the British crime film is a solid enough text to sustain such a multifaceted approach and yet it is one that is very rarely employed to examine it. The Hollywood crime film has been dealt with in a variety of ways, from an examination of its place as a social document to the extent that it details deep fissures in the American consciousness.[16] This book hopes to do the same for its British counterpart and to view the crime film as a valuable source of information about the changing face of the nation's taste and morals.

So, what is a crime film? Can we define its parameters, its characteristics and its tropes? Is crime cinema a genre like the Western or the musical? Does it even exist at all? These are questions that many critics have sought to answer but which most have failed to find satisfactory resolutions to. Nicole Rafter tells us that 'crime films do not constitute a genre (a group of films with similar themes, settings and characters) as Westerns and war films do. Rather they constitute a category that encompasses a number of genres – caper films, detective movies, gangster films, cop and prison movies [etc.]'.[17] Rafter's point is well made; unlike more traditional genres, the crime movie encompasses a whole wealth of different styles of film-making and different types of narrative. If Westerns can be categorised by their semantic and syntactical elements can we really say the same of films as diverse as *The Long Good Friday*, *The Italian Job*, *Performance* or *Harry Brown* (2009)? Each of these films have different settings, *mise-en-scènes* and narrative arcs and yet each is also recognisably a *crime* film. For Rafter, the crime film can be thought of as an overall term that encompasses a whole myriad of sub-sections and types of film. The crime film, then, could be thought to exist alongside terms like the blockbuster or the comedy; categories that describe much larger canvases and are by definition porous and open to slippage.

Thomas Leitch suggests that crime films can be characterised by the interplay between three main reoccurring characters: the perpetrator, the victim and the detective.[18] For Leitch, crime films explore how this tripartite relationship works and how tensions between these three dramaturgical categories are played out during the narrative.[19] Crime films also contain an inherent moral ambiguity regarding illegality that, on the one hand encourage us to identify and sympathise with criminals and, on the other, to feel cleansed by their downfall in the final act. Leitch makes the point that the resolution to the crime narrative, which is usually conservative in nature, is only a feint towards the upholding of the status quo, their ultimate mandate is more seditious. Crime films offer a critique of society by inevitably painting the outsider as more exciting, more interesting and more worthy of interest than the upholders of the law. The criminals become heroes and often the authorities are seen as pedestrian and mundane in comparison.

For Leitch the crime film is as inherently subversive as it is conservative, a point also explored by Rafter, who states:

> Most crime films from the earliest days of cinema have offered this dual satisfaction, enabling us to dwell, if only for an hour or two, in a state of happy hypocrisy.[20]

Carlos Clarens mirrors this notion somewhat, however he characterises the crime film as detailing the process of 'transgression and retribution', suggesting again, the proliferation of the three major character types outlined by Leitch. Benyahia suggests that we might view the crime film as containing a number of different sub-genres including the gangster film, the detective film, the film noir, the thriller the political crime film and the vigilante film and to this Thompson adds puzzle films such as whodunits and heists, erotic thrillers and movies about serial killers. In his early study of the American gangster film, Colin MacArthur takes an iconographic approach, characterising the crime film as one that deals with a specific set of semiotic signs (low key lighting, screaming car tyres, screaming women, etc.) and Steve Neale suggests that the character of the crime film can be shaped by which of the three main character positions it focuses on.[21]

Research on crime cinema, especially that coming out of America, tends to privilege the gangster film and the film noir over all other sub-genres. This was a trend that began with Robert Warshow's seminal essay 'The Gangster as Tragic Hero' but that we see continuing in texts like Clemens, Shadoian, and Leitch.[22] More expansive studies such as Rafter's and Thompson's have expanded out from this to include heist films, psychological thrillers such as *The Silence of the Lambs* (1991) and *Se7en* (1995), and films concerned with trials and the courtroom like *The Pelican Brief* (1993) and *The Rainmaker* (1997). Whereas work on the British crime film has also focused primarily on gangsters and robbery with violence, it also considers the connections between crime and the everyday; therefore we get a series of considerations of the role of the spiv in the 1940s and a wide-ranging cycle of texts that deal with women and crime.[23]

The present book takes its lead from all of these studies but attempts to expand the remit even further by adding the subgenres of juvenile delinquency and prostitution to the umbrella term of the crime film. By way of foundational definitions, this book leans towards Thomas Leitch's notions but attempts a broader base of texts than his book adopts. Although perhaps not wholly endemic to the crime film, Clarens' notion that they also depict crime, not as an isolated incident, but as part of a larger social and ideological mandate also inflects the choices here. We see these kinds of narrative structures present in most, if not all, of the films discussed in this book but such definitions should be used with caution so that they might illuminate rather than constrain and obfuscate.[24]

The chapters of this book can be thought to represent a rogues' gallery of outsiders to mainstream society and, in this way, they also hold a mirror up to the social norms and mores of Britain since the end of the Second World War. There are discussions of the gangster, the delinquent, the prostitute, the thief, the corrupt policeman and, ultimately, that folk devil *par excellence*, the serial killer. Look in any newspaper over the past 60 years and you will find these characters being discussed, variously as bogeymen, as scapegoats and as figures of macabre fascination. Any society gets the criminals it deserves and Britain, it seems, is no exception.

HOW TO USE THIS BOOK

The chapters in this book are divided into sub-genres of the crime film, each of which looks at a specific criminal or behaviour. Each chapter looks at three main films usually from different periods that present the crime film as being in constant flux and re-negotiation. Sometimes, as in the chapter 'Bent Coppers', this periodisation will be relatively small. The 1970s were the heyday of police corruption and so it makes sense to limit our analysis to this one decade; however, for the most part the space between the periods is fairly large.

The films were chosen because they represent something very definite about British society and culture. In the case of *Brighton Rock* for example, it is how post-war privation affected the moral underpinnings of the nation; in the case of *Mona Lisa*, how immigration changed the demographic of the large cities, and so on. This strategy was specifically designed to encourage the view that genre cinema, and crime films in particular, can provide useful inroads into the public consciousness and perhaps might even be a more direct reflector of contemporary ideology than the realist cinema more usually employed as a social barometer. Much of the research surrounding American genre cinema stresses the value of genre films as carriers of ideology and highlights the extent that they can be read through a number of different methodological lenses that both uphold and challenge the hegemonic norms. The British crime film is no different, yet the study of it has often been reduced to fairly narrow historical analysis.

The crime film is a major part of British cinematic culture. However, due to the prejudices that have been highlighted here, it has often been passed over in favour of its documentary or its social realist counterpart. The British crime film is also often criticised for its politics, being seen as overtly misogynistic, too gritty, too violent or too sensationalist for serious academic consideration. Especially in recent years, films like *Rise of the Footsoldier* (2007), *Essex Boys* (2000) or *Kidulthood* (2006) have been seen as pandering to the worst aspects of British society. Peter Bradshaw for example, in his *Guardian* review of the first of these films stated that 'This fantastically boring and misogynistic movie is yet another speculative reconstruction, told from the point of view of a particularly belligerent self-pitying parasite with the face of a bulldog chewing a wasp'.[25]

Such damning statements on a film may well be true but academic film study should not concern itself with such value judgements, or at least should consider what they mean in terms of the wider cultural field. The fact that films like *Rise of the Footsoldier* exist, that they are produced and are consumed for certain audiences, tells us as much (maybe even more) about the state of the nation than a more rarefied work. In other words: we must examine what is there, not what we wish might be there. However the student of the British crime film should be critical of the failings of the films where it is needed and possibly even of the audience that consumes them. A critical stance on a film like *Rise of the Footsoldier*, for example, might well examine its attitude towards women, its glorification of violence, or its aggrandisement of a specific brand of masculinity, but would ask the question: *Why?* Why was it that this was attractive to both film-makers and film audiences at that moment in time? What does this say about British cinema and Britain *per se*? The traditional way of dealing with such films by academia has been to ignore them and perhaps, after a hiatus of forty or fifty years, rediscover them in the BFI library and hail them as a lost masterpieces prime for reconsideration. This book encourages us not to lose sight of the breadth of British cinema and to look, finally, at the whole spectrum of British film-making, from the best to the worst.

FOOTNOTES

1. O' Regan, T., 'Cultural Exchange' in Miller, T. and R. Stam (eds), *A Companion to Film Theory*, London; Blackwell, 2004, p.262.

2. Landy, M., *British Genres: Cinema and Society, 1930 – 1960*, New Jersey: Princeton University Press, 1991, p.11.

3. Thompson, K., *Crime Films: Investigating the Scene*, London: Wallflower, 2007, p.11.

4. Mayhew, H., *London Labour and the London Poor*, Oxford: Oxford University Press, 2010; Dickens, C., *Oliver Twist*, London: Penguin, 2007.

5. Chibnall, S and R. Murphy (eds), *British Crime Cinema*, London: Routledge, 1999.

6. Murphy, R., *Realism and Tinsel: Cinema and Society in Britain 1939 – 49*, London: Routledge, 1992; Spicer, A., *Typical Men: The Representation of Masculinity in Popular British Cinema*, London: I.B. Tauris; Brundson, C., *London in Cinema: the Cinematic City of London Since 1945*, London: BFI Publishing, 2007; Richards, J and A. Aldgate, *Best of British: Cinema and Society from 1930 to the Present*, London: I.B. Tauris, 2001, 2009; Gillett, P., *The British Working Class in Postwar Film*, Manchester: Manchester University Press, 2003.

7. Chibnall, S., *Get Carter*, London: I.B. Tauris, 2003; Chibnall, S., *Brighton Rock*, London: I.B. Tauris, 2004; McCabe, C., *Performance*, London: BFI Publishing, 1998; Brown, M., *Performance*, London: Bloomsbury, 2000; Field, M., *The Making of The Italian Job*, London: Batsford, 2001.

8. Forshaw, B, *British Crime Film: Subverting the Social Order*, London: Palgrave, 2012.

9. Warshow, R., "The Gangster as Tragic Hero", in Silver, A. and James Ursini (eds), *Gangster Film Reader*, New Jersey: Limelight Editions, 2007, p. 13.

10. Hall, S., "Notes on Deconstructing the Popular", in Storey, J (ed), *Cultural Theory and Popular Culture: A Reader*, New York: Prentice Hall, 1998, p. 447.

11. Benyahia, S. C., *Crime*, London: Roultedge, 2012, p. 1.

12. Clarens, C., *Crime Movies: An Illustrated Guide*, London: Secker and Warburg, 1980; Thompson, 2007; Rafter, N., *Shots in the Mirror: Crime Films and Society*, Oxford: Oxford University Press, 2006; Chibnall and Murphy, 1999; Cettl, R., *Serial Killer Cinema: An Illustrated Guide*, Jefferson and London: McFarland and Company, 2007.

13. Murphy, 1992; Hill, J., *Sex, Class and Realism: British Cinema 1956-1963*, London: BFI Publishing, 1986; Spicer, 2001; Leach, J., *British Film*, Cambridge: Cambridge University Press, 2004.

14. *Report of the Committee on Homosexual Offenses and Prostitution (The Wolfenden Report)*, London: HMSO, 1963; *Tougher Regimes in Detention Centres: Report of an Evaluation By the Young Offender Psychology Unit*, London: HMSO, 1984; *The Brixton Disorders, 10-12 April 1981*, Report of an Inquiry by the RT. Hon. The Lord Scarman, O.B.E, London: HSMO1981; Cohen, S., *Folk Devils and Moral Panics*, London: Routledge, 2011; Hebdige, D., *Subculture: The Meaning of Style*, London: Routledge, 1988; Maguire, M, R Morgan and R. Reiner (eds), *The Oxford Handbook of Criminology*, Oxford: Oxford University Press, 2002.

15. Pearson, J., *Profession of Violence: The Rise and Fall of the Kray Twins*, London: Harper Collins, 1995; Morton, J., *Gangland Omnibus, Vols. 1&2*, London: Time Warner Paperbacks, 2003; O' Mahoney, B., *Essex Boys: A Terrifying Expose of the British Drugs Scene*, London: Mainstream Publishing, 2000.

16. Warshow, 1948/2007; Cettl, 2007.

17. Rafter, 2006, p.6.

18. Leitch, T., *Crime Films*, Cambridge: Cambridge University Press, 2002.

19. Leitch, 2002, p.14.

20. Rafter, 2006, p.3.

21. MacArthur, C. *Underworld USA*, London: New York: Viking Adult, 1972; Neale, S., 'Contemporary Crime and Detective Films', in C.A. Bernik (ed), *The Cinema Book*, London: BFI, 1999.

22. Shadoian, J., *Dreams and Dead Ends: The American Gangster Film*, 2nd Edition, Oxford: Oxford University Press, 2003.

23. Murphy, 1999; Wollen, P., 'Riff-Raff Realism' in *Paris Hollywood: Writing on Film*, London: Verso, 2002; Chadder, V., 'The Higher Hell: Women and the Post-War British Crime Film' in Chibnall and Murphy, 1999; Bell, M., *Femininity in the Frame: Women and 1950s British Popular Culture*, London; I.B. Tauris, 2010.

24. Clarens, 1980, p.13.

25. Bradshaw, P., 'Rise of the Footsoldier', in *The Guardian*, 7 September, 2007.

CHAPTER ONE: GANGLAND UK

Brighton Rock (1947)

Unlike Hollywood, British cinema does not have a classical period for the gangster film. Neither does it have a set of movies that could be described as both benchmarks and foundational statements against which all others are measured. From the 1940s onward, American critics soon recognised that the triumvirate of original Hollywood gangster films, Mervyn LeRoy's *Little Caesar* (1931), William Wellman's *The Public Enemy* (1931) and Howard Hawks' *Scarface* (1932), were a kind blueprint for both the form and the style of successive films. Their narrative elements and stylistics were both copied and reinvented time and time again forming a definitive link between these early films and later examples such as *The Godfather* trilogy (1972, 1974, 1990), *Goodfellas* (1990) or *Casino* (1995).

The British gangster film had less obvious beginnings and instead emerged gradually out of the twin straightjackets of strict censorship and outside influence. In the pre-war period the murder mystery and detective film dominated the crime genre in Britain; in 1931, for example, 13 per cent of all films made in Britain were murder-mysteries (Gifford, 2000), as offerings such as Twickenham's *Murder at Covent Garden* (1932) and British Lion's *The Man at Six* (1931) satiated the public's thirst for dark dealings without the need to soil the public conscience with the decidedly working-class criminal activities of gangland.

One of the earliest examples of the British gangster film was William Cameron Menzies' *The Green Cockatoo* produced in 1937 but, due to problems with the BBFC (British Board of Film Censorship until 1984; British Board of Film *Classification* since) not released until 1940. Scripted by Graham Greene, *The Green Cockatoo* has many of the tropes that would come to be attached to the British gangster film and that would serve to distance it from its apparently more sophisticated American counterpart. Whereas the Hollywood film often focused on the rise of the poor immigrant to the heights of mob leadership, *The Green Cockatoo* (like many British gangster films) concentrated largely on the footsoldier, played in this instance by John Mills. Mills' character, Jim Connor, is a nobody in the underworld; he may have pretensions to be a leader or a mobster but ultimately he is a man out of his depth, a pretender, a gangster-manqué. We see his type in post-war films like *They Made Me a Fugitive* (1947), *Brighton Rock* and *Dancing With Crime* (1947) and in the more recent crop of films like *Lock, Stock and Two Smoking Barrels*, *Essex Boys* and *The Rise of the Footsoldier*.

The gangs of *The Green Cockatoo* are not the syndicated Mafioso of *Little Caesar* or *Scarface* – Britain had no such crime networks. Instead they were a loose collection of thugs and criminal fraternities centred on money-making opportunities such as racetracks and unlicensed gambling. The unglamorous nature of gangland UK in the 1930s and '40s is outlined by James Morton in relation to the infamous Sabini family who, he says, 'fought for supremacy on street corners, on trains, on the roads and at the racecourses'.[26] Unlike the vaguely romantic and detached violence of the Tommy-gun toting mobster, the British gangster of the 1940s fought with razors, vitriol and fists, at once a more prosaic and more hands-on method of violence – a reality that was reflected in the cinema.

Allied to the spiv cycle of the 1940s, the British gangster film emerged out of the rubble of the Blitz rather than the glamour of the speakeasy or the big business of prohibition. Although, as with *The Green Cockatoo* and the 1936 film *Crime Over London*, there were sporadic examples of depictions of gangsters before 1939, it was in 1946 and especially with British National's *Appointment with Crime* starring William Hartnell, that a more recognisable cycle or trend in crime film-making began. Perhaps it was the harshness of the 1940s or the promise of a more equitable future under the newly elected Labour government, but the pre-war taste for gentlemen detectives and safe, middle class whodunnits rapidly began to wane. Hartnell's performance in *Appointment with Crime* was described by film critic William Whitebait as:

> a genuine attempt at the popular level to create an English counterpart to the Hollywood gangster legend. Its merits are a certain neatness and speed in its execution, bits of slang, glimpses into the oddly assorted criminal underworld.[27]

This 'oddly assorted criminal underworld' was not merely a construction of British cinema, it was a reflection of the criminal gangs then operating in London, Birmingham and the other large British cities. Hartnell's character is a smash and grab thief, again a nobody who wants to be a somebody. But it is his taunt and tight-lipped performance that was to imbue *Appointment with Crime* with its peculiarly British feel. Indeed, a year later, the young Richard Attenborough would offer a similar performance playing opposite Hartnell in what became a much more celebrated role but the debt owned by the latter to the former is obvious.

In these early examples of the British gangster film, the Godfather or gang leader was often a contingent figure content to sit in the shadows whilst the action was played out by the more lowly gang members and hoods. Frequently they were depicted as cultural and racial others – Italians, Americans or of indeterminate (but recognisably unBritish) nationality. It has been suggested that this was a result of contemporary xenophobia, and that a British cinema-going public would never tolerate a gangland boss that was both evil and British.[28] However, again, this is an over simplification. Since the 1920s, British gangland was dominated by numerous small-time gangs that were headed by exotic-sounding families like the Sabinis, the Messinas and the Mancinis. It seems only natural that such images would find their way into popular cinema. In fact, so prevalent was this image that the comedian Norman Wisdom would parody it in the 1962 comedy *On the Beat* where he played the dual roles of Norman Pitkin and Giulio Napolitani, an Italian mobster.

Of course, as we shall see throughout this chapter, Britain slowly developed its own indigenous mobsters and Godfathers. *Get Carter's* Cyril Kinnear, *The Long Good Friday's* Harold Shand and the *Gangster Number One* (2000) are all examples of how the British gangster can be just as concerned with career development and success as any Michael Corleone. However, it is to the lowly footsoldier or the wannabe gangster that British crime cinema most often turns, whether that is Pinkie Brown or Turkish from Guy Riche's *Snatch* (2000). The British gangster film may often be unfavourably compared with its Hollywood cousin but in its depiction of evolving notions of masculinity, its discussion of social anxieties and its exposition of nationality it is a valuable mirror to a Britain that is both fascinated and repulsed by its dark underbelly.

BRIGHTON ROCK – RACE GANGS AND RAZOR BLADES

> In *Brighton Rock* the bare rooms, smelling of dust and damp, stand as a metaphor for empty, festering minds.[29]

The Boultings' *Brighton Rock* is a film that has been discussed time and time again by British critics. Raymond Durgnat places it favourably alongside Jules Dassin's claustrophobic *Night and the City* (1950) and Alberto Cavalcanti's *They Made Me a Fugitive*, foregrounding its credentials as a British film noir and highlighting how Graham Greene's pessimistic Catholicism invades every shot. Robert Murphy called it the 'first spiv film of 1948' and detailed how contemporary reviewers were divided as to its artistic and ethical merits;[30] and Arthur Vesselo in *Sight and Sound*, provided a fairly representative opinion that it was competently produced and acted but that 'the tale was a sordid one' with an atmosphere that is 'chilled and over-hung by a mood of craven fear'.[31]

Brighton Rock is the story of a seventeen-year-old gangster and spiv, Pinkie Brown (Richard Attenborough), who marries a young, innocent waitress (Carol Marsh) in order stop her from testifying against him for the murder of newspaper journalist Fred Hale (Alan Wheatley). The novel upon which the film was based was published in 1938, just as

Britain was entering the Second World War and much of the anxiety and foreboding of the zeitgeist makes it into the book. Pinkie Brown can be read as both a metaphor for the state of the country and as a universal symbol of man's existential damnation, and on the eve of a war the two must have seemed inextricably linked. In the novel Pinkie is depicted as a Catholic believer, a soul in constant mindfulness of its own dammed position, more knowledgeable of the horrors of hell than the pleasures of paradise (much is made of Pinkie's enforced abstinence where pleasure is concerned). The crimes he commits are not so much the products of socio-economics or even manifestations of psychopathology, but the inevitable actions of a lost spirit. The streets of Brighton might have been full to the brim with holiday makers and sunshine, but they hid the harsh reality of a world that had lost all meaning and was black to the core.

By the time the film was made in 1947 very little had changed. The war was over but the longed for New Jerusalem of post-War Britain had not materialised and, although the film declares in the opening inter-title that it was set in the years before the conflict, contemporary audiences (as Vesselo's review shows) were fully aware that it reflected their own society as much as the earlier decades. If the novel spoke to a Britain preparing itself for a bitter fight, the film spoke to a population attempting to heal itself both economically and socially after it.

In the late 1940s the age of austerity was biting hard and many of Britain's cities were waking up after the enforced cheerfulness of wartime stoicism. Writing about London, Christopher Isherwood eloquently summed up what was a prevailing sense towards both the environment and the population:

> Plaster was peeling from even the most fashionable squares and crescents; hardly a building was freshly painted... London remembered the past and was ashamed of its present appearance. Several Londoners I talked to at that time believed it would never recover. 'This is a dying city,' one of them told me.[32]

In this period, the physical decay of Britain was twinned with its conflicting ethics as it not only tried to recover psychologically after long years of fighting but also suffered some of the worst winter temperatures of the twentieth century. Although the Labour Party election manifesto had declared in 1945 that 'Victory in war must be followed by a prosperous peace', for many people, the housing problems and grinding poverty of the 1930s were still very much a social reality. Some of this bleakness makes it onto the screen in *Brighton Rock* as the *mise-en-scène* of the interiors depict a world that is cramped and decaying, and the stark photography of Harry Waxman is at times both beautiful and demonic. Robert Murphy writes about the films of the 1940s under the subtitle 'morbid burrowings' and this phrase neatly describes both the feeling and the visuals of *Brighton Rock* as it juxtaposes ordinary seaside life with an everyday evil that unsettles the characters and the audience. This sense of foreboding also lurks beneath many other films of the era as titles such as *Mine Own Executioner* (1947), *Take My Life* (1947), *Death in High Heels* (1947) and *Dancing with Crime*; all suggest a Britain that was struggling to come to terms with peace and the criminality that was inevitably unleashed at home by the cessation of fighting abroad.

Ultimately, however, the interest of the Boultings' film for a chapter about the British underworld is its depiction of racetrack gangs and in particular the petty mobster that arose out of the gambling rackets of the pre-war economy and the black market of wartime. Racetracks were a liminal space in pre- and post-war Britain; along with the dog track and the Palais de Danse, they provided a meeting point between the general public and the criminal underworld. Gangs like those led by the Sabinis and, later, Jack Spot and Billy Hill would not only make fortunes from the track bookies through extortion and protection but their exploits were well documented in the popular press, ensuring their place in a particularly British form of gangland folklore.

Up until the *1960 Gaming Act* it was illegal for punters to place bets anywhere other than racetracks. The street betting and small time list shops of the nineteenth century had been eradicated by a number of acts of parliament that were designed to rid the larger towns and cities of the divisive spectre of public gambling, and this remained the case well into the twentieth century. The racetrack, then, became a place beyond the law, where the working classes could engage in activities prohibited in the wider world. Thousands of pounds a day could be made by criminal gangs through a variety of different means, from forcing bookmakers to purchase chalk, boards and sheets of runners to simply demanding protection money. Of course, where there is easy money there is often crime and where there is crime there is often violence and turf war. Devoid of any mafia-like syndication, in the 1930s racetracks became a flashpoint between competing gangs resulting in violent confrontation and an eager public lapped up their tales of razorblade aggression and dangerous glamour.

We see such gang warfare played out in the infamous scene from the Boultings' film shot on Brighton racetrack, overlooking the South Downs. Pinkie has previously arranged with Colleoni (Charles Goldner), the businessman-like leader of Brighton's biggest mob, to kill Spicer (Wylie Watson) who has become 'milky' in the face of Fred Hale's murder. Under the watchful eyes of Colleoni's henchmen, Pinkie seals Spicer's fate by patting him on the back and both men suddenly become surrounded by a vicious mob. Graham Greene and Terence Rattigan's script takes a darkly sinister turn as Pinkie and Spicer exchange pleasantries loaded with double meaning:

Pinkie: Well, I don't think I'll be needing you after all, Spicey, so we might as well be saying goodbye.

Spicer: Well, goodbye Pinkie.

Pinkie: Before you go, I thought you'd like to know I am going to make it up with Colleoni.

Spicer: You are? Well, I'm glad to hear that, really I am. Now, when you've got time drop us a line will you? You know where I'm going.

Pinkie: Yeah, I know where you are going.

(*Looks round at Colleoni's thugs*)

Pinkie: So long, Spicer.

What follows owes more to German Expressionism than the American gangster movie, as Harry Waxman's photography comes close to the look and feel of Fritz Lang's 1931 classic *M*. Instantly we are no longer in the pleasant surroundings of a day's racing but in a thieves' lair. Spicer has become a sacrificial lamb for Pinkie's murderous ambition and it is fitting that the violence meted out is swift, raw and brutal. The crowds on the racecourse only add to the terror of the moment as they swiftly become a moving wall that encircles both men. In the background we catch a glimpse of a zealot's painted banner – 'The Wages of Sin...' – a constant reminder that, for Greene at least, the underworld is home to both gangsters and devils.

It is only when Pinkie himself is attacked by Colleoni's mobsters that we see him for what he really is: a scared child wrapped up in the clothes of a gangster. A razor slash causes him to fall back and scream 'It's not me you want, you mugs, it's him'. His tone of voice is shocked and petulant, the look on his face one of infantile outrage. We will see this face once more in the film, in the last scenes on the pier as he tumbles to his death in the water.

The razor slash that Pinkie receives on his cheek at the racetrack is both a mark of (dis) honour and a brand meted out by the older gang leader. Later, as he is stopped by the gang member Cubbitt (Nigel Stock) sneaking back into the apartment his gang shares, Pinkie tries to hide the cut and we are reminded of its symbolic importance – he has become a man at last, his symbolic virginity taken by Colleoni. Pinkie is now marked by the violence he himself sanctions, the violence that he lives by, and which first wounds and then kills him.

For Steve Chibnall, the scenes at the races are the 'centre-piece of *Brighton Rock*'.[33] They not only allow the Boultings to render visible the ever-present religiosity of Greene's novel but they represent a microcosm of the gangland environment in the immediate post-war period. Spicer and Pinkie are literally overwhelmed by the swift and shocking violence of Colleoni's gang and are saved only by the intervention of, firstly, the crowd and then the police. Bereft of the keystone that was their previous leader Kite, Pinkie's gang falls apart at the seams and as we shall see throughout this book, this image – of the gang falling apart – is a constant one in the British crime film. Colleoni's double-crossing of Pinkie again situates the film within the tradition of the Hollywood film noir, as he suddenly realises he has become a victim of forces beyond his control.

The relationship between Pinkie and Colleoni is at the heart of *Brighton Rock*'s rendering of the British underworld and the scene in which the two finally and calamitously meet is the point at which the film is closest to the classic Hollywood gangster movie. Situated just before the racecourse sequence and filmed on a large soundstage at the MGM studios at Welwyn Garden, it both draws on and distances itself from similar scenes in both *Little Caesar* and *Scarface* where the young pretender marvels at the riches and achievements of an established older Godfather. In the Hollywood gangster movie, this scene usually prompts the rise of the gangster, spurring him on and providing him with the motivation to transcend his own background. Tony Camonte (Paul Muni), for example visits Johnny Lovo (Osgood Perkins) in his apartments, throwing admiring glances at both his clothes and his girl whilst similarly Rico Bandello (Little Caesar, played by Edward G. Robinson) is dwarfed amid the opulent surroundings of Big Boy's hotel suite that looks more Versailles than Pig Alley.

Pinkie, however, is defiant in his dislike for Colleoni who is painted as louche and decadent when compared to the infinitely more ascetic teenage boy. The gulf between the two is emphasised by the relative camera positions adopted by Waxman when shooting their conversation – Pinkie shot from above and Colleoni from below. Pinkie is humiliated by the older man but the latter is no model for the former; instead they form a kind of mirror image – the Godfather and the street urchin, the corrupting influence and the easily corrupted boy. It is easy to tell by their manner, by their mode of dress and by the way they address each other that they come from different worlds and are going to enjoy different fates.

The character of Colleoni is a complicated one, and one that is open to interpretation as Steve Chibnall writes:

> Those commentators who are satisfied with Green's implication that the character is based on Darby Sabini are really missing the point. Those who might note the resemblance to Al Capone, who died just before shooting began on the film, are getting closer. Those who point to the movie mogul Alexander Korda as a referent are closer still. Colleoni is not a shadowy underworld figure, but a representative of the establishment.[31]

The well-known 1930s gangster Darby Sabini, the often assumed prototype for Colleoni, was not the businessman of the Boultings' film. Given to wearing a tweed suit and a flat cap, he seems a world away from Charles Goldner's be-suited, grape-eating sophisticate or the round-bellied effeminate character of Greene's novel. Unlike Colleoni, Darby Sabini was a regular on the race track; he would lead his gang from the ground, not from the comfort of the Grand Hotel. He was born in England but in an area known as Little Italy and was proud of his Italian roots despite never learning the language.

The image of gangster-as-businessman is one that appears in many crime films and Chibnall is right to link Colleoni with Alexander Korda, one of the giants of British film production. However, by 1947 Greene's relationship with Korda was a friendly one and, unlike him, Colleoni manages to straddle or perhaps even erase the boundary line between classes and social positions. Spitting grape seeds into his hand and labelling the wife of Napoleon III 'some foreign polony' characterises him not as an establishment figure, as Chibnall suggests, but as every bit of a social interloper as Pinkie himself. Rather than either a shadowy underworld spectre or an establishment representative, Colleoni is the dream of every footsoldier, the gangster who can rise above the others, who can swap small time violence for big time business and who can lord it over nobodies beneath them. Ultimately, it is money and power that imbues him with his social position, not class, and it is this that Pinkie so obviously both longs for and despises.

Colleoni's assertion that 'you can't damage a businessman' is echoed by another of British cinema's criminal social climbers: *The Long Good Friday*'s Harold Shand (Bob Hoskins) who famously declares his businessman status under the twin towers of Tower Bridge. However, neither Shand nor Colleoni can fully shake off the dirt of the streets from their hands and they are not so much representative of the establishment as perversions of its ideals. In his celebrated essay on the gangster as American hero, Robert Warshow outlines the basic premise of the gangster film as detailing his drive for success and power; in this the gangster is merely following the American Dream to its logical conclusion, swapping legitimate for illegitimate enterprise. Whereas the rise and fall of the Godfather is the focus of many Hollywood movies, the British gangster film often treats this merely as background to a story about a lower, less successful caste.[35] We not only see this in *Brighton Rock*, but it also features in later films like *Performance* and *Get Carter*.

Brighton Rock cannot be seen as an Ur-text in the same way as *Little Caesar*, *The Public Enemy* or *Scarface* and neither should it be considered (as some critics have) merely a copy of those films. It is a snapshot of a period of transition, as the wartime black market racketeer solidified into the post-war gangster. Pinkie Brown is also not so much a copy or ersatz version of Rico Bandello or Tony Camonte but a fairly representative picture of British gangsters of the period who often styled themselves on these Hollywood models. In what will become a common theme in the British crime film, it is the criminal themselves, not their fictional counterparts, who copy the Hollywood image, basing their look and their attitude on the iconography they witness on screen.

Films like *The Green Cockatoo*, *Appointment With Crime*, *Dancing With Crime* and *Brighton Rock* represent a turning point in British cinema, as the fears and anxieties about the political other in the form of the Nazi and the Fascist metamorphosed into a fear of the social outcast in the form of the criminal. Ironically this coincided with a relaxation of censorship laws that began to allow films detailing the criminal underclass to be made and shown. Although never far from the shadow of his Hollywood counterpart, the British gangster would slowly develop into a recognisable cinematic type, fusing Chicago style with a home grown attitude that reflected the shifts of a changing and damaged nation.

VILLAIN – QUEERING THE FIRM

For Jack Shadoian, the development of the American gangster film can be seen to roughly mirror that of the realist novel. There is a classical phase (*Little Caesar, Scarface*) where foundational tropes, characters and ideas are established and proliferated; a phase of decadence (film noir, *The Killing* [1956], etc.) where these forms begin to break down and narratives become darker and more introspective; a Modernist phase (*Point Blank* [1967], *Bonnie and Clyde* [1967]) where narration becomes fractured and aesthetic experimentation serves to distance the audience from the text; and lastly a postmodern phase (*The Usual Suspects* [1995], *Pulp Fiction* [1994]) where images from the past are recycled and reinvented and narrative elements (especially violence) begin to be imbued with a loss of affect.[36]

As we have already seen, the British gangster film followed no such developmental structure. From its very earliest days critics and film-makers were well aware that it was both intertextual and (to a large extent) trans-national, as it inevitably borrowed and adapted films from both Hollywood and Europe. However for the student of the British crime film there are lessons to be learnt from Shadoian's taxonomy. Although we have no classical period, films like *Brighton Rock, Appointment With Crime* and *They Made Me a Fugitive* certainly reflect the decadence and melancholy of American film noir and 1940s gangster movies like *The Killers* (1946) and *White Heat* (1949). On both sides of the Atlantic we see the same search for meaning, the same existential interrogation and the same reliance on chiaroscuro aesthetics to highlight a growing sense of moral ambiguity. British crime films may have been influenced by Hollywood but they were very rarely simple imitations. More often than not they were nationally specific ways of dealing with the same problem or working through the same psycho-social issues.

Later films like *Lock, Stock and Two Smoking Barrels* and *Love, Honour and Obey* (2000) also remind us of the experiments in form that characterised the American postmodern gangster film and that contributed greatly to its reinvention and reinvigoration in the 1990s. However, again, this was not merely a reflection of direct influence. Such films were also products of a particularly indigenous cultural and political zeitgeist that incorporated everything from the election of Tony Blair's New Labour to the publication of lads' mags. As we shall see in Chapter Two, these films can also be seen to belong to a much longer cultural tradition stretching back to William Hogarth, Charles Dickens and Henry Mayhew, that both celebrated and caricatured British working class villainy.

Perhaps the most interesting application of Shadoian's taxonomy to the British gangster film is in the Modernist phase which he roughly dates from the late-1960s to the mid-1980s. He states:

> The label 'modernist' is somewhat voguish and unsatisfactory, but may serve to cover the strategies of films such as *Bonnie and Clyde*, *Point Blank*, *The Godfather*, and *The Godfather II*. The term signifies, in the main, an articulate and consciously conceived

nonillusionistic cinema. The genre from the late sixties on is marked by films that prevent the audience from nursing the illusion that they are watching the real world.[37]

This periodicity is particularly illuminating for British gangster cinema as it covers two of the most widely discussed and popular films in the canon and a further one that has slipped through the cultural net remaining virtually unknown. Between October 1970 and August 1971, British cinema produced three major gangster movies: Donald Cammell and Nicolas Roeg's *Performance*, Mike Hodges' *Get Carter* and Michael Tuchner's *Villain* and over the years, these three films have fared remarkably differently in both the popular and the critical arenas.

Too often dismissed as 'a trendily mindless confection' by contemporary critics, *Performance* has since been revisited and reappraised by writers on cult *and* crime cinema as both a bold statement on the nature of British gangland and a reflection of sixties counterculture.[38] Like the other two films of the era, it details the coming together of two distinct worlds – in this case the underworld of the 1960s gangster and the louche bohemianism of decadent Notting Hill.

James Fox plays Chas Devlin, a violent footsoldier who flees the East End (and his boss Harry Flowers, played by Johnny Shannon) after killing another gang member in a frenzied beating/male rape. Crossing London, Devlin stumbles upon Turner (Mick Jagger) and his bohemian entourage. What follows is part Jorge Louis Borges, part acid trip, as Turner and Devlin begin to transmogrify into one another, merging the loose morality of the West End with the uptight masculinity of the East.

When surrounded by the trappings of countercultural life Devlin looks like a figure from a different time. His smart suit, short hair and taut masculinity represent not only his criminality but, as Colin MacCabe suggests, a version of a staid 'Old England' that stands in contrast to the new, youthful swinging London of Mick Jagger's Turner.[39] Harry Flowers, the indigenous gangland boss, as Paul Dave states, is often depicted holding court from within an oak panelled office in front of what looks like an eighteenth-century pastoral painting, an emblem of his status as traditional patrician and a signifier for an England of rigid class distinctions and old-boy networks.[40] The increasingly avant-garde aesthetics of the film therefore mirror Chas' transition from one world to another, as he is inflected, or perhaps even infected, by the character of Turner.

Performance stands at the intersection of the crime and the art film and its playful treatment of genre allows it to elide simple textual classifications. However, like *Point Blank* or *Bonnie and Clyde*, it draws attention to its own artifice, its own status as fiction. The inclusion of Mick Jagger into the cast was not only a marketing ploy by Warner Bros. (who also distributed The Rolling Stones), it served to distance the audience from the action, evoking ideas like Brecht's *verfremdungseffekt* and creating a work that could transcend the usual limitations of the genre film.

Perhaps even more than *Performance*, Mike Hodges' *Get Carter* has in recent years been canonised by critics and public alike and has come to be seen as a kind of ur-text for lads' magazines and works on classic British cinema. The iconography of *Get Carter* (the suit, the shotgun, the beer in a thin glass) have become clichés of British crime cinema and arguably served to obscure and overstate the film's importance in the development of the form. Although unpopular on its release, a post-feminist popular press saw in its endlessly quotable script and iconographic marketing a return to an age of traditional masculinity, where suits and sawn off shotguns go hand in hand with sizeable amounts of aggression and misogyny. It was also re-released in 1999, cementing its position as a part of the nation's collective cultural consciousness.

Get Carter depicts a country increasingly divided by socio-economics and cultural differences. Michael Caine, fresh from roles in *Alfie* (1966), *The Ipcress File* (1965) and *The Italian Job*, was the archetypal face of 'swinging London' and Mike Hodges uses this to its fullest extent, as Carter travels between classes and across demographic zones. Unlike *Performance*, the gangsters of *Get Carter*, and Caine's character especially, are representative of a new, harsher Britain, where morality and greed have become forces of social progression and the violence is brutal. Much of the power of the film lies in the collision of the old world with the new as Hodges highlights the darker, seedier side of 1960s permissiveness. The urban landscape of Newcastle (specifically chosen by the director for its bleakness) acts as what T.S. Eliot would term an 'objective correlative' for the state of the nation, as the cultural highs of the 1960s slowly slid into the political and social lows of the 1970s.

Jack Carter is both excitingly sexual and disturbingly dangerous as he bursts through the dividing line between the criminal classes and the general public. However, he is less a rounded figure in the spirit of the Realist novel and more like a symbol or cipher from a Modernist text. The figure of Caine and the lack of any real character background (the relationship between Jack and Frank Carter, for example, is explored much more fully in the book than the film) serve as points of distanciation for the audience, taking them outside the narrative and reminding them that what they are witnessing is a fiction. This point is compounded for modern audiences who, since the film's canonisation, can quote passages along with the actors and experience the kind of joyous déjà-vu that cult films encourage.

Both *Performance* and *Get Carter* adhere to the Modernist model proposed by Shadoian; *Performance* in terms of its avant-garde aesthetics and *Get Carter* in terms of Caine's performance and the heavily symbolic construction of the film's characters. Viewed in this way, both films represent the genre experimenting with form, self-consciously mixing generic elements together to form new variations on old themes. *Performance* mixes elements of the musical, the crime film and the art film whereas *Get Carter* fuses gangland with Jacobean tragedy, the everyday banal reality of British life and the cool, hipness of Roy Budd's score.

Michael Tuchner's *Villain* however, as some commentators have stated, has gone virtually unnoticed in the popular forum and is very rarely discussed at any great length in the critical. The reasons for this are, as we shall see, manifold and it is, to some extent, a more interesting film for being overlooked. Like *Performance* and *Get Carter*, *Villain* is quite clearly a depiction of a Britain in transition and yet it has none of the former's aesthetic experimentation and very little of the latter's Jacobean inflected intensity. Its images are hard and uncompromising and its characterisations are stark and unapologetic. Vic Dakin, the film's eponymous villain played by Richard Burton, is both a gang leader and a footsoldier and he displays the harshness of Carter and the naivety of Pinkie Brown. So tied is he to the act of criminality that he refuses to be the business man of the Mafioso, sticking doggedly to the everyday activities of criminality; 'If it's big enough and good enough' he says, 'you do it yourself – 'cause you know why? 'Cause nobody else can do it better.' Dakin is an adult Pinkie Brown, stirred in the cauldron of 1960s permissiveness and boiling over into the heat of 1970s social conflict.

Villain, adapted from James Barlow's novel *The Burden of Proof* by Dick Clement and Ian La Frenais, is the story of a bungled payroll heist carried out by gay gangland boss Dakin. Dakin straddles two worlds: the world of polite working class domesticity and the world of violent perverted gangland. He thinks nothing of having sadistic gay sex with Wolf Lissner (Ian McShane), his sometime boyfriend, in the bedroom of his ordinary terraced house whilst his mother drinks cocoa and reads *Woman's Own* in the next room; in the same way, he sits on Brighton seafront on the Bank Holiday, drives home at 30mph and then engages in violent armed robbery, mindlessly killing, maiming and wounding without a second thought. Unlike Devlin and Carter who move between them, Dakin keeps a foot in both the criminal and the legitimate worlds; an altogether much more divisive and dangerous situation. The pathological nature of Dakin's criminality is made all the worse because it is bookended by a dull quotidian life and because he himself fails to recognise the shock and disapproval that he inspires in others. It is this 'everydayness' that distances Dakin (and many British gangsters) from their Hollywood counterparts and it is this that forms the basis of the British genre.

The Hollywood gangster is a mythical creature, formed out of frontier narratives and the immigrant dream. He has no place in the real world because he is a symbol; in Robert Warshow's phrase, 'a tragic hero'. In this, Jack Carter is more Hollywood than Pinewood. Vic Dakin however, and to a lesser extent Chas Devlin, is most definitely in the British tradition. Their gangster violence is undercut by scenes of domestic dullness that deny them any symbolic value or mythic status. Dakin bringing his ageing mother cocoa in bed, the cramped and ordinary terrace house they live in, the bungled robbery, Devlin sitting in the bath being lectured to by a young girl eating baked beans, and so on, are all part of the familiarity that underpins and undermines the British gangster. As Chibnall details, during the late 1950s and early 1960s the British crime film became heavily influenced by the emerging Social Realist school, as films such as *The Small World of Sammy Lee*, *The*

Loneliness of the Long Distance Runner (1962) and *The Criminal* fused gangland and petty crime with documentary and kitchen sink drama. The British gangster film has a foot in both the mythic and the everyday and the results are sometimes absurd, sometimes disturbing; but they are often noticeably different from Hollywood.

The British press has always had a schizophrenic relationship with gangland – on the one hand vilifying criminality and on the other succumbing to its endless fascination. The race track and razor gangs of the 1930s and '40s, as we have seen, were the subject of many column inches in the popular press of the day and journalists like Arthur Helliwell on the *People* delighted in telling their readership of gangland bosses like Jack Spot and Billy Hill. These figures were already semi-mythical by the time they hit the headlines and they were treated with a mixture of horror and veneration, as events such as the battle of Frith Street (which would claim the career of Spot) were told in colourful language. There were (and are) gangs in all the major cities of Britain, however it was the East End of London that become synonymous with gangland activity from the late nineteenth century onwards. The East End had all the ingredients for the birthplace of gangland Britain: the docks bought ready money and easy pickings, the densely packed housing and grinding poverty bought need and desperation and the proximity to the shining lights of the West End gave a sense of what could and what might be won with hard work, determination and ruthlessness.

Throughout the 1950s and '60s we can recognise a steady rise in what we might think of as indigenous gangland bosses. Slowly but surely the Italian and American Godfathers give way to home-grown villains, as firstly Spot and Hill, and then the Krays and the Richardsons became the archetypal gangster figures from whom cinema drew influence. The Kray twins were brought up in the East End and self-consciously represented a more trans-Atlantic gangster figure, often modelling their clothes and their manner on Hollywood anti-heroes like George Raft's character Rinaldo from *Scarface*. Both Ronnie and Reggie Kray courted the limelight and crossed the line between gangland and clubland, eventually being arrested for the murders of Jack 'the Hat' Mcvitie and George Cornell in May 1968. The Krays' notoriety and in particular the way their lifestyles effaced the boundary line between the criminal and the celebrity classes can be seen to be reflected in all three of the gangster films of the early 1970s. Whereas in the 1940s and '50s, British gangsters were often aloof and asexual, reticent to involve themselves in the difficult and unpredictable world of sex and desire (Pinkie in *Brighton Rock*, Johnny Bannion in Joseph Losey's *The Criminal*, Clem in *They Made Me a Fugitive*), in the late 1960s and '70s, they were imbued with a dangerous and often perverse sexuality that was in part a reflection of Ronnie Kray's own much publicised homosexuality and, in part, a reflection of later anxieties about the permissiveness of the 1960s themselves.

Both *Villain* and *Performance* depict gay gangsters who subvert the usual masculine images of British gangland. Although, ultimately the subversive nature of this depiction is neutered by a reactionary return to the equation of 'homosexuality=perversity', the gay gangster is a peculiarly British invention and one that is very rarely matched in Hollywood. It would be tempting to imagine that gay gangsters like Harry Flowers or Vic Dakin are only reflections of Ronnie Kray and his place in gangland mythology. However, the queer or effeminate gangster is a common sight in the British crime film and was so even before the Krays' notoriety became commonplace. From the feminised and flashy clothing of the wartime spiv to the refined gentleman mobster like Colleoni, the homosexual and the criminal underworlds often collided to create a character that was treated with redoubled suspicion by 'straight' society.

The gay gangster is both a perversion of, and the logical extension to, the homosocial world of the gang. Needing no outside female influence (except perhaps an Oedipal mother) they provide an image of a hermetically sealed masculinity that is left unchecked by the female and by the demands of heterosexual 'normality'. Time and time again we are presented with the image of the gangster 'going soft' and more often than not this is due to a woman and a family. From Hollywood films like *Carlito's Way* (1993) and *Things to Do in Denver When You're Dead* (1995) to modern British films like *Hard Men* (1996), *Gangster Number One* and *Sexy Beast* (2000) the lure of an easy life with a wife and children constantly threatens the delicate cohesion of the homosocial gang. Of course, this is not so with the gay gangster who, like Vic Dakin with Wolf Lissener, is more likely to keep his lovers on the payroll of the firm than look outside of it. The gay gangster becomes the ultimate image of the criminal gang's propensity towards masculine self-sufficiency and is a challenge to both legal and moral boundaries.

This last point is neatly exemplified at the end of *Villain*, where Vic Dakin is surrounded, not by the police as such, but by the mass of 'decent' society. Cornered in the railway arches, desperate and abandoned by his young male lover, Vic Dakin is confronted by Inspector Matthews (Nigel Davenport) who (unlike many 1970s policemen) is indubitably incorruptible. Nodding towards the crowds of onlookers, Mathews declares, 'See them… and them… and them… you can't put the frighteners on all of them, not all the time'. To which Dakin replies 'Why not?', prompting Mathews to conclude: 'You call them punters, we call them witnesses.' Dakin's manic egotism, which has been bubbling under the surface throughout the entire film, finally erupts:

> Dakin: You know, if I looked at one of them, they'd piss in their pants because I'm Vic Dakin.
>
> Mathews: Used to be.
>
> Dakin: And who are you? What do you do? Keeping Britain clean on 30 quid a week. Respect? Respect, you don't know what it is unless you're Vic Dakin – tell him somebody, tell him! A hundred witnesses? There's only twelve men on the jury, you remember that, only twelve men on the jury.
>
> [Dakin looks round to see he is surrounded by police and public.]
>
> Dakin: Who're you looking at?

Given the endings of *Get Carter* and *Performance*, the conclusion to *Villain* is strangely reactionary and reminds us of Ealing films like *The Blue Lamp* and *It Always Rains on a Sunday* (1947), where post-war consensus was explored through the image of a just and cohesive public who were perennially vigilant for transgressions of both a moral and a criminal nature. However, this is no Foucauldian panopticism; it is instead the exercising of the moral majority who are well aware of the power of exposure. Coming just four years after the legalisation of homosexuality, Dakin's last words of the film are a reflection of the anxieties of both the criminal and the gay man – that to be looked at inevitably means to be found out and consequently punished.

Villain concludes on a note of socialistic faith as the individual is controlled and kept in check by the crowd. In the end, Dakin's psychopathology is no match for a morally vigilant public who act as eyes and ears for an overstretched and (as Dakin himself points out) underpaid police force. Coming just two years after the arrest and imprisonment of The Krays and The Richardsons (both of whom were convicted on eye witness testimony) *Villian*'s third act is a prescient reflection of the times and a reminder of the British gangster's outsider status.

The British gangster film of the 1970s was a short-lived but vital strain of film-making, allowing directors and scriptwriters to tackle issues as diverse as homosexuality and the North/South divide. Although the criminal gang would appear throughout the 1970s in both cinema and on television it would mainly be as a foil for an equally corrupt police force (*The Sweeney* (1975 – 1978) being the most popular example of this) and would often be twinned with a distinct operation such as the heist or the armed robbery. The high point of 1960s criminal glamour was all but over by 1972 as the (some would say overly harsh) sentencing of The Krays and The Richardsons strengthened the image of an intolerant legal system and police force in the public imagination.

British cinema also changed irrevocably during this period as dwindling audiences and the withdrawal of funding by the large Hollywood companies prompted many directors and producers to either stick to tried and tested formulae (such as *Carry Ons*, James Bonds and television spin-offs) or to appeal to rapidly lowering common denominators with sequel after sequel of sexploitation comedies or blood-soaked horror films. As we have seen, however, despite what is often (and arguably erroneously) assumed to be a period of declining cinematic quality, the 1970s did produce a series of crime films that not only bucked this trend but also expertly reflected a Britain beset with economic and psychosocial problems. Films such as Michael Apted's *The Squeeze* (1977), Tom Clegg's *Sweeney 2* (1978) and television shows such as *Gangsters* (1976) and *Out* (1978) were a testimony to the fascination that indigenous British gangs held for an eager public during this period. However, it would be almost a decade before British cinema would produce another crop of gangster-heroes and, by the time they came along, the country and the cinema had changed forever.

THE LONG GOOD FRIDAY – GREED IS GOOD

The 1980s provided the seeds for what has become the contemporary British film industry. It was a decade of conflicting fortunes as Thatcherite politics shaped the way films were funded and then inevitably influenced their narratives. In 1985 the Conservative government, via the Films Act, abolished the various tax breaks and levies that had supported the British film industry since the 1940s. Commensurate with the government's lassiez-faire economic policies, this forced British films to fend for themselves in an open market, a move that, as Alexander Walker states '[came] under all party attack as it progress[ed] through Parliament'.[41]

The Thatcherite assumption that the film industry should consider itself merely another form of commerce, without the backing of government subsidy, resulted in massive changes in the way films were funded, causing consternation about the very future of British film-making itself. However, as Leonard Quart states, 'Despite… the industry's economic precariousness and limited resources, the 1980s saw an exciting renaissance of British film' as television companies, especially Channel4 and BBC2, began to fund their production, plugging the gaps in financing that had been left by the removal of state subsidy.[42] By the end of the decade, British films were either financed by Hollywood money (A Fish Called Wanda (1988), The Living Daylights (1987), Hellraiser (1987)) and were more than able to survive in an increasingly multiplex-based market; or were funded by major TV companies (My Beautiful Laundrette (1985), High Hopes (1988), Sammy and Rose Get Laid (1987)) and thus usually had only a brief cinematic release before being broadcast over the terrestrial network. The stringency of the legislation produced by the Conservative government, then, was not as disastrous as many at the time thought and, in the long run, had the effect of solving many of the problems caused by the abuse of the tax system by overseas production companies.

Representations of crime in the British gangster film were not beyond the influence of Thatcherite politics and, during this period, the line between gangster and businessman became increasingly blurred. Whereas, in the 1970s the gangster was a symbol of illicit excess and permissiveness, in the 1980s he became a figure of national pride and free enterprise – the ideal Thatcherite-man. The two main narrative strains that we see in the 1980s British gangster film are: the defence of British values and way of life against some invading outside force (whether that be the Irish in The Long Good Friday or the Americans in Empire State (1987) and Stormy Monday (1988)) and the satirical depiction of excessive consumption usually linked to an abuse of power such as Peter Greenaway's art-house gangster film The Cook, The Thief, His Wife and Her Lover (1989). As John Hill suggests, these two elements (a traditional sense of Britishness and a faith in material success) were also to form the basis of Thatcher's political and economic policies both at home and abroad, as the jingoistic images of the Falklands conflict were mixed steadily with the growing philosophy of the free market.[43]

One of the clearest examples of this is John Mackenzie's *The Long Good Friday*, originally filmed in 1979 but kept back for release until January 1981. Initially the film formed part of a deal struck by Associated Communications Corporation but fears over the levels of violence and political unrest it depicted meant that it was resold to Handmade Films for its theatrical release.[44] *The Long Good Friday* tells the story of Harold Shand (Bob Hoskins), an East End gang boss, who comes under attack from an unknown aggressor at the very moment he is trying to secure American (Mafioso) money for the redevelopment of London's Docklands. Shand is one of the clearest examples of the steady rise in interest in the idea of an indigenous English gangland boss. Where previously such figures were either European or American, in Harold Shand we have not only a home-grown Godfather but one who can be read as a symbol of British nationalism; one who is as much part of the establishment (or at least aspires to be) as outside it. After a series of violent attacks, the aggressors are finally revealed to be a gang of IRA terrorists intent on exacting revenge on Shand's empire for a previous misdemeanour. The film ends with an iconic long shot of Shand, kidnapped and in the back of a car driven by his persecutors, debating who, why and what.

The inclusion of the IRA into the film's narrative immediately suggests parities with the Thatcher Government and their attempts to distance themselves from the colonial violence of the 1970s. Shand's famous speech on the Thames in which he declares that 'I am not a politician... I'm a business with a sense of history' and 'I believe this is the decade in which London will become Europe's capital' comes close to Margaret Thatcher's words in the 1979 Conservative Party manifesto when she states:

For me, the heart of politics is not political theory, it is people and how they want to live their lives.

No one who has lived in this country during the last five years can fail to be aware of how the balance of our society has been increasingly tilted in favour of the State at the expense of individual freedom.

This election may be the last chance we have to reverse that process, to restore the balance of power in favour of the people. It is therefore the most crucial election since the war.

Together with the threat to freedom there has been a feeling of helplessness, that we are a once great nation that has somehow fallen behind and that it is too late now to turn things round.[45]

Interestingly on 12 October 1984, an IRA bomb exploded in the Grand Hotel in Brighton during the Conservative Party annual conference killing five people and providing an eerie example of how life can sometimes imitate art.

Throughout the film, the violence of the IRA is depicted as being beyond the understanding of Shand and his gang. Like the Mafia, British gangland survives through accepted rules of engagement and is based more on greed, power and ambition than idealism and politics. Similar to the Cuban revolutionaries in *The Godfather Part II*, the IRA are depicted as being all the more terrifying for their zeal, as Shand comes to the realisation that no matter how violent he becomes, he can never match the terrorist with a cause and nothing more to lose. The assassination of Airey Neave, the then shadow secretary for Northern Ireland and close ally of Margaret Thatcher, by Irish Republicans in 1979 added an eerie prescience to the narrative concerns of Mackenzie's film. But as Brian McIlroy asserts, the depiction of the IRA in *The Long Good Friday* is heavily depoliticised, transforming what was a bitter and long-running national struggle into little more than a personal grudge against Shand himself.[46] And the casting of a young Pierce Brosnan as an IRA soldier only sweetens the image. The Troubles themselves are de-historicised and personalised making Shand a metonym for the nation, experiencing a problematic return of history.

As Charlotte Brunsdon suggests, *The Long Good Friday* is a transitional work that details the changing physical and economic space of the East London docks, from their place as the vital heart of London's commerce to a playground for the Conservative-created nouveau-riche, or as Brunsdon puts it 'from unloading sugar to eating profiteroles'.[47] In many scenes the docks stand empty, devoid of their former mercantile glory waiting to be redeveloped and turned into waterside luxury flats for stockbrokers and city traders. It is no accident that in the film this redevelopment is headed by Shand, a gangster who rubs shoulders with policemen, politicians and bankers as well as Mafia mobsters and East End low life. Shand is the logical conclusion to the gangster image we saw being proliferated in the 1960s. In order to avoid the fate of Ronnie and Reggie Kray, mobsters like Shand downplay their criminality (if not their vulgarity) and climb up the social scale.

Like Michael Corleone in *The Godfather*, Shand effaces the demarcation lines between the legitimate and the illegitimate worlds. However, whereas Corleone is dragged back into the underworld by his criminal past, Shand is forced merely to look elsewhere for support – moving from America to Europe when the former fails to deliver the goods. In the late 1970s Britain, it seems, was too lawless even for the Mafia. In his last scenes with Charlie, the American godfather/businessman he has been trying to court all through the film, Shand suggests something that twenty years earlier would have been the unthinkable - teaming up with the Germans:

> Shand: What I'm looking for is someone who can contribute to what England has given the world: culture, sophistication, genius... a little bit more than an 'ot dog, know what I mean? We're in the common market now and my new deal is with Europe; I'm going into partnership with a German organisation. Yeah! The Krauts! They've got ambition, know-how, and they don't lose their bottle. Look at you, the Mafia! I've shit 'em.

The Long Good Friday is often seen as anticipating Britain's development through the 1980s in relation to demographics and environment. However, in its depiction of the abandonment of American connections in favour of European ones it would depart greatly from reality, as the 'special relationship' between Britain and the US, in particular Margaret Thatcher and Ronald Reagan, would cause an ever-widening gap to form between the UK and the European continent. The UK's relationship with America would feature in many crime films of the 1980s and early 1990s. Notable examples include Ron Peck's *Empire State*, Mike Figgis' *Stormy Monday* and Danny Cannon's *The Young Americans* (1993). However, as we have seen throughout this chapter, anxiety over the influence of American culture is almost endemic within the form. In the 1940s and '50s, film-makers displayed a concern over the negative effects of the Hollywood gangster film. In the 1950s and '60s we see anxieties over the possible influence of rock and roll, and a particularly American form of teenage delinquency. And in the 1980s, we see the rise of fears over the homogenising effects of American big business and an increasingly globalised culture. In its assertions at the end of the film, *The Long Good Friday* represents a rejection of American imperialism in favour of British nationalism, and it is this perhaps that has endeared the film to indigenous audiences ever since.

Harold Shand is more in the tradition of Vic Dakin and Harry Flowers than Jack Carter; he is monstrous and yet comical, an absurd figure who has no conception of his own absurdity. Whereas Carter is a killing machine who feels very little emotion for those he destroys, Shand is all too human, his violence a product of his failings rather than his strength. Bob Hoskins' intense performance is undercut by his diminutive size, as he is sometimes dwarfed by those he commands. In this way, he reminds us of Edward G. Robinson in *Little Caesar* or James Cagney in *The Public Enemy*. However, his lack of restraint, his belligerence in the face of rejection and his almost childlike sulkiness at the end of the film undercuts any mythic or tragic status he might have – a fact that situates him firmly within the narrative of the British, rather than the Hollywood, gangster. The last scenes of Shand in the back of the car being driven to what we presume is his death resonate with an audience not because we delight in his downfall nor because we share in his fear but because we sympathise with his position.

The British gangster of the 1980s reflected the changes that were happening in the wider society and to cinema itself, as images of the free market and of individual greed were both detailed and lampooned. Albert Spica, in *The Cook, The Thief, His Wife and Her Lover* stands as the ultimate symbol of Thatcherite excess and conspicuous consumption; and yet, interestingly for us, Spica is also a gangster, a criminal masquerading as businessman and restaurateur. In Greenaway's film the greed of the gangster is corporealised and transformed into the greed of the glutton. Spica's criminality however is symbolic of a larger tendency in the 1980s mindset, the target for Greenaway's satire is not the minority criminal element but the prevailing socio-political zeitgeist encouraged by Thatcherite economic policy. *The Cook, The Thief, His Wife and Her Lover* shows the flexibility of the crime film as it blends elements of art house cinema, social satire, gangster movie and love story. This genre mixing is endemic to the British gangster film which has always borrowed from other cultures and other forms whether that is Hollywood or art-house.

Robert Warshow's essay on the American gangster both galvanised and limited the study of crime films. Although Warshow deals primarily with American society, especially of course the immediate post-war period, he uses the term 'gangster' in a universal sense and, very often, this is how it is still used. As this chapter has attempted to show, 'gangsterism' can also be regional and national and, as an image, the gangster allows entry into the specific anxieties, fears and desires of a country or population. For Warshow, the American gangster was a mythical construct, divorced from the everyday reality of crime and conceived along more poetic lines: 'The real city... produces only criminals; the imaginary city produces the gangster.' The Hollywood gangster is both whom we fear and who we want to be.[48]

As we have seen, the British gangster is a more culturally diverse character than his American cousin, one who connects many different narrative traditions at once. We certainly see reflections of the Hollywood archetype – the tragic anti-hero on an inevitable path to destruction and death – but we also see semi-comic inflections that have their roots in the nineteenth-century penny dreadfuls and journalistic accounts, such as Henry Mayhew's portraits of pickpockets, thieves and burglars in the fourth volume of his London Labour and the London Poor or the seedier side of Dickens' Sketches by Boz in which he describes the streets of London as having 'just enough damp... to make the pavement greasy, without cleansing it of any of its impurities'.[49] The British gangster film also slots into the visual tradition of social satirists such as Hogarth and George Cruikshank whose characters are both figures of revulsion and of derision. It is hard to assert that characters such as Harry Flowers, Vic Dakin or Harold Shand are the existential archetypes of Warshow's essay. Instead, they represent something more absurd, more comic than tragic, and audiences are harder on them, mixing fear and awe with derision and pity. One of the reasons why The Long Good Friday has been canonised by subsequent generations is surely Shand's failure to recognise his own comic absurdity; he may believe that he is bigger, harder and meaner than the Mafia but the audience knows better – he is the typical British underdog.

From its beginnings in the post-war period to the epic violence of The Long Good Friday, the British gangster film has always adapted itself to the surrounding social milieu. Very often it has none of the mythic quality of its Hollywood counterpart and is certainly lacking in the budget or the star names. However, it also avoids the sentimentality of the Hollywood film and, aside from a few exceptions, tends to resist the glamorisation of its violence. Death in the British gangster film is brutal and ugly and retribution is often quick.

FOOTNOTES

26. Morton, J., 2003, p.151.

27. Murphy, R., 1999, p.152.

28. Spicer, A., 2001, p.136.

29. Durgnat, R., 'Some Lines of Inquiry into Post-war British Cinema', in Murphy, R. (ed.), *The British Cinema Book*, 3rd Edition, London: Palgrave Macmillan, 2009, p. 255.

30. Murphy, 1992, p.157.

31. Vesselo, A., "Films of the Quarter", in *Sight and Sound*, Autumn, 1947, p.42.

32. Christopher Isherwood, cited in Kynaston, D., *Austerity Britain, 1945- 1951*, London: Bloomsbury Publishing, 2008 p. 191.

33. Chibnall, S., *Brighton Rock*, London: I.B. Tauris, 2005, p.82.

34. Chibnall, 2005, p.74.

35. Warshow, R., 'The Gangster as Tragic Hero', in Silver, A. and James Ursini (eds), *Gangster Film Reader*, New Jersey: Limelight Editions, 2007, pp.11-19.

36. Shadoian, J., 2003, pp.3-28.

37. Shadioan, 2003, p.236.

38. French, P., *Sight and Sound*, Spring, 1971, p.67.

39. MacCabe, C., *Performance*, London: BFI Publishing, 1998, p.42.

40. Dave, P., *Visions of England: Class and Culture in Contemporary Cinema*, London: Berg, 2006, p.103.

41. Walker, A. *National Heroes: British Cinema in the 70's and 80's*, London: Chambers, 1985.

42. Quart, L. 'The Religion of the Market: Thatcherite Politics and the British Film of the 1980s' in Friedman, L. (ed.), *Fires Were Started: British Cinema and Thatcherism*, London: Wallflower, 2007, p.22.

43. Hill, J., *British Cinema in the 1980s*, London: Clarendeon Press, 1999, p.167.

44. See Rockett, K., L. Gibbons and J. Hill, *Cinema and Ireland*, London: Taylor and Francis, 1987.

45. Conservative Party Manifesto, 1979, p.1.

46. McIlroy, B., 'The Repression of Communities: Visual Representations of Northern Ireland during the Thatcher Years', in Friedman, 2006, p.81.

47. Brundson, C., 2007, p.194.

48. Warshow, 1948/2007, p.13.

49. Dickens, C., Sketches by Boz, Oxford: Oxford University Press, 1837/2007, p.13.l Chibnall, S., 'Travels in Ladland: the British Gangster Film Cycle, 1998-2001', in Murphy, R. (ed.), *The British Cinema Book*, London: BFI Publishing, 2001, pp.375-386.li Chibnall, 2001, p.376.

CHAPTER TWO: THE POST-MILLENNIAL GANGSTER FILM

Essex Boys (2000)

Steve Chibnall, in his now ubiquitous essay 'Travels in Ladland: The British Gangster Film Cycle 1998-2001' describes what was a veritable renaissance in the gangster narrative throughout the latter years of the twentieth century as films such as *Lock, Stock and Two Smoking Barrels, Circus* (2000), *Going Off Big Time* (2000) and *Love, Honour and Obey* reinvented and recycled the gangster image for a post-feminist audience, creating a cinema that was rooted more in the criminal activity of 1978 than 1998.[50] As Chibnall says:

> While drug trafficking, money laundering, counterfeiting, forgery, VAT fiddling, vehicle theft and illegal immigration are now the most preferred forms of activity among criminal gangs, British crime films remain preoccupied with protection rackets, armed robbery and unregulated betting and boxing.[51]

For Chibnall, gangster films of the '90s and early 2000s can be split into two basic types: Gangster Heavy and Gangster Light. The former was akin to the realist-based British gangster films of the past; movies like *Gangster Number One, Face* (1997) and *Sexy Beast* offered harsh, gritty narratives that owed a great deal to the mythic lore of the East End underworld and the classic crime film of Hollywood. Gangster Light, however, for Chibnall, was a more comedic affair; it presented its audiences with a faux-criminality that referenced canonical British texts of the '60s and '70s (*Get Carter, Performance* and so on) but had none of their seriousness or gravitas. Films in the Gangster Light mode, exemplified by the output of Guy Ritchie, represented a flowering of late 1990s New Lad culture and mixed a mock-masculinity with decontextualised and heavily edited images of England's cultural and criminal past. Shotguns, greyhound tracks, dog fighting and references to the 'golden era' of the Krays and the Richardsons provided the basic language of these films as they revelled in an ironic and deliberately cartoonish vision of criminal England. Chibnall makes the prescient point that such images added to the cult feeling of such films, as in-jokes and shared cultural references provided points of intertextuality for audiences versed in pre-1980s British cinema. Gangster Light, as some commentators have suggested, was also an inherently conservative grouping of texts that self-consciously constructed a world that was, for the most part, devoid of any meaningful multicultural exchange, positive depictions of women or real human emotion.[52] These films tended to be fast paced, purposefully one dimensional and self-consciously visually and aurally stimulating.

Chibnall's essay is a valuable one in understanding the subtle changes of form the gangster movie took over the millennium. However, since 2000 there has been an explosion of films that disrupt and complicate the simple delineation between his two categories. These films' use of music and editing places them in a history of Gangster Light but their themes and characterisations also reflect its heavier form. We must therefore be careful not to be too rigid in applying Chibnall's taxonomy or extend its use much beyond the textual bounds the author himself sets. To Gangster Heavy and Gangster Light, then, I am proposing a further, much more flexible and changeable form that I have termed 'the post-millennial' gangster film.

The protagonist of the post-millennial gangster film (with a few notable exceptions) comes not from the ranks of the Mafioso or the well-organised criminal fraternity but from the door of the nightclub or the big city back street. They are small time operators or part of a close-knit street crew and unlike their more ethical forebears (admittedly an elastic concept when dealing with crime), their main source of income is drugs usually, but not exclusively, cocaine. Their on-screen violence is often more graphic and detailed than the Modernist period we examined in Chapter One and has none of the balletic quality of the 1970s Hollywood films. It is hard, fast and brutal. The post-millennial gangster film has in more recent years begun to examine street and knife crime and the gangsters themselves have become ever younger, as the surrounding society seeks to come to terms with widely disseminated images of youth gangs and rioting.

This chapter looks at the sons, daughters and even grandchildren of gangsters like Harold Shand and Jack Carter and asks how they fit in with the story of British cinema. What emerges is a depiction of gang culture that is tinged with issues of class, race and gender as British cinema seeks to represent a society shaped by changes in Government, socio-economics and (as the first decade of the new millennium progressed) increasing anxieties over issues such as knife crime, immigration and youth violence.

LOVE HONOUR AND OBEY – 'THAT'S THE THING ABOUT GANGSTERS: WE'RE ALL PERFORMERS'

Ray Burdis and Dominic Anciano's *Love, Honour and Obey* is a good example of what Steve Chibnall refers to as Gangster Light. Funded by the BBC and featuring a coterie of British stars including Sadie Frost, Jude Law and Ray Winstone, it is at once a gangster movie featuring a fairly familiar narrative of inter-gang rivalry and, at the same time, a postmodern statement on performance and identity. Critical opinion however has not been kind to Burdis and Anciano's film: Brian Mcfarlane called it 'appalling[ly] cartoonish', Nick James suggested that it was 'gloriously and publicly inept' and Alexander Walker declared that it constituted 'a scandalous deployment of public revenues' in reference to the fact that the BBC backed its production with licence fee money.[53] However, as it shall be argued here, much of this criticism can be put down either to its failure to conform to existing generic models or to the affront felt by some towards its self-reference, making it a film that is both ironic and flawed in equal measure. In the context of the evolving story of the British crime film, however, it provides us with an interesting turning point: the point at which the gangster film became big business for the British film industry and that, perhaps for the first time since the 1950s, began again to be produced in large numbers.

Love, Honour and Obey deconstructs the rigidity of a concept like genre because it is, at once a crime film – detailing fairly familiar themes like honour, pride, and greed – and an absurdist comedy that features improvised scenes bordering on the farcical and the crude. Each actor is referred to by their first name (Ray, Jude, Jonny, Sadie, etc.) and their on-screen character closely matches their mediated celebrity persona: we are never sure if we are watching the character, the actor, the celebrity or a mixture of all three. The result of this blurring of identities and roles problematises the suspension of disbelief that we usually experience when watching a crime film; we are acutely aware that what we are witnessing are performances - actors playing gangsters rather than gangsters themselves. The subtle process then of being asked to participate in a drama is replaced by the sense that we are voyeurs to an artificial construction, a make-believe rather than 'real-life'. The Russian Formalist critics of the 1920s termed this technique 'baring the device' and it would later form a large part of Brechtian theatre.

The sense of simulacrum, of a narrative based on other texts rather than reality, has been at the root of much of the criticism aimed at Gangster Light generally and of *Love, Honour and Obey* specifically. Critics like Paul Dave see in the film's vision of an exciting but grimy underworld a middle class wallowing in the baser parts of working class existence; a form of cinematic slumming whereby rich film producers, directors and actors assume 'mockney' personae and develop a faux gangster-ness that merely reproduces existing stereotypes and 'provides a problematic vision of unreconstructed working-class man'.[54] The Gangster Light of the late 1990s, he states, harks back to the more reassuring masculinity of the 1960s and '70s and its treatment of racial and gender politics is uncomplicated by considerations of political correctness or sexual equality. It is also self-consciously mythologising, revelling in bad behaviour and outmoded social assumptions.

Dave's criticism is convincing but it misses the generic specificity of the gangster film and its place within British cultural history. There is no doubt that the characters of Gangster Light are grotesques, they are intentionally one-dimensional and picaresque, existing somewhere between folklore and caricature. However condemning them for this misses the essential relationship between the gangster film and the real-life gangster, one that has always been a two way process of influence. Burdis and Anciano's film continues a theme begun with Cammell and Roeg's *Performance*: that the gangster, especially the British gangster, is as much a performer as he is criminal. We saw the flowering of this with The Krays in the 1960s but, by the year 2000, with high profile gangsters such as Lenny McLean, Mad Frankie Fraser and Charlie Kray publishing autobiographies and appearing on chat shows and in films, the line between the gangster and the celebrity became inextricably blurred. Gangland biographies, for example, read more like a Guy Ritchie script than a Social Realist crime film of the 1950s; their narratives are self-mythologising and often unapologetic as they depict a gangland every bit as consciously constructed as *Snatch*. The inclusion of many famous villains in Guy Ritchie's films and the many famous faces in *Love, Honour and Obey* further complicates the dividing lines between art, life and gangland folklore.

Britain, in the late 1990s, sought to reinvent itself in the wake of the New Labour victory of 1997 and, as Andrew Marr details, 'Tony Blair arrived in power... in a country spangled and sugarcoated by a revived fashion for celebrity'.[55] As Michael Foley details the Blair administration was seen as inherently presidential, a concept that not only suggests a personalisation of the decision-making process but an increasing reliance on image and celebrity.[56] The confidence with which New Labour suggested it could lead Britain into the twenty-first century can be seen to be reflected in the cocky swagger of the protagonists of Gangster Light. Crime films became increasingly slick, fast paced and set to a modern soundtrack that was as important to the experience of the film as the narrative or characterisation.

Films like *Snatch* and *Lock, Stock and Two Smoking Barrels* used their soundtracks not only to suggest mood or to underline a narrative point but as a foreground to the visuals; like a pop video, sound and vision have equal importance in a film that asks only to be looked at and enjoyed. Compare this to the use of Roy Budd's music in *Get Carter*, a score that begins by mimicking the rattle of the train tracks and punctuates the narrative throughout with dissonant chords played on the zither; or Francis Monkman's electronic score for *The Long Good Friday* that exists as a suggestive counterpoint to the narrative, highlighting and underpinning the emotions the audience experiences but always in a supporting role to the visuals. Like the use of hip–hop in the New Black Realism of the 1990s, Gangster Light employed contemporary bands and popular songs to not only add colour to the visuals but to appeal to a specific audience – the soundtrack to the lives of the protagonists becomes the soundtrack to the life of the audience member. Again, as

Chibnall suggests, this underpins Gangster Light's modes of consumption that were, by and large, based on communality over individuality and the experience of domestic DVD viewing rather than cinema going.

Like its other aspects, the soundtrack to *Love, Honour and Obey* toys with the boundaries of traditional mainstream cinema by continually erasing the distinction between diegetic and non-diegetic sound. In the final climactic scenes set at Ray's wedding, Matthew (played by Rhys Ifans, not using his real name) begins by listening to Oasis' *Force of Nature* through headphones in readiness for his assault on the wedding party and on Jonny (Jonny Lee Miller) in particular. Here it is his sonic experience that we share, knitting the audience into a subjective soundscape. However, this diegetic use of sound is quickly turned into a non-diegetic one as it takes on the more familiar cinematic role of punctuating and highlighting the excitement of the narrative. The change from one state into the other is signalled by an alteration in the quality of the sound itself as the tininess of the Walkman's headphones is replaced by the high fidelity of a modern filmic soundtrack. Aural theorist Michel Chion uses the term 'acousmatic' to describe scenes like these; an audience initially sees the source of the sound but then this visual cue is removed foregrounding the artificial nature of the cinematic text and exposing the film to be a constructed reality.[57] We see the same in moments where, for example, we are presented with a character talking on camera only for their voice to then act as a voice-*over* for another scene.

Love, Honour and Obey, however, also uses music in the opposite way as an obviously pre-recorded soundtrack to sporadically punctuate the narrative. Throughout the film, each of the major characters is shown singing to a karaoke backing-track, or rather we might say (tellingly) *miming* to a karaoke backing-track. This not only adds to the sense of postmodern self-reflexivity, once again prompting the identities of the actors and the characters to become blurred, but also allows the songs themselves to switch from diegetic to non-diegetic as they serve as the soundtrack for successive scenes. The central metaphor of karaoke again evokes the theme of identity confusion and performance and erases the distinction between what is inside and what is outside the narrative. It also serves to humanise the central characters as the gulf between their leisure activities and their violent working practices becomes apparent. As Jonny first sees Ray singing in the club he is advised that 'Nothing comes before the karaoke', a statement on the nature of the gangster-performer if ever there was one: nothing comes before the performance, all is performance in this tale of wannabe stars and wannabe criminals.

Gangster Light, unlike its heavier cousin, sets up a virtual gangland that exists beyond time and space. Although set in the present day and in fairly recognisable British cities (London, for example, in *Love, Honour and Obey*, Brighton in *Circus*, Cardiff in *Rancid Aluminium* (2000)) the environments and visual references are drawn from the genre's past rather than contemporary real-life locations, as Chibnall asserts:

Locations are chosen for their generic suggestiveness rather than their specificity of place. This gives the *mise-en-scène* a pared down minimalist feel that separates it from most London films and contributes to the sense that we are witnesses to an urban folk tale. Instead of expansive tourist vistas, we are shown the more claustrophobic village London of television's *Minder* (1979–94) a world of minicabs and sex-shops, spielers and lock-ups…[58]

Chibnall's ideas relate only partly to *Love, Honour and Obey* that depicts a variety of different settings and thus a variety of different Londons: from the impressive vista seen from the windows of the gangland boss' office to the dingy interiors and backstreets of the cocaine deal venues. London is not only depicted as a gangster's playground, with its associated pubs, clubs, and garages, but also as a place where families lead ordinary domestic lives, once again undercutting the seriousness of the crime drama and suggesting a more postmodern self-reflexive project. The criticism levelled at many of the Gangster Light films – that they depict 'an almost Dickensian vision of a city gone to seed, surviving as a grown up playground for hustlers adept at "picking peanuts out of poo"' – is untrue of *Love, Honour and Obey* as it sets its action in a series of socially varied environments that, together, form a fairly faithful representation of contemporary London.[59] The scenes set in Ray's lock-up, or the fire fight at the film's conclusion are arguably its most 'Dickensian' locations; however these are constantly opposed with scenes set in ordinary domestic houses, back gardens, suburban streets and even a supermarket car park. The overall impression of *Love, Honour and Obey* then is of the gangster as father and family man as well as hard man and criminal.

If the more well known texts of Gangster Light (*Snatch* and *Lock, Stock and Two Smoking Barrels* especially) present worlds that are inherently homosocial, the gang coming before any female or heterosexual relationship, in *Love, Honour and Obey* the opposite is true. Throughout the narrative, the masculinity of the gang is constantly enhanced by the relationships they have with women: Ray and his wife Cathy's (Kathy Burke) relationship, for example, although mostly played for comic effect, is both touching and two dimensional as they struggle to overcome his impotence using a variety of different means. Cathy is at times understanding, at others frustrated, but they both deal with the matter in their separate ways (Ray talking with the others in the gang; Cathy suggesting a sex counsellor). This subtlety is not present in any of the classical British gangster films except perhaps (as we have seen) *Villain*.

The relationship between the professional and personal life of the gang member is exemplified in a montage that occurs around an hour into the film. After being taken by the South London mob, Bill (William Scully) and Fat Alan (Perry Benson) are beaten and tortured in a scene that is disturbing as it is violent. Bill escapes the torture room (incidentally yet another suburban house on an ordinary street) by biting the neck of one of the opposing gang members and jumping out of the window to the bemusement of the workaday neighbours. This scene, that reminds us of a similar one in *Get Carter*, is intercut with shots of Ray and Sadie talking in their well maintained back garden after a domestic argument. Again, these snapshots of a gangster's home life are tender and believable as the older man seeks the forgiveness of the younger woman until they finally make-up to the coos and sighs of their watching family. The homosocial masculinity so endemic to the British crime film is set aside for a moment and Ray becomes an ordinary fiancé apologising to a loved one. Again, sound is used to draw the two scenes together as Laila (Laila Morse), Ray's sister, is heard to say 'Look, he is just like all the geezers, his bark's worse than his bite' at the exact moment we hear the animalistic sounds of Bill sinking his teeth into the jugular vein of the rival gang member; men are revealed to be both animals and romantics in equal measure.

Love, Honour and Obey, then, constructs but then unravels the myth of the gangster so important to Gangster Light, on the one hand playing on and clearly aping the image of the hard man but on the other suggesting that this could be just a front, a façade for a more human, softer core. Women, although contingent to the narrative, are an important part of this process. Unlike many crime films of both the Gangster Light and Heavy variety, the female characters extend beyond the stereotypes of stripper, nagging wife or prostitute and, whilst their presence does at times interrupt the masculine bond of the gang, this is more productive than problematic as the gangsters are shown up to be men merely playing games of war.

Gangster Light, as a term, is both useful and misleading when viewing the British crime film. It does offer us a way of categorising and classifying a group of films that were made whilst Britain was riding high on the back of a new government and happily exporting its cultural goods abroad. It also serves to distinguish a group of films that played with the generic conventions of the crime film and that referenced, but did not necessarily follow, the feel of their older, more established counterparts. However, we must be careful not to use the term too freely. A film like *Snatch* for example, easily fits the various elements of Gangster Light (comedy, pastiche, British crime simulacra, the use of music and so on), however many of the others in the genre do not; it is more difficult to state with any certainty that a film like Rob Walker's *Circus*, with its homage to classic American film noir and its strangely avant-garde *mise-en-scène* is even in the same tradition as Guy Richie's work at all, much less thought of as part of the same cycle.

Love, Honour and Obey both fits and deconstructs the concept of Gangster Light. It certainly 'approach[es] criminal violence with comedic intent' and offers a postmodern, self-reflexive vision of gangland and its culture.[60] However it is also a statement on celebrity, a successful examination of the dividing line between myth and reality, an experiment in film form (especially the use of sound and vision) and a self-indulgent exercise in improvisation and the relationship between on and off screen personae.

In his chapter on the relationship between contemporary British film and American funding, Nick James bemoans what he sees as the gangster movie bandwagon that occurred at the turn of the century.[61] Following on the coattails of *Lock, Stock and Two*

Smoking Barrels and perhaps the earlier *Shallow Grave* (1994) and *Trainspotting* (1996), in the late 1990s and early 2000s it was certainly chic to be criminal. However, as has been argued here, these texts (that were largely ignored or even derided in their time) can yield up interesting information about the period in which they were produced and the genre that they both draw from and attempted to break down. Many of these films may not be considered classics of the form but this fact alone means that they are often deeply rooted in their time, allowing us access into the values of the film-makers and their audiences. If nothing else, they exist as texts in the world and so should be studied and considered along with other, more canonised works.

We see a diminishing number of mainstream films that could be considered Gangster Light after 2001; mainly, we could assert, due to an increasing weariness on the part of a public for its generic type, or perhaps an increased wariness on the part of funders (be they private or public) after a run of critical and commercial failures. After a number of high profile critical duds like Dave Stewart's Lottery funded *Honest* (2000), a film that was pulled even before its general release, and Edward Thomas' Wales-based *Rancid Aluminium*, producers were less likely to fund big money projects about crime and the crime film was relegated to the cheaply produced straight-to-DVD market. However, as we shall see in the next section, these films too have a part to play in the story of British crime cinema as they fused much of Gangster Light's postmodern, sexy *mise-en-scène* with the seriousness and grittiness usually associated with the classic period. These post-millennial gangster films are more problematic than those produced in the 1990s and early 2000s; they have a moral bleakness and a cynicism to them that is, at times, unsettling and unattractive. They have their roots in a definite stream of British culture that again stretches back to Dickens and the Victorian melodrama. However rather than the semi-comic overtones of Fagin or Mr Macawber, we are presented with the sexual violence of Bill Sykes.

ESSEX BOYS, RISE OF THE FOOTSOLDIER, BONDED BY BLOOD – A TALE TOLD THREE WAYS

On 17 December 1995, in a secluded country lane in Rettendon Essex, three men – Pat Tate, Tony Tucker and Craig Rolfe - were found dead in a Range Rover in what was to become known as the Essex Boy murders. The full significance of this event would only later become apparent when it was linked to the recent high profile death of teenager Leah Betts who had died only a month earlier after allegedly taking Ecstasy. The Essex Boys case has since spawned four films, numerous books and countless newspaper and magazine articles. Its mixture of drug-fuelled violence and small town glamour can still be felt today in contemporary crime cinema, where the highly stratified hierarchy of the 1970s and early '80s gangster film has slowly given way to a genre that examines the fine lines that exist between gangland and clubland and between the underworld and mainstream societies.

The real Essex Boys story has all the ingredients of a Jacobean or Shakespearean tragedy and needs very little in the way of dramatic enhancement; three small town gangsters became embroiled in a plan to import a large quantity of drugs from abroad unaware that they are secretly being set-up by an associate in return for making death threats against him. Contemporary news articles and subsequent factual accounts suggest that the gang, who worked as doormen but who also dealt in Ecstasy and cocaine, suffered from that most classical of crimes, hubris, as they gradually span out of control on a diet of drugs, steroids, money, and reputation. Local rivals Michael Steele and Jack Whomes were later convicted for the murders although both strenuously denied the charges. In all four films detailing the case their deaths are seen as necessary revenge by an increasingly intolerant underworld that took steps to police itself and to remove unwanted characters from its midst.

The murders of Tate, Tucker and Rolfe inspired films that sit neither with the fanciful imagery of Gangster Light, nor with the semi-mythical realism of Gangster Heavy. Terry Windsor's *Essex Boys*, the first of the films that would deal with the incident, is both violent and non-naturalistic, the narrative situated somewhere between docu-drama and film noir. Borrowing heavily from the Hollywood crime movie, Windsor's film plays with the truth and manipulates reality so that the line between what is factual and what is fictional becomes hard to discern.

The three Essex Boys films produced between 2000 and 2010 allow us insights into how the same basic story can be presented in three distinctly different ways.[62] As Andrew Spicer details, Windsor's film is the most visually stylistic and cinematic of these works and, both in its *mise-en-scène* and in its characterisation of the femme fatale, is more reminiscent of 1940s Los Angeles than mid-1990s Southend.[63] The film employs considerable artistic licence at its conclusion, transforming a heavily masculine storyline of gangland violence into a noir-esque tale of female manipulation and revenge, as the partner of Pat Tate, one of the murdered men, is revealed to be the mastermind behind the killings.

Of the four films, *Essex Boys*, had the widest release; produced by the television company Granada it was distributed initially by Miramax, the major independent, and Buena Vista Home Video, the adult arm of the Disney Corporation. Such a pedigree, and the bankable name of Sean Bean, might have suggested that it was destined for a wider release than it actually got; it opened on 54 screens in the UK, grossing an opening revenue of only £111,548. Many contemporary British critics missed the film's attempts to situate itself alongside film noir rather than the British gangster film, typical of which is Keith Perry in *Sight and Sound*:

> Windsor's refusal to invest his characters with any degree of psychological complexity ironically secures his film a distinct place in the roll call of British gangster movies.
>
> The Essex locations - its sand flats and marshlands - are as well chosen as the grotty

northern locales of *Get Carter* (1971). Even Jason's scheming wife Lisa (the equine Alex Kingston) is as much Essex girl as femme fatale.

But ultimately *Essex Boys* is depressingly similar to the two film versions of '70s television police series *The Sweeney*.[64]

Essex Boys is self-consciously noir inspired. Although Perry here references the femme fatale of the American genre, he situates Windsor's film in a British rather than a transatlantic tradition, missing the main textual aims of the film itself. Perry also confuses form and location; it is little wonder that a film called *Essex Boys*, that details the rise and fall of notorious gangsters in Southend would be set in the grotty sandflats and marshlands of that county. However, in its structure and its placement of characters it is clearly closer to *Double Indemnity* (1944) than *The Sweeney*.

2007's *Rise of the Footsoldier*, a film based on the autobiographies of Carlton Leech is arguably a more traditional gangster film than *Essex Boys*. As the title suggests, it charts the rise of a gang member from the football terraces of West Ham United to the clubs of the West End and from there to gangland. If contemporary reviews of *Essex Boys* were sometimes begrudgingly positive about its cinematography and performances then they were almost unilaterally damming about *Rise of the Footsoldier*'s mixture of realism and masculine ultra-violence. Phillip French in *The Observer* called it 'an ugly story of sadistic, foul-mouthed psychopaths, and singularly unilluminating' and suggested that it can be read in the tradition of Martin Scorsese's *Goodfellas* whereas *The Guardian*'s Peter Bradshaw asked 'do we really need another fatuous, naïve, violent, Groucho-club-mockney-geezer fantasy on the same subject? [as *Essex Boys*].'

Of course, what both critics fail to grasp here is the distinction between the Gangster Light of the 1990s and the post-millennial gangster film of 2007. Whereas, indeed, films like *Circus*, *Rancid Aluminium* and *Snatch* could be seen to fit in with the concept of faux-gangsterness (what Bradshaw calls a 'Groucho-club-mockney-geezer fantasy') this can hardly be used as a term to describe *Rise of the Footsoldier*. Not only is *Rise of the Footsoldier* based on true events, it clearly goes to great lengths to ensure that these are told in as direct a way as possible, sometimes shockingly so. Autopsy and crime scene photographs were used to lend similitude to some of the scenes, especially those in the mortuary and the Range Rover, and Carlton Leach himself appears part way through to lend an authenticity to the film. The murders here are used as a climax to a clubland culture that has spiralled out of control; although there is a glamorisation of violence it is also depicted as being inevitably linked to death, paranoia and domestic unhappiness.

Carl Neville is correct in suggesting that *Rise of the Footsoldier* should be seen as being a part of a more recent attempt to depict the anxieties and frustrations of a post-Thatcherite working-class that reveals 'the desire for radical social change, for the release of pent up energies, on the one hand, and the catastrophic effect of what you have brought down upon yourself on the other'.[65] The central characters in *Rise of the*

Footsoldier exemplify the contemporary cult of the gangster, enshrined in the popular imagination through books like Leech's own or those of Bernard O'Mahoney and television programs like Kate Kray's *Hard Bastards* and Danny Dyer's *Deadliest Men*. Whereas more traditional gangster figures like The Krays tended, when under the glare of the public gaze, to downplay their criminality and their violence, contemporary gangland focuses on this, playing-up the hyper-masculine aspects of its culture in a heavily mediated form of contemporary gang folklore. It is difficult not to see in the condemnatory words of the film's mostly middle class critics a reflection of the same distrust and disgust of working class culture that prompted negative reactions against crime films of the post-war period.

Rise of the Footsoldier also once again highlights the generic instability of the contemporary British gangster film. At times it reminds us of the classic Hollywood movie with both Phillip French and Carl Neville noticing its debt to Scorsese; however its *mise-en-scène* meanders between the blue and green filtered colourisation of the modern horror film and the starkness of documentary realism. We can also note, especially in the early sections that detail Leech's involvement with the football gang the Inner City Firm, the influence of Gangster Light and Guy Ritchie signified through the use of a loud soundtrack, face-paced editing and a voice-over narration.

The film borrows its aesthetic style from a number of different sources and nowhere is this more apparent than in the disturbing opening scene which draws heavily from US crime dramas such as *CSI* (2000–) and *The Wire* (2002–2008). Three bodies are laid out on the mortuary slab, their faces a mess of blood, bone and mangled flesh, beside them a mobile phone rings and a voice, that we later learn belongs to Leech, is heard. The nature of the scene is far from romanticised, the victims of the shooting are an age away from the stylised depictions of shootings in Scorsese or even recent Hollywood gangster movies, where shots are fired and blood is shed but the bodies of the victims remain unaffected by the force of the gun's blast. *Rise of the Footsoldier* presents the trauma of violence in its profound ugliness, as special effects are used not to fetishise and beautify the injured body (as it does in Scorsese, see for example *Raging Bull* (1980)) but to make it seem uncanny and beyond (or perhaps even beneath) human. The close resemblance of the victims' bodies in the film to the real life autopsy photographs that became widely available both online and in print after their deaths allows the viewer to become acutely aware of the sheer physical trauma of gangland violence which, on the whole, leaves the body broken and destroyed.

The most powerful example of the film's exploration of bodily trauma comes at its denouement, as Tate (Craig Fairbrass), Tucker (Terry Stone) and Rolfe (Roland Manookian) are shot by Steele (Billy Murray) and Whomes (Frank Harper) in the Range Rover. Although we are offered three possible endings to the narrative each culminates in a violence that is both visceral and sudden, as the director acutely avoids the clichés of the crime film and chooses instead to shoot the deaths in real time with no intrusive soundtrack or music. The lighting in these scenes is more reminiscent of contemporary horror than the gangster film, as the blue filter darkens the blood that sprays on the faces of the killers and stains the clothes of the victims. Again, Gilbey avoids the trap of glamorising either the victims or the killers, as the former die scared, in pain and traumatised and the latter are reduced to simple executioners with none of the mythologising gravitas associated with a St Valentine's Day Massacre or a *Godfather* hit. The violence at the end of *Rise of the Footsoldier* is brutal and raw but its brutality comes from the act itself, not from the camera or *mise-en-scène*.

The penultimate film to be born out of the Essex Boy murders was *Bonded by Blood*, produced in 2010 and directed by Sacha Bennett. If Terry Windsor's film drew from film noir and Julian Gilbey's from contemporary horror then Bennett's drew from the romance and the love story. The underworld dealings of Tate (Tamar Hassan), Tucker (Terry Stone) and Rolfe (Neil Maskell) are framed, in *Bonded by Blood*, by the growing relationship between Mike Steele (Vincent Regan) and Tate's girlfriend Kate Smith (Kierston Wareing), and it is this that provides the film with its tension and its narrative conclusion. Produced by Gateway Films who also produced *Shank* (2010) and *Anuvahood* (2011), *Bonded by Blood* not only continued the cycle of films dedicated to the Essex Boys story but also used many of the same actors in a process that, as Carl Neville states, has overtones of the B movie production houses of the 1930s and '40s. Many of the later films even reference the earlier ones in their advertising, as *Bonded by Blood* and 2013's *Fall of the Essex Boys* cite *Rise of the Footsoldier* on their DVD covers and promotional material. This set of films constitutes a cycle in the true sense of the word, as they each react to and are influenced by those that have gone before. United by a common narrative, however, they each also add a subtly different style and thus constitute a subtly different text.

In its use of music, lighting and cinematography *Bonded by Blood* reflects a more consistent aesthetic than *Rise of the Footsoldier* which is a more stylistically varied (perhaps even confused) text. The characters of Tate, Tucker and Rolfe in Bennett's film are merely generic types with none of the menace and threat of the earlier work; they are one dimensional and unapologetic about their actions. The *mise-en-scène* is slicker, the narrative faster and often complicated by the use of dream sequences that distance the audience from the plot. We see similar traits in earlier films like Julian Gilbey's *Rollin' With the Nines* (2006), Neil Thompson's *Clubbed* (2008), Alex DeRakoff's *Dead Man Running* (2009) and Robert Cavanah's *Pimp* (2010). This strain of post-millennial gangster film reminds us of the aesthetics of the video game, where lives are lost and violence is carried out but the moral dimensions of such actions are never explored. The ethical questions and moral positioning of *Rise of the Footsoldier* are neatly sidestepped by concentrating on the romance between Steele and Smith and the former is depicted as a knight in shining armour rather than a scared and desperate thug. The love story sweetens the sting of gangland violence but it also removes some the moral complexity as the deaths are seen not as the inevitable outcome of a drug culture for which society is also partly responsible but the result of an isolated and personalised situation. As viewers we are spared any complicity we might have with the narrative through the employment of a storytelling device.

If we compare the murder scenes from all three films we can detect how the same narrative can be played three entirely different ways. The Range Rover murders in *Essex Boys* are dramatically realised, with Darren Nicholls transported into the car itself (Nicholls claims he was, in fact, in another car waiting for Steele and Whomes), the shooting is quick and clean and although Tate is shot at close range by a 12 bore shotgun, Sean Bean's handsome face remains untouched as he slumps forward dead. As already discussed, the same scene in *Rise of the Footsoldier* is depicted with a much more visceral visual sense; not only is there blood, but the bodies of those shot are twisted and blown back with the force of the gun blast, their faces ripped open. In *Bonded by Blood*, the scene is more drawn out, the music more dramatic and Tate manages to remain defiant in the face of death; the plot to kill him switches from one based in gangland drug deals to one founded in romance and jealousy.

The three films we have looked at here present us with an interesting insight into the development of the post-millennial gangster film. Spanning ten years they chart the evolution of this most maligned of genres, from the postmodernity of the early 2000s to the cynicism and melancholy of the end of the decade. Each film borrows tropes from other genres and yet in each case presents the story in a fairly conventional way. We have the same characters, the same basic elements and even sometimes the same actors playing the roles; however, despite this, each film is noticeably different and clearly reflects the breadth that the British crime film can achieve. The post-millennial gangster film has production and consumption practises that differ notably from those of either Gangster Light or Gangster Heavy and therefore should be thought of as being intrinsically different in both construction and reception.

Ultimately, the popularity of the British gangster film continues to fuel its production. Films like *Pimp* (2010), *Dead Man Running* (2009), *Rollin' With the Nines* (2006) and *Clubbed* (2008) are made fairly cheaply for the DVD market rather than a wide theatrical release, a fact that inevitably affects their quality as texts for critical analysis. However, like the B movies of the 1940s, '50s and '60s, their sheer abundance makes them difficult to ignore, if not to take seriously. By and large these films (we can safely assume) are specifically designed to be consumed by men and their narratives and characterisations reflect this; their real-life models however, whether consciously or not, are quite clearly Tony Tucker, Pat Tate and Craig Rolfe, the victims in the Essex Boy killings.

I DAY, HARRY BROWN – STREET GANGS AND THE NEW BRUTALITY

The post-millennial gangster film, as we have seen, departs in crucial ways from that of Gangster Light and Gangster Heavy as outlined in Steve Chibnall's influential article. The slew of films that emanated from the Essex Boys case is representative of a style of film-making that has characterised a number of works since the turn of the century. As we have seen, these films are quickly produced, are often released straight to DVD and present audiences with a familiar set of aesthetic characteristics, thematic concerns and character types. They feature none of the postmodern self-awareness of the 1990s crime film and have been largely ignored by the vast majority of critical opinion that, presumably, sees them as either continuations of Gangster Light or manifestations of an unsavoury strain of unreconstructed male culture. Of course, whereas this latter point may well be true, the sheer numbers of these films mean that they need to be taken seriously as cultural artefacts, if not high art, in their own right.

A separate strain of film-making that has slowly emerged since 2000 has been concerned with depictions of the street gang. Although we can trace attempts to represent similar cultural anxieties and folk devils back to the early 1950s and '60s with films like *Cosh Boy, Serious Charge* (1959) and *The Frightened City* (1961), recent depictions of gang culture are problematised and complicated by high profile discussions in the popular media about the role of youth, race and poverty in the formation of contemporary social problems. Recent political and media-led discourse has tended to demonise and overstate the presence of gangs on Britain's streets, seeing in them embryonic beginnings of the widespread gang membership that characterises life on the streets of large American cities like LA and New York.

The media has tended to assume that British and European street gangs work along similar lines to their American counterparts and the cinema that depicts them has reflected this; British gang films like *I Day* (2009), *Bullet Boy* (2004), *Kidulthood, Adulthood* and *Life and Lyrics* (2006) have clear antecedents in the films of Spike Lee, John Singleton and Albert and Allen Hughes. As Paul Gormley suggests, films like *Menace II Society* (1993) and *Boyz n the Hood* (1991) are complicated texts that both challenge and uphold the stereotype of the young black American youth; on the one hand playing on the accepted image of the violent Afro-American gang member and, on the other, expressing and giving voice to social issues and concerns that are particular to that group (the tag line for *Menace II Society* for example was 'This is the truth, this is what's real').[66] As Gormley states, the New Black Realism drew attention to white cinema's inability to fully capture the inherent violence that was felt to be an everyday occurrence in places like Compton and the Bronx during the mid-1980s; such violence would eventually find its way into white cinema in the form of *Reservoir Dogs* (1992) and in what Gormley calls 'the 'hood films' of the late 1990s.[67]

Whereas the New Black Realism of the 1980s gained some of its power by accurately portraying the reality of gang life in large US cities, its British counterparts have often been criticised for drawing too heavily on these American models. Anthony Quinn in *The Independent*, for example, summed up what was a fairly widespread reaction to Penny

Woolcock's film of Birmingham gangland *1 Day*:

> Penny Woolcock's Birmingham-set drama seeks to meld the black gangsta flick with a hip-hop musical, which some will find a challenge.
>
> The one day in question finds Flash (Dylan Duffus), a drug dealer, desperately scouting the mean streets of Brum to raise a whole lot of 'scrilla' (cash) for his hot-out-of-jail boss. The street patois is at times incomprehensible, the plot is a joke and the music is absurdly aggressive, but there are good things too, including Duffus's brooding performance and an interesting sidelight on generational respect: the only person the gangs step back from is Flash's stern-faced, church-going nan (Monica Ffrench). Make this lady drugs czar now.[68]

What we notice in this review, and in similar ones like it, is the observation that the aesthetic of New Black Realism seems incongruous when applied to inner city locales in Great Britain. The gun crime, gang culture, hip-hop soundtrack and linguistic register of *Menace II Society*, for example, works because it is deeply rooted in the social milieu of LA or New York; as soon as it is translated into a British context it becomes disingenuous and false.

One notable scene in *1 Day* takes place in a local fast food restaurant: Flash (Dylan Duffus), a local gang leader and his crew, enter the restaurant only to elicit suspicious stares from the other, mainly white diners. In the background we can hear hip-hop music but it is never made explicit whether this is diegetic or non-diegetic. The members of the gang are aggressive to the assistant behind the counter as they order a series of individually tailored burgers, the air in the restaurant is instantly threatening and tense and clearly demarcated along racial lines. Once seated, the gang begin to talk loudly within earshot of the other diners; eventually one of them plays a tune on his phone and one of the raps that pepper the narrative begins:

> Oi, what you starin' at
>
> You don't like me cause I'm wearing black,
>
> You don't like me, I don't want to be hearing that,
>
> You don't like man cause I'm wearing black,
>
> Like woman, I don't mean to be rude,
>
> But you don't like me 'cause I'm eating food.

The lyrics of the song highlight the sense of the scene: that Flash and the other members of the gang are simply misunderstood by the rest of (mainly white, middle class) society. They may talk differently, they may have different priorities, they may look different but they are victims of a society that fosters a racial and criminal underclass and that bars certain sections of society from more legitimate socio-economic pursuits. The chorus of the song makes this explicit:

I'm gonna flip and I hate you

Trust me if you hate me then I hate you

No point in being fake too

Cause trust me if you hate me then I hate you.

The moral weight of scenes such as this in *I Day* are problematised by the director's own personal and cultural background; middle class, white and female, Woolcock only began work on the screenplay for her film after she was attacked by a street gang in North London, as she told BBC Birmingham:

> I was mugged violently late one night in North London. I struggled with the young man who punched me to the ground and kicked my head to get my handbag.
>
> He was prepared to hurt me but that was not his intention; he was doing a job, he just wanted my handbag. And I wanted to know who the hell he was and how he had ended up at a place where he thought it was acceptable to bash women in the middle of the night for 30 quid.[69]

I Day then began its life with an act of intimidation and much of this is carried over onto the screen. Although there is a clear distinction between Afro-Caribbean and gang culture (the church group is consciously contrasted with the street gang for example) the film does depict street gangs as being intimately connected with race and with blackness. Contemporary Afro-Caribbean society is depicted as either being rife with social problems (promiscuity, drugs, violence and crime) or its polar opposite (church going, preachy and paternal); both ends of the spectrum delineate it from white middle-class society, as the directorial gaze comes closer to social anthropology than the self-knowing portrayal of everyday life that characterises US New Black Realism. Portrayals of the Black and Asian gang experience in Britain are still predominately filmed by white directors (Richard Laxton's *Life and Lyrics*; Julian Gilbey's *Rollin' With the Nines*; Eran Creevy's *Shifty* [2008]; Matthew Hope's *The Veteran* [2011], etc.) and British cinema has yet to produce high profile Afro-Caribbean auteurs like Spike Lee, Albert Hughes and John Singleton. Black British directors have approached the subject of youth violence and crime but this has often been in the area of documentary (Black Audio Film Collective's *Handsworth Songs* (1986) for example) or as a background to a social realist narrative like Noel Clarke's *Kidulthood* and *Adulthood* (2008).

Since the mid-noughties there has been a sharp increase in the number of films that deal with youth violence and the image of the out of control teen. Beginning in France in the 1990s but carrying on into the new millennium, films like *La Haine* (1995), *Base Moi* (2000), *Ils* (2006) and *Marytrs* (2008) all deal with violence and terror as it relates to the younger generation and this has also been reflected in contemporary British cinema. Films like *F* (2010), *Eden Lake* (2008), *The Estate* (2011) and the aforementioned *Kidulthood* and *Shank* all deal with the disquieting concept of hoodie children taking over polite society.

Such films reflect the anxieties of a heavily mediated zeitgeist that constantly demonises its youth. Although such films are clearly closer to the truth of life on British streets than films that take New Black Realism as their model, they often draw upon surrounding fears however phantasmagorical they may be. The British Crime Survey (BCS) taken in 2010 reveals that public anxiety over the threat posed by teen gangs and street violence still persist despite a drop in the actual numbers of crimes reported. Twenty-six per cent of those surveyed for the BCS for example stated that 'teenagers hanging around on the streets' were a big anti-social problem in their area (note: there is no suggestion of a crime being committed, merely that teenagers are perceived as 'hanging around') whereas only 13 per cent worry about violent crime, 10 per cent worry about car crime and 10 per cent about burglary. The reality of the situation is that assaults by knife (clearly the biggest area of crime linked to the young and youth gangs) actually *fell* by 6% in 2010 and homicides fell by 16 overall from 102 in 2009 to 86 in 2010. Gun crime in England and Wales also is still very uncommon: in 2010 there were 40 deaths caused by a firearm.[70]

This is certainly not the situation portrayed in recent British cinema where the streets are reimagined as a wasteland of guns, violence and warring gangs. In Daniel Barber's 2009 film *Harry Brown*, for example, Michael Caine plays an aged SAS soldier who is held under siege on his estate from a group of violent teenage thugs. Contemporary reviews of the film praised Caine's performance and drew attention to the meta-textual nature of the narrative – the irony of Jack Carter being terrorised by a group of hooded gang members was not lost on audiences or critics. What characterised the film most however was its sense of melancholy and isolation, as Martin Ruhe's cinematography highlighted the maze-like quality of the inner city housing estate that is full of subways, tunnels and dark corners.

Harry Brown is an everyman and it is his isolation and frustration that we are made to feel, it is his fear that drives the narrative to its ultimate conclusion: a blood bath amid the red brick and underpasses of modern Britain. Harry's fear is used to justify his own extreme behaviour later on in the film as the old scared man turns vigilante in a criminal display that far outweighs that of the young people he fears so much.

In one particularly telling scene, Harry gazes out of a broken, fire stained window at a gang of youths massing below in an underpass. The camera cuts between Harry's point of view and Caine's own haggard and pained face as ominous music plays underneath the visuals. The gang of youths in the underpass engage in petty criminal behaviour (some pass drugs to each other, others intimidate a couple who walk past, others merely 'act up') until a gun is shown and the scene instantly becomes imbued with more seriousness and a sense of menace – all of which is registered on Harry's face as he stands in for the concerned eyes of the audience. The key element to this scene, the point of real tension, is not that the gang are engaging in potentially violent and criminal behaviour but the evocation of the relative social positions of the gang and the ageing and vulnerable Harry (who, of course, is our representative). It is clear here that it is the gang's world, their

49

streets, they are the comfortable ones, it is they who own the underpass that Harry is too scared to walk through even though not doing so will make him late for his hospital appointment. The gang here have become kings, they rule the estate and Harry can only stand and watch. He has lost all agency.

This is a noticeable shift from films like *Essex Boys* and the Modernist phase of the British gangster film where we have the clear delineation between two worlds – an underworld and a mainstream world. In films like *Harry Brown*, the underworld has now completely taken over mainstream society. Harry is caught between a lawless youth and an ineffectual and liberalised police service that can offer no help to the ordinary citizen; it is of course this that prompts the spiral into a greater and greater violence. *Harry Brown*, then, is also in the tradition of the revenge movie like *Death Wish* (1974) and *Falling Down* (1993) that have been seen as providing a voice for the 'silent majority' in contemporary western society and ipso facto a large part of mainstream cinema's core audience.

As has been argued already, *Harry Brown* (and films like it) can be read as both representative and productive texts; representative, in that they present the fears of society on screen for them to be worked through; and productive, in that they simultaneously encourage such fears in the first place adding to the paranoia and anxiety that, statistically at least, have no basis in fact. In this way, cinema can be seen as a publicly shared space where ethics can be negotiated and moral positions re-worked, as Wanda Teays suggests:

> Movies can be vital to our intellectual and moral development by offering us insights into the human condition and shining a light on the dilemmas we face.[71]

However, as in most films, the moral resolution of *Harry Brown* is complex and polyvocal. In the final scenes of the film, we are presented with a series of shots of Harry's estate in peaceful repose: children play, a postman delivers his letters, a mother walks along with her pram and the buildings of the estate, though stark and grey, harbour a strange calm as if after a storm. As we watch we hear the voice of the police commissioner commenting on the narrative we have just watched; he talks of the reduction in crime, the on-going fight against the criminals and the great strides that the authorities are making against gangs and youth offending. We then cut to Harry staring into the subway as if meeting his own destiny and the inference is clear: it is Harry's actions that allowed the area to live in peace, not the police's, his actions that restored law and order when it was threatened. The violent vigilante has won despite the ineffectual actions of the authorities.

Unlike the end of a Greek tragedy where the death of the protagonist removes the guilt by association attached to the audience, the ending of *Harry Brown* forces us to align with his position. Harry's survival at the end of the film's shoot out asks more questions than it answers and legitimates the violence that he uses against the local criminal gangs. The end image of him once again being able to walk into the subway is a morally complex one that problematises the ethical position of the film itself. Do we condemn or support

Harry? Is he a hero or a criminal? Is Harry's violence more or less justifiable than the gangs?

Neither *Harry Brown* nor *1 Day* are gangster films in the vein of *Brighton Rock* or *The Long Good Friday*. The gangs they depict and that form a central part of their narrative are looser; they are unorganised and are located in one specific geographic area. Rather than being centred on criminal activity as a business, the crimes committed tend to reflect their wider socio-economic position, and are petty in comparison with the large-scale concerns of the firms of the 1960s or the Mafiosi of America and Italy. The post-millennial gangster film reflects contemporary British gangland organisation which, as John Pitts outlines, is a much more ad hoc, fractured system than the regimented structures of the past.[72] As stated earlier, we must always be aware that images of contemporary gangland are both representative and productive, they both depict and create the fears and folk devils of modern society, allowing us insight into how we see ourselves. From the drug-fuelled excesses of the Essex Boys to the hooded teenagers of *Harry Brown*, gangs and all they stand for provide a constant fascination for modern British film-makers and their audiences. Gangs provide us with ready-made objects of fear and intimidation; they exist as semi-autonomous bodies that represent societies within societies. They have their own morality, their own support systems, their own modes of dress and their own codes of honour. They are strange and dark organisations that are also seem increasingly present in our very streets. Perhaps it is this that provides the key to their continuing place in cinema both in Britain and abroad. Gangs exclude us, excite us and terrorise us – is it our world or theirs?

FOOTNOTES

50. Chibnall, S., 'Travels in Ladland: the British Gangster Film Cycle, 1998-2001', in Murphy, R. (ed.), *The British Cinema Book*, London: BFI Publishing, 2001, pp.375-386.

51. Chibnall, 2001, p.376.

52. Chibnall, 2001; Monk, C., 'Monk in the '90s', in Murphy, R. (ed.), *British Cinema of the '90s*, London: BFI Publishing, 1999, pp.156-166; Dave, 2006.

53. McFarlane, B. 'The More Things Change…British Cinema in the '90s', in Murphy, 2001, p. 369; James, N., 'British Cinema's US Surrender – A View from 2001' in Murphy, 2001, p.22; Walker, A., cited in Chibnall, 2001, p. 380.

54. Church Gibson, P. cited in Dave, 2006, p.17.

55. Marr, A., *A History of Modern Britain*, London: Pan, 2009, p.514.

56. Foley, M. 'The Blair Presidency: Tony Blair and the Politics of Public Leadership', in Chadwick, A and R. Heffernan (eds), *The New Labour Reader*, London: Polity Press, 2003, p.276.

57. Chion, M., *Audio-Screen: Sound on Screen*, New York: Columbia University Press, 1990, pp. 71-72.

58. Chibnall, 2001, p.378.

59. Chibnall, 2001, p.378.

60. Chibnall, 2001, p.380.

61. James, 2001, p.22.

62. As of writing, the fourth Essex Boy film, *The Fall of the Essex Boys* (2012) has been released.

63. Spicer, A., *Film Noir*, London: Longman, 2002, p.200.

64. Perry, K. 'Essex Boys', in *Sight and Sound*, August, 2000.

65. Neville, C., *Classless: Recent Essays on British Film*, Winchester: Zero Books, 2010, p.43.

66. Gormely, P., *The New Brutality Film: Race and Affect in Contemporary American Cinema*, London: Intellect, 2005.

67. Gormely 2005, p.131.

68. Quinn, A., 'I Day', in *The Independent*, 6 November 2009.

69. Woolcock, P. 2009, 'I Day the movie – an interview with Penny Woolcock', available online at http://www.bbc.co.uk/birmingham/content/articles/2009/10/29/1day_interview_with_penny_woolcock_feature.shtml <accessed 06, 2012>.

70. The British Street Crime Survey, 2012, available online at http://www.homeoffice.gov.uk/science-research/research-statistics/crime/crime-statistics/british-crime-survey/ <accessed 06, 2012>.

71. Teays, W., *Seeing the Light: Exploring Ethics Through Movies*, London; Wiley Blackwell, 2012, p.13.

72. Pitts, J., *Reluctant Gangsters: The Changing Face of Youth Crime*, London: Willan, 2008.

CHAPTER THREE: THE HEIST

The League of Gentlemen (1960)

The heist film is a sub-genre that is both easily recognised and difficult to define. Allied to the gangster film, the war film and the film noir, its ingredients were set early on in its development and have remained reasonably stable ever since. Often featuring complicated plots, the heist movie is also about simple human emotions – pride, jealousy, paranoia, greed, lust – making it the cinematic descendent of the medieval morality play or the children's cautionary tale. The heist movie can be tragic (*The Town* (2010), *The Asphalt Jungle* (1950), *Face*) or it can be comic (*How to Steal a Million* (1966), *The Great St Trinians Train Robbery* (1959), *Topkapi* (1964)) it can be gritty and realistic (*Armoured Car Robbery* (1950), *The Killing* (1956), *Payroll* (1961)) or it can be cool, stylish and aspirational (*Ocean's 11* (1960/2001), *The Bank Job* (2008), *Croupier* (1998)); it has been used to discuss issues as wide ranging as Irish nationalism (*The Day They Robbed the Bank of England* (1960)), the failure of post-war masculinity (*The League of Gentlemen*) and the existential malaise of the middle classes (*Perfect Friday* (1970)). However, as we shall consider in this chapter, what lies at the heart of the heist sub-genre is not so much greed and avarice but a compulsion to play the game, to outwit the authorities and their technologies; in its purest form, the heist is about psychological rather than financial gain and more about reputation and ego than pounds, euros or dollars.[73]

Cinema has always had a fascination with crime and easy money. The earliest narrative fiction film, Edwin Porter's *The Great Train Robbery* of 1903 was a heist movie of sorts and, for an art form that was primarily designed to satisfy the desires and wishes of a largely impoverished population, the prospect of a sudden financial windfall, however illegal, must have been attractive. British cinema was no exception and early film-makers and producers such as Clarendon, Warwick Trading Company and the Hepworths were not averse to depicting diamond heists, bank jobs and train robberies as well as the more traditional fare of comedies, musicals and fantasies.

The heist movie, however, is more than a film about robbery and financial gain; it is a carefully constructed generic type that developed in the late 1950s and evolved from both Hollywood and European cinema. The image of the gentlemen crook, the jewel thief, or safe breaker who remains undetected whilst carrying out their crime is an important one in both English and French crime fiction with characters such as E.W. Hornung's Raffles and Maurice LeBlanc's Arsène Lupin being successfully translated from the printed word to the silver screen in the 1920s and 30s. As Alastair Phillips details, however, it was Jules Dassin's 1955 film *Du rififi chez les hommes*, more succinctly known as *Rififi*, that set the tone, structure and aesthetic for the heist thriller and ensured that it would become 'an international cinematic genre'. [74]

Rififi contains the three main narrative stages that will come to typify the heist thriller. As we shall see, these stages (that correspond roughly to the three acts of classical dramaturgy) although often varying in length, are present in most, if not all, heist thrillers and not only shape the audiences' expectations but propel the narrative forward. It is from these three basic elements that films as diverse as Steven Soderbergh's *Ocean's Eleven* and Gilliat and Launder's *The Great St. Trinian's Train Robbery* are formed, and yet within them there are a seeming endless number of variations. This makes the heist movie ideal when studying the workings of narrative and plot.

ACT ONE: THE PLAN

In the anatomy of the heist movie the plan is key. Like Hitchcock's famous MacGuffin, it is that which sets the narrative in motion, that motivates the characters and drives the plot, and yet ultimately it is merely a feint for the film's real concern: the relationship between the gang members. As Alastair Phillips details, the plan, and knowledge of it, is also that which ties the audience into the action and creates the specific emotional experience of the movie itself. Once the audience is familiar with the plan, they are mindful of how it can go wrong and how it can endanger the characters, setting up the tension that is so much a part of the genre.

The first Act, then, not only introduces us to the characters, their relationships and their environment (as with classical Aristotelian analysis) it also takes us through the plan and how it is to be carried out. In *Rififi* for example, the plan is subtly suggested through a series of 'trial runs' and reconnaissance exercises where Tony le Stephanoise (Jean Servais), the heist leader, and his gang formulate how they are going to rob a jewellery store. In the early Steve McQueen vehicle *The Great St. Louis Bank Robbery* (1959) the perpetrators discuss the heist and the movements of the beat policemen and security guards over a carefully prepared timetable that (we assume) will add a temporally-based tension later on in the narrative. In *The Italian Job*, the plan is partially explained through a series of semi-comic rehearsals where we are made aware of the dangers of the operation as well as the likelihood that things might go wrong ('You were only supposed to blow the bloody doors off!'); and, as we shall see, in Basil Dearden's *The League of Gentlemen*, there is a preliminary operation that, although not a blueprint for the final heist does allow the audience to see how the gang works together and thus how the robbery will be played out. Sometimes, as in Jim O'Connolly's 1963 British B movie *The Hi-Jackers*, the action starts *in media res* and we are presented with what turns out to be a merely a rehearsal for the major heist that will occur later on the film. Again however, straight away the audience is made complicit in the crime, a factor that shapes both the narrative and the viewer's experience of it.

The working of the gang is also explored in Act One, as they are first sourced and then assigned roles. We see this clearly in John Houston's *The Asphalt Jungle* (itself an obvious influence on Dassin's *Rififi*), as Doc Riedenschneider (Sam Jaffe), the brains behind the outfit, strives to find the suitable personnel for his perfectly planned heist. Much of the early part of the film is dedicated to this search as he interviews and assigned various roles to those taking part (the banker, the safecracker, the driver, the strong-arm and so on). The heist gang is a working unit where each man plays his part; it is the criminal equivalent of the division of labour and the success of the entire operation depends upon the skill and commitment of each member. The members of the heist gang are specialists and have clearly defined roles within the operation; as with *The Asphalt Jungle*, these roles are often hierarchised socially and financially with highly skilled jobs like the safecracker or the jelly-man commanding more respect and a bigger share of the pay-off than more lowly positions like the driver or the look out. As Fran Mason states:

> The heist gangster is just a hired hand, as alienated from gang labour as he is from social labour and the gang is no longer a substitute family that allows the gangster to escape from social alienation. The heist gang industrialises and corporatises the gangster, becoming a corporation in miniature. Individual desire, however, reasserts itself as soon as the heist is over...[75]

The heist gangster, then, is merely a cog in a wheel, a team-player and only in the third act, when the team breaks down, does he become an individual again.

Act One also introduces us to what is personally at stake in the heist. With notable exceptions (*Honest, How to Steal a Million, Perfect Friday*) the heist gang is primarily male and many early examples of the form centred the narrative around issues of the masculine decline that occurred as American and European societies attempted to assimilate large numbers of ex-service men after the class and gender shifts of the war. As we shall see, the 1950s and 60s heist gang was littered with broken men – the hen-pecked, the closeted, the redundant, the unemployable, the excluded and the emotionally disabled. Such social problems appear to legitimate and excuse the sometimes desperate foray into criminal activity. Unlike the gangster, who stands as a symbol of a willing flouting of society's rules, the heist gangster has been pushed into his criminality through circumstance, a point that makes them at once more human *and* more pathetic.

ACT TWO: THE EXECUTION

After the planning comes the execution. In films such as *Armoured Car Robbery, Rififi, Robbery, The Bank Job* and *Heist* (2001) the execution is central to the narrative structure and demands a reasonable percentage of screen time; *Rififi*, for example features a famous 25 minute near-real-time heist sequence in which there is no speech and no non-diegetic sound resulting in an intense identification with the characters as we witness their unfolding endeavours. The images are almost balletic as the robbers' ingenuity is pushed to its limits.

In films such as *Daylight Robbery* (2008) and *Dog Day Afternoon* (1975) the heist takes up most of the diegetic time and we are not even made party to the crucial early planning stage at all. This creates a spectatorial experience all of its own as we are suddenly thrust into the action without forewarning and asked to situate ourselves immediately within an unfolding criminal drama. In Antonia Bird's *Face*, a film as much about the problems of Thatcherism and masculinity as the execution of a crime, the robbery itself takes up only five minutes of screen time leaving the rest of the film dedicated to exploring how the gang breaks down and how individual greed takes over.

In many heist films the execution of the crime has a set of aesthetic concerns all of its own and, again here it would be instructive to quote from Alastair Phillips' book on *Rififi*:

> The second and arguably most important aspect of the film's handling of vision and time rests in the way it provides a template for how popular cinema should treat the aesthetics of the heist genre. Here, the central points of tension for the thieves are clearly temporal and spatial. We are constantly being made aware, for instance, of the process of time passing and the significance of the impeding deadline of dawn – of time literally running out.[76]

The tension engendered in the heist is based, states Phillips, on two main concerns: the temporal (how long the operation is going to take, whether they will achieve it in time and so on) and the spatial (whether the gang will remain hidden, whether they will be discovered by the authorities, etc.). Audience member and on-screen character are knitted together in a shared obsession over time and space as we are made to feel complicit in a crime to such extent that we abandon our usual morality and root, not for the heroic lawman, but for the transgressive criminal. *Mise-en-scène* and shot selection underlines the spatio-temporal anxieties that form the basis of the heist experience as images of ticking clocks, watches, passing shadows and suspiciously loitering policemen litter the heist environment. We can see an ideal example of this in Norman Harrison's 1963 film *Calculated Risk*, the story of a gang of robbers who tunnel into the vaults of a bank through a disused bombsite. The bank is regularly patrolled by the local police who check its security just feet above the heads of the tunnelling gang who inevitably have to stop in silence at set intervals to avoid detection. The gang are constrained both by time and space as they walk a tightrope between imprisonment and plenitude. The result is pure heist tension that not only allows the audience to experience some of the vicarious thrill of the robbery but subverts and deforms the usual morality of popular cinema.

Act Two ends with the appropriation of the loot in scenes that often display both a jubilant childishness and a sense of satisfied approbation. A crucial feature of the heist is the encounter with financial plenitude and, whether this takes the form of the opening of safety deposit boxes (*The Bank Job*), the stacking of gold bullion (*The Italian Job*) or the counting of money (*Robbery*, 1967) it is always accompanied by a euphoric high that will, if generic conventions are to the played out, be followed by a desperate low as reality, and the law, begin to close in.

ACT THREE: THE AFTERMATH

The aftermath of the heist has the most variations and is the stage that most closely reflects the surrounding society's cultural mores and ethics. Very few heist films allow their protagonists to remain unscathed throughout the process; often the money is lost, they are arrested, killed or the gang breaks up leading to paranoia, anxiety and in-fighting. Even when a gang member does make a clean getaway, such as Gene Hackman's character Joe Moore in David Mamet's *Heist* or Paul Clifton (Stanley Baker) in Peter Yates' *Robbery*, their futures are uncertain and the audience is invited to wonder what pleasures a life on the run must hold and whether the money will bring them happiness at all. Films as early as Ealing's *The Lavender Hill Mob* (1951) have dealt with the problems of being an ex-pat criminal living off the earnings of the one big job, waiting for either money or luck to run out.

In *Rififi*, Tony Le Stephanoise's gang are terrorised by a local mob family, the Grutters, until the money becomes a curse rather than a blessing. Tony meets his end in the middle of a busy thoroughfare after saving the son of a fellow gang member in a conclusion that absolves him of any moral guilt and transforms him from criminal to hero. It is the money that singles Tony out as a target and that sets in motion the playing out of his hubris, as he makes what is almost an Aristotelian journey from happiness to misery. Like most heist gangsters, Tony never gets to spend or enjoy his money and his death is a bittersweet end to a well-formulated plan.

We must be careful, however, of the somewhat naive assumption that the overriding moral of the heist film is that 'crime does not pay'. Although it is true that, either through fate, jealously or the law, the criminal very rarely escapes with the money intact this is more of a generic trope than a reflection of social morality or the flexing of the censor's muscle. The loss of the loot at the end of the narrative only serves to highlight the fact that the heist is a ludic activity, a game of wits between the criminal and the authorities. Charlie Croker's coolness at the end of *The Italian Job* when faced with the loss of the gold is entirely understandable when we consider that he has already successfully carried out the plan to steal it in the first place. Similarly at the end of *The League of Gentlemen*,

Hyde and his gang give themselves up willingly to the police because they have already succeeded in fulfilling their identities as successful criminals; the acquisition of the money becomes irrelevant. For the heist gang, getting away with it is always a greater motivation than greed or avarice.

Ultimately, then, the heist film is a celebration of human ingenuity rather than a cautionary tale about greed. Adopting elements from the war film, the film noir and detective fiction, the heist movie is both varied and reassuringly the same, as directors and screenwriters take what is a basic plot structure and use it to articulate the concerns of the day.

We can divide the *British* heist film up into three loose areas each divided by two high profile crimes. Up until 1963, the British heist film was centred largely on the bank raid. Films like *The Day They Robbed the Bank of England*, *The Lavender Hill Mob* and *Calculated Risk* often feature the gang tunnelling, breaking or otherwise forcing themselves into the vault of either a local or (more often) a national bank. In Vernon Sewell's *Strongroom* (1962) for example, not only do the raiders break into the bank, steal the money and lock the manager and his secretary in the safe, they attempt to break into it *again* to free them when they realise the staff will suffocate.

After the 1960s however, the heist movie became more mobile, inspired by one, widely publicised event. In August of 1963 £2.6million pounds (almost £32,000,000 in today's money) was stolen from a Royal Mail train on the Bridego Bridge in Ledburn, Buckinghamshire. 'The Great Train Robbery' was almost instantly absorbed by popular culture and the robbers themselves immediately mythologised by the popular press and media. We see the influence of this event on crime cinema within a few years of it happening as the British heist film begins to transform itself to reflect robbery on wheels and tracks; films like *The Great St Trinian's Train Robbery*, *Robbery*, *The Italian Job*, *The First Great Train Robbery* (1978) and *Buster* (1988) all depict robbery on the run and movement, speed and excitement become an intrinsic part of the heist experience.[77]

The spatial topology of both of these types of crimes (the bank raid and the train robbery) is noticeably different — one features the gang stealthily penetrating the defensive walls of an authoritarian institution (sometimes *the* symbol of British economic power, the Bank of England) and the other disperses the criminal activity into society, often using the weight of the crowd to make their getaway.[78]

More recently, and especially after the high profile Brink's-Mat robbery of 1983, where £26million worth of gold bullion was stolen from a depot in Heathrow airport, we have not only seen a resurgence in cinematic bank raids (*The Bank Job*, *Daylight Robbery*, *Tuesday* (2008)) but also a link with the concept of criminal retirement and the proverbial 'one last big job' (*Sexy Beast*, *Face*, *The Business* (2005)). Inspired by images of the Costa Del Crime, post 1980s British heist movies dwell on the figure of the gangster gone to seed, the ex-pat criminal who is either living off the proceeds of or is dragged back into one last heist.[79]

Although we should be careful not to simply reduce the British heist film down to reflections of current crime, a taxonomy like this is useful when periodising what is a rarely studied area. The British heist film was inevitably influenced by its Hollywood and European counter-part; however, like the gangster film, the reality was also often influenced by the fiction, as criminals attempted to mirror what they saw on screen in real life situations.

THE LEAGUE OF GENTLEMEN – A VERY BRITISH HEIST

Basil Dearden's *The League of Gentlemen* was in production at the same time as Lewis Milestone's *Ocean's 11*, John Guillerman's *The Day They Robbed the Bank of England* and the B movies *The Dover Road Mystery, Jackpot* and *The Professionals* in a year (1960) that must be considered a bumper one for heist films.

The League of Gentlemen was one of the most popular British films of the year; costing £192,000, as Alexander Walker details, Bryan Forbes' script was originally sent to Cary Grant but was eventually taken up by Dearden and producing partner Michael Relph. Dearden and Relph made their name with thoughtful, socially relevant films like *The Blue Lamp, The Ship that Died of Shame* (1955) and (later) *Victim*.[80] It was little wonder then that *The League of Gentlemen* would constitute more than a mere heist film; rather, it would deal with relevant social issues and present them in a liberal humanist manner. It is the story of a daring daylight bank robbery by a disparate group of ex-service men, each of whom has a secretive past. The leader of the group, Colonel Hyde (Jack Hawkins), brings them together and explains that they have been specially chosen for a criminal operation that is itself inspired by a fictional American pulp novel, *The Golden Fleece*. In a piece of ironic logic that would permeate the rest of the script Hyde explains:

I brought you all together because I have a certain proposition to make. Now what do we all have in common apart from an urgent need for funds? We were all trained, at great public expense, to do certain things with the utmost efficiency, such as how to kill a man with a minimum of effort and other arts and crafts which, while frowned upon in peace time, are acclaimed in times of war. Well I've got a social conscience and I think it's a crying shame that so much public money is wasted so I intend to put it to some practical peace time use.

In the opening scenes, Hyde provides the gang and the audience with brief biographies of each man as he explains the plan to them at their inaugural lunch. Major Race (Nigel Patrick) had to resign his commission just before a black market ring was discovered in post-war Hamburg; Lieutenant Lexy (Richard Attenborough) sold information to the Russians; Captain Porthill (Bryan Forbes) was cashiered for shooting Eoka suspects in Cyprus; Captain Stevens (Kieron Moore) is a closeted homosexual and 'fascist back room boy'; Captain Weaver (Norman Bird) was found guilty of being drunk on duty and causing the deaths of soldiers under him; and so on. Each man has been somehow excluded from polite society, trained by the army, sent to war and then forgotten in peacetime, they are misfits and yesterday's men through no fault of their own. Hyde finishes the biographies by explaining his own position:

> I served my country well as a regular soldier and was suitably rewarded after 25 years by being declared redundant.

The term 'redundant' here can of course apply to each man, as they have all become surplus to requirements in a Britain that, by 1960, had moved on from the war both economically and psychologically. It is not only their status as ex-military that determines their marginalised social position, each man is powerlessly trapped within a society that neither cares for nor respects them: Weaver lives in a dull and loveless marriage, Race is beset with financial worries, Rutland-Smith (Terence Alexander) is married to an unfaithful wife, Lexy is stuck in a dead end job, and so on. Hyde and his fellow gentlemen are symbolic of a middle-aged masculinity that, by the beginning of the swinging '60s, was quickly being seen as old fashioned and out-moded.

Like many Dearden vehicles, *The League of Gentlemen* is quietly subversive. Although, in essence, it is a heist caper, it is also a comedy of manners, the central players all both gentlemen and scoundrels and their characters as questionable as their legal logic, as Raymond Durgnat states:

> These officers and gentlemen, unprepossessing as Simon Raven's fictional characters, are a pressgang of moneygrubbing or dishonest scoundrels, largely caddish, seedy and mean.[81]

One illuminating moment occurs in Hyde's country house where the league is trained. Major Race is inquiring about Hyde's wife whose portrait he spies on the wall: 'Is she dead?', he asks the Colonel; to which Hyde replies, 'No, I am sorry to report the bitch is still very much alive'. Such misogyny is endemic within the gang who view women as either harpies or dolly birds. The blame for their own emasculation is laid firmly at the feet of the female. In this, Dearden's film offers at first glance a conservative vision of social relations in Britain in the mid-twentieth century but it is also one that that the director is critical of; we are presented with a fairly obvious picture of a country and a society in a period of transition – from a post-war austerity to a post-50s affluence. However, as Durgnat suggests, this picture is a more complicated one that we might first imagine as the men of the league are far from deserving of our sympathies: they are, in Hyde's words, merely a bunch of crooks of one type or another. Their marginal status is revealed as being partly due to their own inability to change with the times and to relinquish the power and privilege that comes with a King's commission. A film that at first sight seems to legitimate the bad behaviour of its central male characters also subtly undermines them and exposes their failings.

We can compare this subversive image with 1960's other great heist movie, *Ocean's 11*. Although based on the same premise (ex-soldiers conducting a bank raid using organisational skills and techniques they learnt in the military) the two films pose remarkably different moral portraits. *Ocean's 11* has an equally blinkered view of gender relations, as the male characters are pursued by money grabbing wives, overly protective mothers and beautiful but largely silent showgirls. But possibly due to the public personae of the high profile cast (Frank Sinatra, Dean Martin, Sammy Davis. Jr.), there is none of the dangerous and seedy sexuality that dogs the league of gentlemen. Danny Ocean and fellow gang members are as exciting, as bright and as superficial as the Vegas casinos they rob. Milestone's film has none of the tacit critique of a fading masculinity that Dearden's has. If the league of gentlemen are a picture of a masculine past that is inevitably failing, *Ocean's 11* have yet to experience their fall from grace; at the end of the caper they remain as brash, cocky and conceited as when it began.

As Kirsten Moana Thompson details, *Ocean's 11* began a trend amongst Hollywood heist films for depicting the heist gang as a sexy, well drilled unit that either successfully steals the loot or, at the very least, avoids detection.[82] We see this most obviously in Steven Soderbergh's remake and successive sequels but also in David Hamet's *Heist*, Brian Hutton's *Kelly's Heroes* (1970) and even Ben Affleck's *The Town*. The British heist film, however, is rather harsher on its protagonists whose characters are more often than not noticeable for their ineptitude rather than their skill. Paris Leonti's 2008 heist movie *Daylight Robbery*, for example, continues a trend of depicting British bank robbers as incompetent marginals rather than outlaws, an idea that we can trace back to *The Lavender Hill Mob* over 50 years earlier.

The heist in *The League of Gentlemen* roughly conforms to the Three Act structure outlined above, although the stages are unequal in their length and narrative importance. There are in fact two robberies in the film, the major assault on the bank that occurs roughly an hour and twenty minutes into it and an earlier raid on the army barracks that enables the gang to arm themselves for the bank job proper. As detailed earlier, the first raid offers a way of orientating the audiences' sympathies towards the gang; we become familiar with their working methods, we can detect any weak spots in the team dynamic (we know for example that Weaver is slow, that Hyde is dependable, and so on) and we can use this information to anticipate how the heist will go in the latter parts of the film. Forbes' script calls for parts of the plan to be presented to the audience throughout the central section of the narrative; we know, for example, that smoke and explosives will be used somehow, we know that a truck will be needed, we know that the gang plan to steal the money inside the bank rather than outside of it and we know that the getaway will be made through busy rush hour traffic. The heist then becomes a ludic process of piecing all these elements together as it unfolds before our eyes.

Both heists highlight the film's extended trope of subterfuge and pretence. In the first raid the league not only masquerade as British army officers but affect Irish accents in an attempt to pass their actions off as the work of the IRA; in the second they don gasmasks to disguise themselves in an act that lends a touch of surrealism to the raid itself. Of course, such masquerade also extends into the men's pre-league life as they are all revealed to be leading a double life of one sort or another (Mycroft (Roger Livesey) poses as a priest, Rupert as a dutiful husband, Lexy as a radio repairman, and so on). In a society that was slowly beginning to question the hierarchy that had carried it through a world war and had taken it from austerity to affluence, the image of the middle-aged man with a secret was a powerful one.

Ultimately however, it will be the league's reliance on subterfuge that will be their undoing, as Hyde's real identity is betrayed, not by another gang member or an outside threat, but by his own car, the number plate of which is taken down by a small boy during the raid. Meticulous in its planning, ruthless in its execution, the league of gentlemen's robbery is foiled, tellingly, by a child, a symbol of the new generation that will eventually sweep away their particular form of patrician-led social order for good. The early 1960s saw a change in both the political and the social landscapes of Britain as the old guard of cliques and traditional hierarchies began to be overtaken by swinging London and the counter-cultural turn. By the mid-60s, Britain had lost face over Suez, had experienced corruption at the heart of government with the Profumo scandal, had been introduced to pop culture via The Beatles and had begun to sell itself abroad as a culturally fertile country that was young and 'happening'. As Arthur Marwick details, the 1960s signalled what might be thought of as an end to the Victorianism that had been so much a part of the British character since the nineteenth century.[83] The League of Gentlemen is a heist film but it is also a social document, a snapshot of a social class and a way of life that was quickly falling out of touch; although Dearden's film is sympathetic towards the league it is also quietly critical and their resignation at the end, as they all sit in the back of the police truck, their caper over, is of a generation whose time is well and truly up.

ROBBERY AND THE ITALIAN JOB – SELF-PRESERVATION SOCIETIES

What is it that makes one film a national treasure and another almost virtually forgotten? We began to ask this question with Get Carter and Villain in Chapter One and will consider again here. The 1960s and early '70s were the high points for heist films in both Britain and Hollywood. In the latter there was Bonnie and Clyde, Topkapi, How to Steal a Million, Who's Minding the Mint (1967), The Getaway (1972), Charley Varrick (1973) and The Sting (1973); and in Britain we had A Prize of Arms, Strongroom, Calculated Risk, Gambit (1966), The Great St. Trinian's Train Robbery, Perfect Friday and 11 Harrowhouse (1974), each of which put their own spin on what was fast becoming a distinct sub-genre. As well as cinematic heists, the 1960s provided a series of real life robberies that would not only hit the headlines but would quickly be inculcated into popular mythology. The Plymouth Mail Truck Robbery of 1962 was at the time America's largest haul; this was followed by the Great Train Robbery in 1963, the Airfrance Robbery in 1967, the Baker Street Robbery in 1971 and the Great Bookie Robbery in Australia in April 1976. Every year, it seemed, records for heists were being broken. This was a time when large amounts of currency and bullion needed to be transported to keep economies alive and so became prime pickings. In the 1980s and '90s however automated banking would remove the need for the transportation of cash and the age of the heist gangster would be over.

In the heyday of the British heist movie two films stand out, one of which has stayed in the public consciousness, the other is barely remembered at all. *Robbery* and *The Italian Job* share cinematic DNA; both films were produced by Michael Deeley and both stars, Stanley Baker and Michael Caine respectively, had previously worked together in Cy Endfield's *Zulu* (1964). Stanley Baker had been playing major roles in British films since the early 1950s; his hard man persona and rugged good looks had proved popular in working class parts such as Truman in Basil Dearden's *Violent Playground*, Tom Yately in the lorry driving social realist film *Hell Drivers* (1957) and the taciturn police inspector Harry Martineau in *Hell is a City* (1960). Caine, on the other hand, was fresh from such iconic successes as *Alfie*, *The Ipcress File* and *Gambit* (1966) and would widen his cinematic appeal yet further with the much harder, morally duplicitous Jack Carter in the years to come.

Robbery, made two years before *The Italian Job* and directed by Peter Yates, anticipated the grittier harsher world of 1970s crime dramas like *The Sweeney* and *The Squeeze* rather than reflecting contemporary swinging London. It tells the story of a train robbery that is strikingly similar, although not identical, to that carried out by Buster Edwards and co. in 1963. However, unlike the much more sentimental film *Buster* released in 1988, *Robbery* situates its gang firmly within a harsh underworld of professional thieves and career criminals, its *mise-en-scène* has none of the flashy jingoism of *The Italian Job* but instead displays a colour pallet and lighting style that is more in keeping with film-making that would come to characterise the next decade.

As Robert Shail details, Yates' film also reflects Baker's own socialist politics as it respectfully documents a working class masculinity that populates urban spaces like the football ground, the pub, the train station and the prison.[84] The men of *Robbery* are old lags who are good at their job; their thoroughness, however, is matched with a ruthlessness that avoids the sentimental mythologising of later depictions of the train robbers. Although Yates and Baker understand the reasons behind the robbery, the violence and intimidation that is shown to the postal staff working on the mail train is a reminder that the crime was the act of a determined and well-rehearsed criminal gang rather than a band of modern day Robin Hoods.

Like a great many '60s heist films, *Robbery* depicts theft on the move. The crime is no longer secreted away in a bank vault or safe but is carried out in the open, albeit under the cover of night. We also begin to detect a shift in the dynamic between the criminal and the police that, again, will continue to be explored in the crime dramas of the 1970s. In *The League of Gentlemen* the police are a benevolent and necessary force and the arrest of the gang at the end of the film is a form of inevitable justice more reflective of

British fair play than legality. By 1967, however, the police have been transformed into hard working coppers, forced to slave over paperwork late into the night, squeezed between the underworld and the media. We saw this with the character of Bob Matthews in *Villain* but we also see it in *Robbery*'s Inspector George Langdon (James Booth) who is less Dixon of Dock Green and more Jack Regan, blurring the line between criminal and lawman to get the results society demands of him. Only Stanley Baker's character is allowed to escape the arm of the law and this time the robbers do not come willingly, they run and fight to avoid arrest.

Robbery was praised by a number of critics both in Britain and abroad upon its release. Vincent Firth in the *ABC Film Review* of 1967 called it 'the finest motion picture of its kind' and Roger Ebert of the Chicago Sun Times stated that 'it's good, it doesn't get sidetracked by a lot of cute dialog and psychoanalysis like *The Thomas Crown Affair*'.[85] However, time and culture have not been kind to Yates' film and it has, to a very large extent, been relegated to a footnote in British crime cinema. It barely gets a mention in Chibnall and Murphy's seminal collection of essays or Barry Forshaw's monograph; it doesn't feature at all in Alexander Walker's equally influential *Hollywood England* and in Robert Murphy's *Sixties British Cinema* it is described as 'disappointingly colourless'.[86] As Murphy also details, however, *Robbery* did valiantly attempt to add a seriousness to crime drama that was missing in a number of the more comedic heist films produced in this era.

Peter Collinson's *The Italian Job* exemplifies this other, more comic, mode; it is fast paced, colourful, cool and has none of the gritty realism of *Robbery* or other early 1970s gangster movies. Produced by the same team as *Robbery* and featuring a scriptwriter (Troy Kennedy Martin) whose next work would be the war-cum-heist movie *Kelly's Heroes*, *The Italian Job* and its distinctive attempts to both prolong and concretise the swinging 60s has, like *Get Carter*, not only passed into the national consciousness but has also largely eclipsed other contemporary texts. As Chibnall details however, the intentions of the film's scriptwriter, director and producers were somewhat at odds with how the film has come to be received by successive audiences:

> Clearly, the allegorical intentions of the film were present from the beginning; but the tone in which they were handled would change considerably in the transition from script to screen. Collinson would play up the satire of English chauvinism already evident in the screenplay, and add a dose of camp excess that was not entirely of the author's taste.[87]

By 1969 the myth of 'swinging Britain' was beginning to fail. American producers soon grew tired of the cinematic images that had formed so much a part of the British brand since the middle of the decade and began to pull funding from projects at an alarming rate. The withdrawal from the British film industry by the big Hollywood companies was twinned with severe political and economic unease at home in relation to Europe and in particular France's vetoing of Britain's entry into the Common Market (now the EU). Both in terms of cinema and in terms of its economy, Britain was being asked to stand alone, cut off from both Europe and America.

Much of this finds its way into *The Italian Job*, which, if nothing else, is about British spirit in the face of foreign interests abroad. However, as many commentators have stated, the irony of Collinson's film is that the national character is left in the hands of crooks, swindlers and petty hoodlums as Britain is transformed from a league of gentlemen into a gang of thieves.[88] *The Italian Job* details a post-colonial Britain desperately renegotiating its place on a world stage. No longer was it the Empiric power it was in the nineteenth century nor was it the symbol of Stoicism that it became during the Second World War and it certainly was far from the apex of cultural cool that it had presented itself as five years earlier. Britain, according to *The Italian Job* at least, was a country living off its wits; the patriotism that had served it so well during the Blitz had been reduced to a campy show of empty signifiers that could be called up at will and just as easily dropped. The class system, that many felt provided the backbone for a country at war, was shattered forever by upwardly mobile social climbers like Charlie Croker and his gang, and, as Barry Miles states, 'Even in 1969, *The Italian Job* looked dated'.[89]

As Chibnall suggests, originally *The Italian Job* was intended as a gentle satire on the state of the nation; its images, although lovingly drawn, suggested mild lampooning rather than jingoistic celebration. The older characters in the film (Bridger, Keats, Birkinshaw) are presented as bluff patriots, xenophobically distrustful of 'Johnny Foreigner', while the younger characters are chancers and wideboys out for what they can get. We get the impression, for example, that Croker is less concerned with the British interests in Europe and more concerned with his own pocket, and that even the national pride attached to a football match is merely a cover for an altogether more self-serving mandate. The subtext of *The Italian Job* seems to be, despite all of its red, white and blue flag waving, that Britain was fast becoming more self-preservation and less of a society. All of this is at odds with how the film has been reinvented and revisited in the popular arena, where it has come to stand for a form of nostalgic Britishness in TV commercials, pop videos and on the football terraces. The degree to which filmic texts are rediscovered and canonised by successive audiences is a testimony to their ever-changing status as carriers of meaning and reflectors of the public consciousness. A consideration of a how a film has been received over time reveals audiences to be much more than passive recipients of a film's message; there is a constant dialogue between the text and the culture that surrounds it – a dialogue that is in constant movement and change.

Robbery and *The Italian Job* represent two sides of the heist coin: one a serious exposition of a crime and how it was carried, the other what we might think of as a 'caper', a comic fantasy in which the acquisition of vast sums of money becomes a feint for car chases, wish-fulfilment and flights of cinematic excess. Both of these films herald from the war movie and the film noir but each also reflects how flexible crime cinema can be, how two remarkably different but virtually contemporaneous texts can deal with essentially the same thing: the state of the nation and, perhaps more importantly, how it views its own values, morals and ethics. Moreover, the extent that one film has been entered into the public canon and the other has been virtually forgotten allows us insight into what British audiences demand of their films, how they both construct and read their own identity into texts and how they are used to bolster national homogeneity. In recent years *The Italian Job*, like *Get Carter* and *The Long Good Friday*, has entered the pantheon of British national cinema, an act that says more perhaps about contemporary Britain's need for simple cultural iconography than any intrinsic textual worth. Films like these are vital to British cinema and to crime cinema in particular but they should always be viewed alongside the more morally and thematically complex texts that they often obscure.

SEXY BEAST — THE RETURN OF THE REPRESSED

Jonathan Glazer's *Sexy Beast* is a film that defies easy categorisation. It *is* a crime film, a heist film to be precise, and yet it is also an existential and psychosocial parable that negotiates the borderline between art house and popular cinema and that achieved a modicum of popular and critical success. Its images are both disturbing and comic and yet it conforms to many of the generic structures and tropes that we have highlighted in this chapter. Roger Ebert located *Sexy Beast* firmly within a tradition of 'movies about Cockney villains' and cites *The Long Good Friday* and *The Limey* (1999) as antecedents; yet Desson Howe in *The Washington Post* called it a 'Molotov cocktail of a movie" in an obvious allusion to both its power and its stylistic heterogeneity.[90]

Partly funded by Film Four, Glazer's was the latest in a cycle of crime films produced in the 1990s that attempted to broaden the genre and create a cinema that was both popular and challenging, coming close to the stylish output of American indie cinema at this time. *Lock, Stock and Two Smoking Barrels*, *Hard Men*, *Gangster No. 1*, *Circus*, *Love, Honour and Obey* and *Rancid Aluminium* can all be viewed as attempts to mirror the kinds of cross-fertilisation that had occurred between Hollywood and independent cinema in the US, especially with films like *Reservoir Dogs* and *The Usual Suspects*. In the absence of a major independent distributor like Miramax, however, the results in terms of British output made less of an impact on mainstream audiences. *Sexy Beast* however was an exception and received a wider US release than British, making a relatively healthy $10,000,000 in its first two years. It also garnered critical recognition with an Oscar nomination for Ben Kingsley and a BAFTA nomination for Best British Film.

Sexy Beast's central character Gary Dove (Ray Winstone) has swapped a career in crime for retirement in the Spanish sun. With his wife Deedee (Amanda Redman) and friends H (Cavan Kendall) and Jackie (Julianne White) he lives the dream of every British footsoldier and petty crook: a life of leisure on the 'Costa-del-Crime'. Detailed lovingly in the opening scenes, he spends his days sunning himself by the pool and his nights drinking and eating in the local restaurants. Gary's body, like his ambition, has grown loose and out of shape; lured by the sensual pleasures of an easy life, he has become a figure of contented inactivity. In an opening monologue accompanying images of Gary's prone and bloated body floating on an inflatable sun lounger, he lazily extols the virtues of his idyllic retired life: 'Ahhh, who wouldn't lap this up? It's ridiculous, tremendous, fantastic. Fan-dabby-dozy-tastic.' Gary is instantly recognisable as a gangster gone-to-seed, an ageing, perma-tanned and ultimately harmless ex-pat criminal.

However, one of the unwritten rules of the heist gang is that you can never fully leave and this is brought home to Gary when his ex-comrade, Don Logan (Ben Kingsley), arrives on the scene. Logan is not only an unwanted face from Gary's past, he is symbolic of everything he has left behind in England; he is the return of the repressed forces of violence, aggression and criminality that retirement in Spain attempts to expunge.

Logan tries to persuade Gary to carry out 'one last job' back in England but he refuses and an argument ensues, leaving him shaken and humiliated. Rescuing her husband from a further beating, Deedee shoots Logan, leaving Gary with no choice but to travel to England to carry out the heist and to cover up Logan's death. England is depicted as a grey and rainy country, full of aggressive criminals and corrupt aristocracy. The interiors of England are a world away from the bright, sunny sensuality of the Spanish villa that Gary has left behind, as Glazer's camera style reminds us of both Scorsese and Tarantino and the *mise-en-scène* takes on a paranoid, neo-noir quality. The scenes where Gary and the gang eat their pre-heist meal, for example, are shot so as to make their faces a low-life phantasmagoria reminiscent of Eisensteinian typage. Gary the ex-pat criminal becomes the noir Everyman, as Teddy (Ian McShane) interrogates him about Don's death.

The gulf between what Gary has become and the life he has left behind is made painfully obvious when he phones Deedee just before the heist is about to take place; in a moment of intimacy that carries him through the crime, Gary asks his wife to say his name. Her voice is a reminder of the more feminine spaces of mainland Europe and of the life he has made for himself away from the smoky backrooms and pubs of the London underworld. The image of Britain in the closing decades of the twentieth century is a largely negative one and for Gary it becomes the dark place of repression, anxiety and paranoia that he has to return to in order to exorcise the demons within and around him. *Sexy Beast* is not the only contemporary British film to use Europe as an adjacent paradise where Britons can experience some form of escape and liberation; we see the same for example in Lynne Ramsay's *Morvern Callar* (2002) and in Shane Meadows' *Somers Town* (2008).

Sexy Beast is a heist film in that it features the planning, execution and (to a certain extent) the aftermath of a robbery. The tension, however, comes not from the theft itself but from the relationship between protagonist and antagonist. As Jim Leach states, Glazer's film plays with the personalities of its actors, subverting their usual types and challenging its audience's preconceptions.[91] Making his name in notably masculine roles like Carlin in Alan Clarke's *Scum* (1979), Ray in Gary Oldman's *Nil By Mouth* (1997) and the father in Tim Roth's *The War Zone* (1999) Ray Winstone's performance is uncharacteristically docile; Gary Dove is not the hard man so typical of Winstone's repertoire, but a caring, vulnerable Everyman who leans on his wife and friends every bit as much as they lean on him. Moments of genuine affection and tenderness between Gary and Deedee are accompanied by scenes of deliberate sentiment as their love story is depicted in a magical-realist cinematic style.

Conversely (or perhaps even perversely) Ben Kingsley, who is better known for characters like Gandhi in Richard Attenborough's biopic (1982) or the timid Jewish account Itzhak Stern in Steven Spielberg's *Schindler's List* (1993), imbues Don Logan with a terrifying ferocity that stands in complete opposition to Winstone's character. His wiry physical stature (especially in relation to Gary) only serves to highlight the air of threatening intensity that accompanies him on screen; again, something that is in total contrast to Kingsley's usually more relaxed, understated acting style.

Such postmodern self-reference distances the audience from the action, undercutting the realism that is so endemic within the British crime film, and asking us to view it as a text rather than a reflection of reality. The small touches of avant garde visual experiment and surrealism (the Rabbit-man, the boulder, the underwater camerawork) that Glazer inserts into the narrative only add to the sense that what we are witnessing is a constructed world rather than a reflected one, distancing the audiences from the realism of the movie. *Sexy Beast* not only draws on a cinematic tradition of crime and heist films it asks its audience to make intertextual connections to works outside of this to its actors' previous roles. As Carl Neville suggests, Don Logan is more than a symbol or a figment of Gary's imagination, a hallucination in the vein of films like *Fight Club* (1999) or *A Beautiful Mind* (2001), he is a part of Gary's past and therefore, inevitably, a part of his psychological make-up:

> Whereas in *Fight Club*, for example, Tyler Durden doesn't actually exist, for Glazier [sic], quite rightly, the people we know, the people to whom we cleave, so become part of us and do function as agents in the psyche.[92]

Watching the first act of *Sexy Beast* we are reminded of the taut intensity of a Beckett or Pinter play but it also conforms to the opening stage of the heist movie, where the gang is assembled and given roles by a paymaster. The paymaster is Teddy Bass and, like many heist gang leaders, his presence is shadowy and covert, pulling the strings from the safety of England and ultimately controlling the division of the spoils when the operation is over.

As Neville states, Glazer's film constantly draws on the psychological differences between England and Spain, as one is painted as a land of sensuality and pleasure and the other as a dark and rainy storehouse of aggression and barely suppressed violence:

> In *Sexy Beast*, Spain and England are both real locales with the film and also contradictory and warring elements within the central character Gal's psyche, just as his nemesis Don Logan is a real figure and also a manifestation of everything within

Gal that must be overcome so that he can be liberated fully and finally embrace the world of pleasure and get away from the destructive demands of Englishness.[93]

The image of Spain as a haven of peace and sensuality is a noticeable one in modern British culture. Whereas, in the 1940s and '50s we witness a series of references to the dangers and pleasures of British coastal towns like Brighton, Skegness and Blackpool, from the 1970s onwards we see a distinct twinning of places like the Costa del Sol and Magaluf with the notion of an escape from the everyday drabness of British life. As Dominic Sandbrook states, the rise of package holidays and the removal of the limit on currency that could be taken out of the country meant that, increasingly, families were opting to travel abroad for the summer, securing forever the association of Spanish sun with relaxation and the shedding of responsibility.[94]

However Spain was also the destination of choice for the criminal fraternity 'on the lam' during the 1970s and '80s, as international relations between the UK and Spain cooled over the ownership of Gibraltar. Michael Newton states that by July 2002 almost 230 British criminals were living 'in high style' on what had been dubbed the Costa-del-Crime due to the Spanish authorities' reluctance to extradite.[95] Crime, then, becomes both that which allows Gary to escape the harsh realities of England and that which drags him back; the narrative takes on Faustian overtones as we realise Logan is but a minion of the real Devil of the piece, Teddy Bass.

For Gary, pleasure comes at a price and it is one that must be continually paid. The gang and, more specifically, the crime itself become the secret that must be repressed. We can see this Faustian trope in a number of gangster and heist films of the 1990s both from Britain and Hollywood. Brian De Palma's 1993 film *Carlito's Way*, *Things to Do in Denver When You're Dead*, *State of Grace* (1990), *Face* and *Hard Men* all deal with the character of the criminal who 'wants out' but who is eventually and inevitably drawn back into an abusive and threatening underworld from which they can never fully escape.

In *Sexy Beast*, the underworld is both literal and figurative as the physical landscape is divided between above and below ground, first in the swimming pool of the villa and then as the gang tunnel into the vaults to carry out the bizarre heist on the bank. Water and drowning become an important visual trope as Gary struggles to breath in a world that is increasingly claustrophobic. His near-death experience at the beginning of the film, as a boulder narrowly misses him and smashes into the swimming pool, provides the opportunity later on for him to cover up the death of Logan, suggesting that, in order to truly defeat his demons Gary has to first confront death and self-destruction himself. The split, then, between the subterranean and the surface world mirrors Gary's unfolding psychology as he battles against his demons both real (Don Logan) and imaginary (the Rabbit-Man) in an attempt to overcome his own history. This split, of course, is accentuated by the prevalence of a *mise-en-scène* that alternates between depicting the blazing Spanish sun and the overcast British weather.

The answer to the unsatisfying masculine aggression of England and its criminal underworld, so *Sexy Beast* tells us, is love. In the final scenes of the film and after being conned by Teddy Bass into taking only £10 for his part in the heist, we discover that Gary has buried Don Logan under the entwined hearts of his and Deedee's swimming pool. The poetic symbolism is obvious: hatred and aggression can be buried beneath love and understanding. The exploration of love is common to *Sexy Beast's* scriptwriters Louis Mellis and David Scinto, whose other works, *Gangster No. 1* and *44Inch Chest* (2009), also deal with the degree to which hard men grapple with strong emotions. We also see this in several other films of the period, most notably Antonia Bird's *Face*. In *Sexy Beast* however, love becomes the primary healing agent and the force that allows Gary to transcend his own demons.

Sexy Beast, however, is ultimately a crime film. It may be startling different to many we have looked at this chapter and it may be infused with an art house rather than a popular cinematic ethos but it is a crime film nonetheless. We can note that it has a planning stage (the first act as the gang is being assembled), an execution stage and, ultimately, an aftermath as Teddy attempts to discover the truth about Don Logan. *Sexy Beast* is a testimony to the heist movie's flexibility, as it not only adopts but adapts the generic conventions of the form, creating a postmodern commentary on performance style and aesthetics whilst offering a familiar narrative.

The British heist film is as popular as ever. Films like *The Bank Job*, *Daylight Robbery*, *Layer Cake* (2004) and *Tuesday* all attest to the fact that, for British audiences, robbery is still a fascinating topic. The films we have looked at in this chapter all feature a central theft of some sort and all the narratives deal, more or less, with the playing out of this. However, as we have seen, this can come in many forms, a point that raises difficult issues when dealing with topics like genre and film traditions. Is a film such as *The Great St. Trinian's Train Robbery*, for example, a heist film or a comedy? Does it fit into the tradition of British comedy cinema or crime cinema? The answer, of course, is that it fits into both; a text's place in one generic history does not immediately preclude it from existing within another.

FOOTNOTES

73. As will become obvious during this chapter I am not making the distinction between a 'caper' and a 'heist' film; the one denoting a comic version of the other. Part of the interesting aspect of the heist movie is its capacity to take on a wide variety of forms and yet retain the same basic generic tropes. When I use the term 'heist' then I refer both to films like *Robbery* and *Face* and to films like *The Big Job* (1965) and *The Great St. Trinian's Train Robbery*, which are (it could be argued) emanating from different aesthetic traditions.

74. Phillips, A., *Rififi: French Film Guide*, London: I.B. Tauris, 2009, p.41.

75. Mason, F., *American Gangster Cinema: From Little Caesar to Pulp Fiction*, London; Palgrave Macmillan, 2003, p.99.

76. Phillips, 2009, p.44.

77.	It is an irony of British cinema that the comedy *The Great St. Trinians' Train Robbery* is perhaps the first cultural responses to The Great Train Robbery, an indication of comedy's role in the larger social discourse.

78.	It should be pointed out that this taxonomy is a loose one, Sidney Hayers' 1961 film *Payroll*, for example, clearly influenced by Richard Fleischer's *Armoured Car Robbery* (1950, USA), presents robbery on the move 2 years before *The Great Train Robbery* made it a popular image in mainstream cinema.

79.	Chibnall, S., 'The Italian Job', in Ward Baker, R. and B. McFarlane (eds), *The Cinema of Britain and Ireland*, New York: Columbia University Press, 2005, p.382.

80.	Walker, A., *Hollywood England: The British Film Industry in the Sixties*, London: Orion, 1988.

81.	Durgnat, R., *A Mirror for England: British Movies from Austerity to Affluence*, London: Faber and Faber, 1970, p.35.

82.	Thompson, 2007, pp.46-47.

83.	Marwick, A., *British Society Since 1945*, London: Penguin, 2003, p.133.

84.	Shail, R., 'Stanley Baker and British Lion: A Cautionary Tale', in Newland, P. (ed.), *Don't Look Now: British Cinema in the 1970s*, Bristol: Intellect, 2010, p.35.

85.	Firth, V., *ABC Film Review*, November 1967; Ebert, R. 'Robbery', in *Chicago Sun Times*, 29 August 29 1968.

86.	Murphy, 1997, p.217.

87.	Chibnall, 2005, p.147.

88.	See for instance Chibnall, 2005; Powell, D., *Studying British Cinema: The 1960s*, Leighton Buzzard: Auteur, 2009.

89.	Miles, B., *The British Invasion: The Music, The Times, The Era*, London: Sterling Publishing, 2009, p.177.

90.	Ebert, R., "Sexy Beast", in *Chicago Sun Times*, June 22nd, 2001; Howe, D., "A Beauty of a Beast", in *The Washington Post*, 22 June 2001.

91.	Leach, 2004, p.180.

92.	Neville, 2010, p.75.

93.	Neville, 2010, p.72.

94.	Sandbrook, D. *State of Emergency: The Way We Were, Britain 1970-1974*, London: Penguin, 2011, p.141.

95.	Newton, M., *Gangsters Encyclopaedia*, London: Anova Books, 2007, p.154.

CHAPTER FOUR: BENT COPPERS

The Offence (1972)

As Robert Reiner suggests, the police series, and consequently the police film, has always relied on verisimilitude for its impact.[96] Even the ageing and avuncular image of *Dixon of Dick Green*, that perennial portrait of British paternalism, framed its narrative within a broadly realist structure that owed as much to 1950s kitchen sink drama as it did the middle class consensus exemplified by the output of Ealing Studios. It was in the 1970s, however, that the police drama came of age and began to be infused with a high octane masculinity that was to make it both iconic and problematic for future generations and their film-makers. Prompted by numerous influences that ranged from the Hollywood maverick cop film to several high profile police corruption cases, films such *Sweeney!*, *The Offence*, *All Coppers are...* (1972) and *The Squeeze* blurred the line between the criminal and the lawman by depicting the police as inherently corrupt, morally flawed and personally vulnerable. Gone was the image of the kindly and solid copper on the beat and in came an altogether tougher, more violent professional whose behaviour was every bit as a questionable as the criminals they pursued. The age of the bent copper had arrived.

Whilst it is difficult to historicise precisely, the rise of the fictional bent copper can be seen to coincide with a number of developments both in British society and its culture. In 1969 reporters from *The Times* investigated claims that several high profile detectives from the Metropolitan Police Force's Flying Squad (the real life inspiration for *The Sweeney*) were guilty of framing small time crooks and taking bribes in return for dropping charges; and in the early 1970s, Soho pornographers like Bernie Silver and Tony Mifsud were revealed to be inextricably linked to members of the London Metropolitan Police's vice squad. No longer was it the case that police corruption could be thought to rest with a 'few bad apples'; now it seemed the whole barrel had gone sour and, as

Alwyn Turner details, even high ranking members of the constabulary admitted to certain criminals that 'We've got more villains in our game the you've got in yours'.[97]

The most infamous of these real life bent coppers was Detective Sergeant Harold Challenor, a decorated army veteran and member of the Flying Squad. As James Morton details, Challenor's mental state was always in question and throughout his career he constantly flouted the line between legality and criminality.[98] At his trial for corruption in 1964, the prosecuting council declared that:

> On the evidence which I heard from the doctors when he was arraigned, it seems likely that [Challenor] had been mentally unbalanced for some time, and the evidence which I heard from Superintendent Burdett in the case worried me a great deal. It seems to me the matter ought to be looked into further.[99]

The concept that a British bobby could be considered not only corrupt but also mentally unstable was to provide an injection of paranoia and desperation to a genre that had always relied on the comforting binary of hero and villain. As this chapter will attempt to show, the story of the British police film after the 1960s becomes one of anxiety and fear both of and for the place of the constabulary in British culture.

The perception of escalating police corruption was reinforced in the late 1960s and early '70s through media images of uniformed bobbies holding back armies of desperate striking miners and colliery workers at places like Saltley near Birmingham; we could also add to this countless news images of British soldiers firing on civilians in the Bloody Sunday massacre in Derry and the increasing use of the police as battering rams by a series of governments that were struggling to maintain control of social unrest. The racial make-up of the police force also prevented it from truly reflecting the changing demographic nature of modern Britain; in 1976 there were just 70 black or Asian police officers in a force that had grown to over 22,000. To make matters worse, the 1971 *Select Committee on Race Relations and Immigration* found that most British policemen assumed black youths to be more criminal than their white counterparts.[100]

The image of the paternal PC Dixon, with his local knowledge and firm but friendly hand seemed more and more unlikely towards the end of the 1960s and the cinema began to reflect this. The policemen of the '70s were often shown as being caught between an out of control public and an ineffectual government. They were the last line of law and order and they often, as in Sidney Lumet's *The Offence*, buckled under the strain. Like the character of Joe in Sidney Hayers' *All Coppers Are...* (whose full title, tellingly, was originally *All Coppers Are Bastards* but was changed to avoid censorship issues) the individual police officers in these films were just as fragile in terms of their morality as they were in terms of psychology; unlike their happily married cousins of 20 years previous, they had affairs, drank too much and were generally flawed in an all too human way.

To this state of affairs we can also add the influence of two distinct media cultures: British TV and Hollywood. As Susan Sydney Smith has successfully argued, the relationship between the cinematic copper and their television counterpart is a complex one of mutual influence and joint evolution. At no point is this more obvious than in the 1970s, where due to a number of factors (financial, cultural, social) the TV cop show began to influence its widescreen partner.[101] Shows like *Softly, Softly* (1966–1969), *The Sweeney* (1975–1978) and *The Professionals* (1977–1983) provided blueprints for representations of a harder-edged police force that was not only reflective of the change of mood in Hollywood but also mirrored the general mood of a country that was slowly becoming divided by internal strife and a distrust of the police and the state.

We have to be aware of placing too much emphasis on the cultural place of 1970s dramas like *The Sweeney*, which, like many über-macho texts of the period have been endlessly reinvented and re-envisaged for the post-feminist era. Although vital in the development of the British TV cop show it was, in many ways merely an extension of what was happening already with shows like *Z Cars* (1962–1978), *Softly Softly*, and *Special Branch* (1969–1974). It was these texts of the late 1960s that provided the impetus for the changes in public attitudes towards the British police show; like *The Blue Lamp*, they stretched the boundaries of public acceptability without ever threatening to break it apart and they offered a familiar, if quietly subversive, view of authority. A contemporary review of *Softly Softly*, authored in 1966 by Peter Knight of *The Daily Telegraph* for example and cited by Susan Sydney Smith gives us some insight into how the series was seen:

> The BBC's new television crime series *Softly Softly* which opened on BBC1 last night, is a legitimate, well-bred offspring of its predecessor *Z Cars*. It has the same rough, abrasive realism, the same sharp prickly dialogue, the same terse economy of style. But it is also a development of the original [*Z Cars*] taking some of the better qualities and moulding them to a new format. It will not have the same impact that *Z Cars* made when it first appeared for the new ground has already been broken. All the new series can do now is explore the tracks.[102]

New ground then had already been broken by June 4th 1974, the date of the first airing of *Regan*, the pilot that would become *The Sweeney*. *The Sweeney*, however, would represent a concretisation of the new direction for the British cop show and moreover would inspire countless imitators, pastiches and copyists and ensure that, once explored, television would never again lead back to the paternalism of PC George Dixon. The public cynicism that was born out of almost daily retellings of police corruption, brutality and fallibility found a place on both the small and the large screen. To this end, we will visit the two *Sweeney* films towards the end of this chapter. The popularity of *The Sweeney* and its continuing resonance in the British cultural psyche can be attested to by the BBC series *Life on Mars* (2006–2007) which purported to be a wry look at the 1970s cop show but could just as easily have been read as an excuse to revel in the non-PC nature of its treatment of women and ethnic minorities. The character of Detective Inspector Gene Hunt (Philip Glenister) drew heavily on *The Sweeney*'s Carter and Regan as well reflecting the attitudes of a less socially aware era and, as always with such a portrayal, it is difficult to know if audiences were responding to the irony or enjoying the licence to engage in bad behaviour.

The other area of specific influence on the formation of the modern cop show was Hollywood and more specifically the raft of anti-heroes and broken psyches that came out of the New Hollywood of the early 1970s. Films like *Serpico* (1973), *Dirty Harry* (1971), *Magnum Force* (1973) and *The French Connection* (1971) reflected America's feeling that it too was beginning to the feel the strain of social and political unrest. Events like the Attica prison riots of 1971, protests surrounding race relations, the Vietnam War and, eventually, Watergate would, as Geoff King asserts, produce some of the finest cinema the world has ever seen.[103] However it would be a cinema with a hard edge, one that blurred the lines between the criminal and the police and that would be unerringly dark and morally complex. The underlying sense of this generation of cop films would be of a society under siege from the criminal, that the war for law and order was being hopelessly lost and that the lawman had to become as heartless and as corrupt as the murderer or thief to survive. Dirty Harry's famous entreaty to 'make my day' encouraged audiences to join in the dismantling of the basic freedoms of the US citizenry; the lawman had become judge, jury and executioner – but he had been pushed into the role by the very society he was charged to protect.

Although diluted somewhat, it was undoubtedly this sense of an increasingly fraught social scene that provided shows like *The Sweeney* and *The Professionals* with their underlying moral compass. Visuals were also borrowed from New Hollywood as outside locations, restless camera work and realistic lighting imbued the images with a sense of urgency and aggression that was matched with an appreciation of the humanness of the police. No longer were they seen as infallibly moral, they were everyday men and women with everyday flaws. The 1970s were a decade that buzzed with aggression and violence and this was inevitably reflected in the films and TV shows that depicted law and order.

This chapter will look at three of the most socially reflective police films of the 1970s: *All Coppers are...*, *The Offence* and *Sweeney 2*. None were major box office successes or have been extensively covered by British cinema criticism; however all constitute an interesting snapshot of how Britain in the 1970s (that most fractious of decades) saw itself and its relationship to the police and authority.

ALL COPPERS ARE... – THE TROUBLE WITH THE 1970S

Hints that the role of the policeman was changing by the late 1960s can be evidenced in the various police training videos that were produced by the Central Office of Information (COI), the information dissemination bureau that succeeded the wartime Ministry of Information. We can detect in many of these short films, which were designed primarily for public relations and recruitment purposes, subtle shifts in the way the police saw themselves and were in turn seen by the wider public. Early films like *Help Yourself*

(1950), a short that depicted a light-fingered thief who is eventually caught by a vigilant public, are reminiscent of depictions of criminality that came out of the Ealing Studios in the 1950s (John Salew who plays the central character of Joe was a fairly regular Ealing performer). They also have the sheen of the informational films of the war period that often mixed paternalism with a light-hearted comedy that was designed to both inform and entertain in equal measure. The police in these early shorts are always seen as being in control and familiar sights on the beat, their uniforms acting as a symbol for a paternal authority.

By the 1960s and '70s the police public relation film had taken on a different character; the job of the policeman was now depicted as inherently difficult, morally complex and, at times, almost impossible. Eric Marquis' 1970 film *Police Station* depicts the sheer variety of activities and challenges that faced the constabulary in a busy metropolis. The audience is presented with a series of increasingly difficult scenarios from petty thievery to rape, from burglary to riot control and it is the uniformed copper who always takes the brunt. The underlying position of the police force has changed in this film; although still trustworthy, the policeman is now a figure under pressure and their role is not to maintain the law as such but to provide a thin blue line between chaos and order. Rather than paternalism and a firm hand, the constable relies on good training, courage and dedication to his job. He is presented as a consummate professional rather than a kindly uncle. The 1975 film *Challenge of a Lifetime* also suggests that the policeman faces a constant battle for everyday survival in city streets that are rife with violence and aggression.

If these docudrama public relations films present the life of the policeman on the beat as being one of managing increasing social antagonism then we can detect the same in narrative film. One of the earliest examples of this trend was *The Strange Affair* (1968), a film that Robert Murphy has called 'the first of a new generation of crime films which use the permissiveness of the Swinging Sixties to display a more explicit treatment of sex and violence'. [104] It is also instructive, and highly relevant to what will happen in the next decade, that the chapter in which Murphy discusses the film is called 'Degenerate Britain'. The film details the downfall of an ordinary policeman, P.C. Peter Strange (Michael York), from upstanding trainee recruit to prisoner in a narrative that sees him come into contact with pornographers and criminals.

One noticeable manifestation of the changing times in *The Strange Affair* is the depiction of the urban environment that, by the late '60s was irrevocably changing. We still see glimpses of the old London with its partially demolished houses and its narrow three floored tenements; however by the late 1960s this has largely given way to what Murphy describes as 'concrete office blocks, multi-storey car parks, garish modern pubs and a heliport crowded with the white clad supports of an Indian guru'. [105] This change in physical vista provides a metaphor for the change in public morality, as Britain is depicted as being awash with a mixture of degenerate, drug-taking hippies and bent policemen on the take. PC Peter Strange provides us with the innocence against which all of this decadence and corruption is contrasted as he is lured into an increasingly immoral underworld by girlfriend Fred, played by Susan George.

Whereas *The Strange Affair* clearly addresses police corruption, its main thrust is the sense of overall permissiveness that threatens the innocence of the younger generation. In what will be a common thread in the 1970s, individual policemen are seen as being as weak and as vulnerable as the public they serve. Strange is seduced by a 15-year-old girl; another policeman, Det. Sgt. Pierce (Jeremy Kemp) grows evermore obsessive throughout the film until the final scenes show him as a snarling, monomaniacal madman; and his superiors are corrupt and in the pay of the gangsters. No one, it seems, is infallible.

The permissiveness of *The Strange Affair*, however, is strictly for mainstream consumption; its drug addicts laugh manically and talk about 'taking a trip' wear velvet loon pants and sport neatly trimmed bowl haircuts, its gurus are clad in white robes and have flowers draped around their necks and the pornographers are louche quasi-aristocrats who seduce young boys into their expensively furnished flats only to film their exploits through a two-way mirror. This is British permissiveness at its most cartoon-like, seen through the eyes of the outraged middle-Englander. *The Strange Affair* has none of the dangerous crackle of Nic Roeg and Donald Cammell's *Performance* that would appear two years later or the world-weary degradation of *Get Carter* or *Villain* that would herald the true arrival of '70s culture. It was an altogether safe form of subversion.

The picture we get of sexual permissiveness in Sydney Hayers' 1972 film *All Coppers Are...* is noticeably more prosaic, as if the heady exoticism of the late '60s had given way to the grubby verisimilitude of the '70s. Hayers worked variously in low budget films and television from the late 1950s until the 1990s and could boast credits on shows as diverse as *Airwolf* (1985), *The Professionals* (1978) and *The Famous Five* (1979). In terms of crime, Hayers had a solid background, directing the 1961 film *Payroll*, the psychological thriller *Assault* (1971) as well as nine episodes of *The Avengers* between 1965 and 1967. *All Coppers Are...* was Hayers' fifteenth film in a career that established him as one of the great unsung journeymen directors of British genre cinema.

Produced by *Carry On* impresario Peter Rogers and distributed by the Rank Organisation, *All Coppers Are...* has none of the social commentary of *The Strange Affair* and is a less ambitious text overall. It does, however, share some of the earlier film's concern with a society whose moral boundaries are inevitably changing and whose figures of law and order are being questioned. The central character, Joe (Martin Potter), again represents the innocent man tempted by an attractive and sexually promiscuous young woman, Sue played by Julia Foster. Sue also has an affair with Barry (Nicky Henson), a local small time crook and, as the narrative plays itself out, the two storylines inevitably cross as Barry and Joe meet whilst the former is on a job. The film ends with Joe dying in the yard of a haulage firm after being shot by Barry.

What is noticeable about the moral positioning of *All Coppers Are...* is that Joe's transgressions are purely carnal. Unlike PC Strange his sins do not extend into corruption or falsification of evidence; he does not plant drugs, does not take bribes and is, as far as we can tell, a model police officer, making him a far more complex figure in terms of the police film's moral evolution. What he is is fallible and open to temptation. It is not the law of the land he flouts but the law of polite society. He leaves his young wife and child at home, for example, while he visits Sue for sex and he lies to both until he is found out in an awkward scene in a pub. Joe's corruption is one of propriety rather than legality but it is no less finely drawn for this.

The sexual permissiveness of *All Coppers Are...* is centred firmly on the character of Sue who provides the object for many of the male gazes in the film and typifies the misogynistic characterisation of many crime films. She is allied firstly to Joe, then to Barry whilst at the same time being ogled and mauled by Jock (Glynn Edwards), her mother's boyfriend. Sue is also frequently equated with alcohol: we first see her surrounded by the detritus of a party as she wakes up in a body stocking after a hard night's drinking; her easy sexuality is at odds with the cheap domesticity of her mother's flat as she roots around for an aspirin to ease her hangover. The next time we see Sue for any length of time is at the wedding where she meets Joe and Barry and again she is linked with alcohol and partying. She is clearly depicted as the temptress, the image of the female as a siren that lures Joe away from his safe family and his secure job.

Sue's permissiveness however has none of the freedom of earlier '60s films like *Darling* (1965) and *The Knack... and How to Get It* (1965). Sexual proclivity is seen as very much a precursor to sin and crime. If *The Strange Affair*'s subtext was that morally suspect policemen can be blackmailed into greater criminal activity, then the message of *All Coppers Are...* is that policemen are just as human as the rest of us. However, as the narrative shows, this, too, can lead to trouble and there is the suggestion that this itself is symptomatic of larger fissures in the public psyche.

Sue's characterisation reminds us of that other staple of 1970s British cinema, the sexploitation film. Her scantily clad body is more reminiscent of *Confessions of Window Cleaner* (1974) than *Alfie* as the camera scans her curves through the gaze of the various men she encounters. She is constantly held in comparison with Joe's wife who is motherly and sisterly in equal measure. Like many police films of the 1970s, *All Coppers Are...* is problematic in terms of its gender politics, seeing women variously as either dolly birds or dutiful wives.

The title of *All Coppers Are...* has an obvious irony. In the final scenes of the film, and just after Joe has been shot in the course of his duty, Barry is seen running past a wall with the full title of the movie sprayed in garish pink letters – 'All Coppers Are Bastards' it proclaims. The film's underlying sense is that Joe is anything but a bastard, he is merely a young family man caught up in the excitement of the permissive age, led astray by an attractive scantily clad girl. Joe becomes a victim of an immoral society that cares little for its authority figures and where the police on the beat are facing an ever more violent criminal fraternity that are, increasingly, armed and dangerous.

In essence, of course, the conclusion to *All Coppers Are...* mirrors the narrative of Basil Dearden's *The Blue Lamp*, a film made almost 20 years earlier in supposedly more innocent times. Both depict the shooting of a policeman by a small time crook and both explore the relationship between crime and the larger community. However, in the 1972 film Joe's death is seen as an inevitable outcome of a society that has lost its moral heart. In *The Blue Lamp*, PC Dixon's death is the catalyst for a typically Ealing-like ending as British society heals its own wounds by coming together and confronting its criminal elements, the gunman is surrounded and arrested. In *All Coppers Are...* Joe dies in an abandoned yard alone and the gunman escapes. All that is heard is the report of his death over the police radio. It is as if this is a natural outcome of the mounting violence that provides the film's subtext – the gangland figures, the rioters, the sexual permissiveness all provide a backdrop to the young PC's shooting. This is subtly different from the communality of *The Blue Lamp* and the austerity of post-war Britain.

The Strange Affair and *All Coppers Are...* should be seen as transitionary films, films that begin to trace the implications of the permissiveness that characterised the 1960s into darker, more cynical times. As Alwyn Turner suggests, the public still had a basic faith in the police force in the 1970s and this is reflected in the media. TV shows like *Softly Softly* and *Special Branch* still clung to images of the good copper fighting a difficult battle against increasingly impossible circumstances and this was carried over into cinema. Turner writes:

> For the public, acceptance of police corruption was still perhaps a step too far...
> for there remained a need to believe that someone somewhere was holding the line,
> defending society against what was seen as a rising tide of violence.[106]

The sense of transition, in both films, extends into space and place. In his influential article on the New Wave Realism of the 1960s Andrew Higson characterises British Social Realism as continually experiencing a tension between the narrativising tendency of depicting a psychologised and mythical space and the more historicised place of traditional realism.[107] The former presents space as subordinate to narrative and character and the latter offers real settings that can be appreciated on the level of visual pleasure (Higson discusses this with examples taken from *Saturday Night and Sunday Morning* (1960) and *A Taste of Honey* (1961) that present both narrative spaces and socio-historical places).

All Coppers Are... can be read in this tradition: on the one hand, its images of London have a psychologising function (the cramped and messy interiors especially can be taken as being intimately connected to the development of the narrative) and on the other it depicts recognisable landmarks such as Battersea power station, the Savoy and the Thames embankment. Generalised space is replaced, intermittently, with historicised place as we are taken on a tour of London's thoroughfares. The effect not only adds specificity to the film but also suggests that it might point to more national issues. London is clearly the setting for the action but this particular London is one that can be taken as representative of the country as a whole.

Taken together, *The Strange Affair* and *All Coppers Are…* can be read as examples of a genre in change and transition. Neither displays the kinds of contempt for the police that we will see in *The Offence*, *The Sweeney* or, in particular, *The Squeeze* but they do represent a country coming to terms with its own internal fissures. Both films feature young attractive male leads in what can also be considered a reflection of the country's concern for its youth and therefore its own future.

The state of the British film industry in the 1970s inevitably shaped its output. The abandonment by the large American studios, general socio-political tension, the relative importance of TV drama and a series of desperate attempts to spice up what were largely uninspiring texts meant that money was perennially short and interest in the British product was continually waning. We certainly see this in a film like *All Coppers Are…*, a film that is unambitious in both its themes and its look. What it does show, however, is that despite the many problems in the British industry films were still being made. They may not have had the big stars and intensity of contemporary Hollywood counterparts but they do successfully capture a time, a place and a culture in transition. Especially with regards the police and the relation between the mainstream society and the law, what we see in these films mirrors what was being printed in the newspapers and what was seen on the evening news.

As Dominic Sandbrook details, decades rarely fall into neat historical divisions and *The Strange Affair* and *All Coppers Are…* go some way to proving this. Although from the late '60s and early '70s respectively, they present us with a picture of both change and continuity, a snapshot of a society dealing with transition but still reflective of the morals and ethics of the past.

THE OFFENCE – THE LONG NIGHT OF THE SOUL

For every image of easy permissiveness that occurred in the 1970s there was one of a darker, blacker hue. For every *Confessions of a Window Cleaner* there was a *The Wicker Man* (1973). It was a decade when the relaxation of social and moral boundaries took its toll on the public morals and the devil-may-care attitude of the Swinging Sixties began to have consequences.

Sidney Lumet's *The Offence* was described by the director himself as 'a failure' although whether this referred to a lack of critical or financial success is unclear.[108] United Artists certainly failed to capitalise on marketing what, in 1972, was a meeting of considerable talent. Sean Connery had just been tempted back into playing James Bond in *Diamonds Are Forever* (1971) and Lumet himself had just released *The Anderson Tapes* (1971) (with

Connery as well) and would go on from this to film *Serpico* a few years later, launching the career of Al Pacino.

Given the subject matter of *The Offence* it is perhaps unsurprising that United Artists balked at fully committing to its distribution. It is the story of Detective Sergeant Johnson (Connery), a tough British policeman who is charged with investigating a series of child murders and in particular the recent abduction of Janie Edwards, a young schoolgirl. With little evidence to go on (just a sighting by a witness who saw Janie being taken by a man in a distinctive coat) Johnson arrests, questions and beats suspect Kenneth Baxter (Ian Bannen) in a show of physical force that acts as a visual trope throughout the film. As Frank Cunningham states, Lumet blurs the line between the criminal and the lawman by making Johnson a noticeable psychotic driven mad by the daily grind of witnessing the crime and degradation of 1970s Britain; in a broken society it is lawmen like Johnson who take the full brunt.[109] There is a psychological connection between Johnson and Baxter that muddies the moral waters of the film as the audience is invited to speculate upon Johnson's own possible involvement in the crime. He too wears a noticeably distinctive coat throughout, his anger is ready to erupt at any moment, and the scenes in which he finds the beaten and raped girl in the woods are clearly shot so that the audience is left unsure as to the Detective's own sexuality and frame of mind. As Cunningham states:

> No film in Lumet's canon is more uncomfortable to watch than his relentless *The Offence* (1972); yet none shows so strikingly how the director can confront the most controversial and horrifying themes without resorting to gratuitous violence or sensationalism. Perhaps lines from Eliot's 'Sweeney Agonistes' introduce most compellingly the theme of *The Offence*:
>
> > I knew a man once did a girl in
> >
> > Any man might do a girl in
> >
> > Any man has to, needs to, wants to
> >
> > Once in a lifetime, do a girl in.[110]

The violence shown by Johnson to Baxter is revealed not to be an indication of their difference, but an outcome of their similarity. Johnson is a victim of a social and political war and Lumet paints his psychosis in stark, disturbing colours. Again, as Cunningham details:

> [He] has stored unbearable memories of the hideous sadism, violence and inhumanity he has been forced to witness through his grim duties. But he has continually repressed these horrors…[111]

Johnson is no everyman in the sense of Joe or PC Strange; he is an exceptional case, a man under enormous strain. He is also caught between the needs of the public and the needs of the authorities. In a protracted dialogue between Johnson and Detective Superintendent Cartwright (played by a time-ravaged Trevor Howard) we see the untenable position of the jobbing policeman working in trying times. Cartwright is transformed into the role of interrogator, as Johnson recounts his reasons for arresting Baxter, reasons which amount to little more than gut feeling and the infamous policeman's intuition. Years later, in TV shows like *The Sweeney* and *The Professionals*, Johnson's actions will become valorised and even celebrated but in *The Offence* we are left in no doubt that what we are witnesses to is a perverting of the law and the legal process. It is Johnson's mind that is at fault, however, not his morals. Lumet's concern, as he himself states, is the corruption of the spirit not of law and order.[112]

One of the most notable influences on the narrative and the visual sense of *The Offence* was the Moors Murders case of the mid-1960s. Between July 1963 and October 1965, Ian Brady and Myra Hindley abducted and killed five young children ranging between the ages of 10 and 17 and buried the bodies of four of them on Saddleworth Moor, near Manchester. The case quickly entered the public consciousness and would haunt the British psyche for the next half-century (Hindley died in custody in 2002; Brady is still imprisoned and in poor health at the time of writing). There are several scenes in *The Offence* that seem to directly refer to the large-scale police searches that occurred on Saddleworth Moor. The police searchers and tracker dogs that adorned the front pages of the popular press found their way into the tense, anxious scenes where Johnson desperately tries to find Janie and, for contemporary audiences, memories of Brady and Hindley must have been fresh in their minds.

Detective Johnson then becomes reflective of a specific image in the post-1960s police film: the professional under pressure. This is most noticeable in Hollywood with films like *Serpico*, *Dog Day Afternoon* and *The French Connection* but certainly makes itself felt in British cinema as well. Johnson becomes a scapegoat for modern society, absorbing all of its inhumanity, all of its evil, so that the rest of the population can continue its day-to-day life. True crime would produce its fair share of similar individuals, real life coppers who would endure and sometimes buckle under the strain of some secret dark knowledge they were forced to carry around with them; policemen like Superintendent Bob Talbot of the Moors Murders case or Assistant Chief Constable George Oldfield of the Yorkshire Ripper case who would retire early through the strain of leading such a high profile investigation.

The dramatic structure of *The Offence* reflects the fact that it was based on a stage play, John Hopkins' *This Story of Yours*. Lumet adds some cinematic flourishes in terms of camera work (using a fish eye lens at various points to punctuate and highlight Johnson's mentality) but, by and large, what the audience is presented with is three acts consisting of three separate dialogues between Johnson and Baxter, Johnson and his wife (Vivian Merchant) and Johnson and Cartwright. Lumet, however, alters our sense of narrative flow through use of flashbacks as we gradually learn the truth of what happens between Johnson and Baxter in the opening scenes of the film (the end scenes are also the beginning). However, what concerns Lumet is Johnson's state of mind and, more particularly, how it unravels. In the tense scenes between Johnson and his wife we are never sure as to how the former will react; the *mise-en-scène* is deliberately dark and shadowy and Maureen Johnson is purposefully dowdy and ill at ease. Their flat is cramped and furnished cheaply and Johnson constantly helps himself to scotch from the melamine drinks cabinet. The walls are bare and beige and the three-piece suite is covered in brown nylon candlewick. It is a domestic environment that, a few years later, would be mercilessly lampooned in plays like Mike Leigh's *Abigail's Party* (1977) or sitcoms like *The Fall and Rise of Reginald Perrin* (1976–1979). For Johnson, though, this lower middle class environment is merely a foil for the degradation he sees daily played out in front of his eyes. In several shocking flashbacks we see the cause of his existential misery – the images of child murder, rape, death and dismemberment that haunt him and manifest themselves in his own violent behaviour.

What is noticeable about *The Offence* is precisely this interrogation of a police officer's mind. This would arguably have been unthinkable 10 years earlier when audiences were asked to associate the copper with a cheery smile and a friendly wave. It was never thought that behind the smile could lurk a madness more profound than any criminal's, that the strain of being the thin blue line could irrevocably damage the psyche of the policeman forever making them far more dangerous and far more deadly.

Although it is questionable to assert that *The Offence* is a British film at all (Lumet was an American director, it was funded by United Artists) it does provide us with several interesting insights into the evolution of the police film and the culture of British society in the post-permissiveness of the 1970s. The character of Johnson would be reflected in countless policemen, women and detectives in the popular media throughout the rest of the century. Not only would shows like *The Sweeney* depict their officers as flawed and vulnerable but later detective shows like *Cracker* (1993–1996), *Prime Suspect* (1993–2006) and even *Inspector Morse* (1987–2000) would feature protagonists imbued with the requisite number of character flaws and peccadilloes. Johnson's dark and brooding relationship to his suspect would also find a place in texts like Boris Starling's *Messiah* (2001) but never again would it reach the kinds of intensity displayed by Sean Connery and Sidney Lumet.

SWEENEY II – GET YOUR TROUSERS ON, YOU'RE NICKED!

2012 saw the release of Nick Love's *The Sweeney*, a film that was loosely based on the 1970s original. Starring Ray Winstone and Ben Drew, *The Sweeney* had very little of the urban realism that characterised the TV series and was less a homage and more a re-telling or perhaps even re-booting for the twenty first century. The drab, litter-strewn and smoke filled offices of the Metropolitan police flying squad were replaced by the glass and chrome of the City's contemporary architecture and the coshes and sawn off shotguns were replaced by handguns and computer profiling. It is, however, difficult to ignore the subtext of the film, which pits the strong-arm tactics of Regan against the officious and middle-class DCI Frank Haskins (Damian Lewis). Love's film is an *adaptation* of the original TV series and whereas it attempts to offer connections to Ian Kennedy Martin's initial conception (such as snatches of dialogue and character names) it has very little in common. Nick Love's *The Sweeney* more closely reflects the aesthetic sense of films like *Bonded By Blood* and the director's *The Football Factory* (2004) than the original series, fusing elements of masculine lore with twenty first century visuals.

The Sweeney then has become an ideal barometer for the British cultural zeitgeist, providing us with a glimpse of how the culture deals with issues like masculinity, gender and violence. When the television series was first produced in 1975 many critics saw it as the latest in gritty realism, offering a realistic slice of London life through the eyes of the world weary coppers that kept the chaos at bay. A special edition of the journal *Screen Education*, for example, was dedicated solely to using high level critical tools to examine the series and cultural writers as renowned as John Tullock and Ed Buscombe contributed.[113]

This was an example of critical theory taking *The Sweeney* seriously. Everything is examined – from its ideological stance on consensual policing to its structure and narrative. Reading the essays now, almost 40 years later, it is as if the writers were talking about *Hamlet* and *Macbeth* rather than Regan and Carter and it is difficult to imagine the same tribute being afforded to Love's film. Ed Buscombe's closing remarks in the journal display an obvious sense of caution towards the show and in particular its treatment of women but ultimately he sees it as quietly subversive. Regan's humour, he states, quietly mocks authority whilst at the same time forging working-class bonds between those with whom he works:

> *The Sweeney* isn't a comedy show, but much of its appeal derives from the repartee between Regan and his colleagues, Regan and his superiors, Regan and his crooks. Risking generalisation, one might say that Regan's wit in the presence of his superiors is bitter, cynical, intended to wound. With his equals or those below him, the wit is more gently ironic, often turned against himself or the job.[111]

As Pat Gilbert suggests, by the late 1970s the image of *The Sweeney*, with its smoky pubs and armed robbers, was losing its appeal.[115] The heirs to Regan and Carter were younger, slimmer and flashier. They would come from the US, like Starsky and Hutch, or be virile, more obviously heroic figures like Bodie and Doyle of *The Professionals*, who were fit and well trained in equal measure. By the 1980s the wheezing frame of Jack Regan seemed anachronistic to say the least.

Regan would have to wait over 25 years before he would be canonised by a generation of young men eager for heroes that harked back to a more consoling time. In January 2000, the magazine *Loaded* (arguably *the* ur-text of the New Lad) featured (as part of its Millennium celebration) Regan and Carter on its cover beneath the strap-line 'For men who've had no dinner', a slogan referring to the infamous line in the pilot. Leon Hunt outlines that, by the 1990s, *The Sweeney* had been adopted as one of those few typically British examples of masculinity that, like *Get Carter*, could be used by a generation eager for a post-feminist answer to masculine identity.[116] With Ray Winstone as Regan and Ben Drew as Carter, this is surley what we see in the remake.

For a figure that has been seen as heralding a new era in the cop show (see, for example, Richard Paterson in the *Screen Education* edition) Jack Regan was always behind the times. In the pilot of the show this is directly articulated by Det. Chief Supt. Maynon (Morris Perry) when he states: 'He's an odd sod, Regan. Twenty years ago he would have been the perfect cop, in the days of individualists. Now he's out on a limb.'

As we saw with the COI films, the official police answer to the rising wave of crime and disorder in the 1970s was an increased professionalism and what Stuart Hall writing at the time called 'the control culture' of law and order.[117] This was twinned by an increase in the levels of middle management and organisational structure as exemplified in *The Sweeney* by the various images of the busy body pen-pushers and those with second-class degrees from red-brick universities. Regan, whose detection methods consisted mainly of informants, hunches and lying in wait for 'blags' to be carried out harked back to a simpler age before computers and time and motion studies threatened to disrupt the more instinctual process of police work. Even in the 1970s, Regan cuts an isolated figure as he pursues his own personal mandates against the criminal fraternity. He is also, however, inextricably tied to the same immoral rot that he tries to cut out.

The two films of *The Sweeney* were made in 1977 and 1978 between series 3 and 4 of the show. Both films feature the familiar set of characters; however, they are also surprisingly different. As Pat Gilbert outlines, *Sweeney!* was conceived to specifically capitalise on the popularity of the television series and secured a reasonably hefty budget of £900,000 from Nat Cohen at EMI. The promise would be that the big screen version would have more thrills, more violence and more sex than the television show could ever deliver and the X certificate awarded to it seemed to underline this.

Sweeney! does stray into areas not explored in the television series. The narrative is played out against the background of the middle-eastern oil crises that were constantly newsworthy in the early 1970s. A perennially drunk and sexually promiscuous cabinet minister (Ian Bannen) is blackmailed by a morally corrupt press agent, McQueen (Barry Foster) into selling the country's oil reserves cheaply. Sexual intrigue in the form of a series of high class prostitutes is mixed with gangland violence and big business as Regan (John Thaw) and Carter (Dennis Waterman) become caught up in a narrative that would be more at home in a John Le Carré novel or *The Sweeney*'s precursor, *Special Branch*.

The opening scenes of *Sweeney!* clearly declares its cultural intentions and reflects the international concerns of a feature film rather than the narrower focus of the television serial. In terms of location, as we saw with earlier films such as *The Offence*, police films in the 1970s were often noticeably contemporary showing the modernist architecture of the day with its concrete police stations, schools and town centre vistas. The TV series of *The Sweeney*, however, always relied on a more mythological, nostalgic London of smoky pubs, dockside warehouses and betting shops. The patrons of the pubs where Regan and Carter did their drinking were always more likely to break into a Cockney sing-song than sip white wine or listen to David Bowie.

The 1977 film shows another London entirely. This time we are presented with an image of a tourist's playground. Exterior scenes are often shot against notable London landmarks such as Tower Bridge or the Houses of Parliament and the Thames ceases being a place of grimy dockworkers (as it was in *Regan*) and becomes instead the picturesque front for a riverside hotel where the manicured lawns are ringed by white rope fences that lead to the private dock. The London of *Sweeney!* is, we could assert, seen through the eyes of the tourist rather than the beat policeman. Regan and Carter mix with politicians and businessmen rather than the bank robbers and prostitutes that litter the TV series.

One of the most notable ideological outcomes of this textual 'social climbing' is the juxtaposition of major and petty crime. In one impassioned speech (set in yet another smoky pub) Regan articulates to his partner Carter what is an implicit subtext of the film:

> Listen – why do you think we get such a free hand on the Sweeney? I'll tell you... they need us death or glory boys to take on the violent criminals... the blaggers... Big Tiny... that wages truck... All over the papers: 'The forces of law and order continue to combat major crime.' Major crime! How much was on that wages truck? Twenty grand! A good accountant could make that in half an hour fiddling some toff's income tax.

The meaning here is clear: the real criminals are not those with sawn-off shotguns, stocking masks and transit vans; they are the governments, the big businesses and those who work in the City. In fact *Sweeney!* goes further than this and suggests that there is an unspoken allegiance between the petty criminal and the police that is both familiar and (as far as it can be) honourable. The armed robber, the gangster and the diamond thief play the game of law and order in which there are rules and accepted consequences. There is a mutual dependence between the policeman and the thief that is broken by the white-collar crime of the City gent or the tax fiddle of the politician. In an episode of *The Sweeney* called *Poppy* (1976), for example, Regan is asked by a colleague if he is still an inspector: 'I don't play golf' is his world weary reply, showing a level of self-awareness about his own (lowly) social position that belies a cynicism directed towards those in power.

This last point is exemplified by the ending of *Sweeney!* where Regan uses Johnson and Johnson, McQueen's own hired guns, to kill him. In scenes that display an artistic formalism very rarely evident in the rest of the film, George Carter screams at his boss

'They didn't kill him… you did', and Regan is caught in a grainy black and white freeze frame that accentuates this dramatic denouement. Ever since the original pilot, Carter represented a form moral conscience for the flying squad – if Regan was morally corrupt, then Carter was only partially so and in moments of crisis like this, George would sometimes provide a dissenting and ethical voice, as audiences were are asked to view Regan's actions through the eyes of the younger man. The effect is dramatic and the freeze frame at the end of the film is reminiscent of other great uses (Truffaut's Les quatre cinq coups (1959), Scorsese's Taxi Driver (1976)).

Other than providing a rare moment of visual formalism in what is otherwise a fairly straightforward realist depiction, this moment highlights Regan's complex relationship to crime – on the one hand upholding, but one the other, bending and sometimes breaking the law if he believes true justice will result. This point, however, must always be seen within the context his character as a whole and the depiction of Britain in the rest of the film. Regan's actions, although criminal, are, the film suggests, a necessary evil in a world that is beset on all sides by corruption and dishonesty. It is also interesting that the true villain of Sweeney! is not a politician or a bank robber but a press secretary – the faceless middle-man who became so much a part of the Heath Conservative government of the early 1970s. McQueen is not so much reflective of figures like Profumo or even Challenor but the men in grey suits that permeated what Private Eye magazine called 'Heathco' and that sought to run Britain by committee.

This then is the major socio-political subtext of Sweeney! and was perhaps why it proved surprisingly popular with audiences and, according to its director David Wickes, made a thousand per cent profit.[118] It was different enough from the television series in terms of soundtrack and visuals to lure audiences into the cinema but it was also noticeably familiar, allowing the producers to promote what was an already established brand to a market schooled in its characters and narratives. The huge profits made from the original film meant that within a year another was filmed; however, this would be far more within the mould of the original show.

With Sweeney 2 we find ourselves in familiar territory. Once again we see the same basic narrative elements (Regan as a man on the borderline between criminality and legality, the homosocial relationship of the Flying Squad, the dichotomy between Regan's method and that of the modern police force, and so on), however this second film becomes a much darker, more introspective text whereby the daily toll of London's underworld and its sights begins to affect Regan intensely. In a scene at the end of the film, for example, which would not look out of place in The Offence, Regan breaks down after seeing the leader of the robber gang that he has been pursing shoot himself in the head with a sawn-off Purdey shotgun.

Sweeney 2 exemplifies many of the issues that we have been looking at in this chapter. It begins with what will become a familiar theme in the film: movement and transport. Since the 1960s, depictions of police activity moved further and further away from the officer on the beat and concentrated more and more on the squad car. In part this was a result of the changes in the force (and, of course, the Flying Squad's reliance on the vehicle) but it was also the pervasive influence of high speed police movies like *The French Connection*, a film which had a direct impact on creators of *The Sweeney* Ted Childs and Ian Kennedy Martin.

The opening scenes of the 1978 film are as fast moving as any that came out of Hollywood at the time. We hear the sound of George Carter talking on the police radio as the camera follows a green Mercedes through a non-descript English town centre. Tony Hatch's score gives the images a decidedly cinematic feel as we become aware that the diegetic voices are referring to the car we are observing; we are on a stake-out and from the very beginning we are part of the squad. It is Regan's perspective that we will follow throughout the film but his voice is strangely absent here; this is a routine operation, the tone of the voices is unhurried, unaffected. When we learn that the criminals 'have gone to ground' it is merely a matter of retiring to the café to phone back to the office. The true meaning of why we are following this car and this group of men will not be revealed until later.

This technique, of keeping information from the viewer, was a mainstay of the television show where audiences would be presented with a three-minute prologue before the main titles began. In *Sweeney 2* the opening shots not only intrigue us but prepare us for our dominant viewing position – as a member of the police. Throughout the film we will inhabit many different points of view – at one stage, for example, we will see through the eyes of a bank robber, at others the Chief of Police but, mainly, it is Regan and Carter's perspective we are given. The opening scenes condition us to this and prepare us for the moral position the film asks us to take (imagine, for example, if the film opened with the camera situated in the watched car – this would offer us a different perspective and result in a very different film).

While Carter and the rest of the Squad are on the stake-out, Regan is at the Old Bailey after being subpoenaed to give evidence in defence of his former superior, Det. Sup. Jupp (Denholm Elliott). Jupp (who Regan himself describes as being 'so bent that it's been impossible to hang his picture straight on the office wall for the past twelve months') provides an interesting contrast to Regan, for whereas Regan bends the rules Jupp breaks them for his own profit (later we learn that he took money to frame a bank robber) providing an altogether more disruptive image of police corruption. This storyline highlights the complexity of *The Sweeney*'s evolving moral framework. Regan refuses to testify in defence of his former boss and in doing so is forced to weigh up the personal with the political. The suggestion however is not that Regan's actions are moral but that they are selfish; any officer defending corrupt colleagues is likely to be seen as corrupt themselves and so suffer the consequences. Again we are made witness to what is personally at stake for the police officer caught between the criminal and a rotten system.

The last images we have of Jupp before his trial are tinged with poignancy as he is photographed in long shot across from where Regan stands. Through shot/reverse-shot, the camera unites the two men as they gaze at each other, both aware of the necessary betrayal that Regan's actions signify. In the look between the two men we read their shared alienation from the rest of society; without the job Jupp is nothing, a situation of which Regan is only too aware.

Sweeney 2 introduces a further layer to the simple moral framework of the earlier film and television shows as we see the effects of increasing violence and alienation on the mind of Regan. In the first episode of series 4 (made immediately after Sweeney 2) Regan's drinking now seems out of hand and the even the limited affection he displayed for women in the earlier series and film is all but abandoned. The relationship he has with the hotel telephonist he woos in Sweeney 2 has nothing of the fleeting but heady romance shown in his fling with Bianca (Diane Keen) in Sweeney! a trait that extends into the other relationships he has with colleagues. By the second film Regan is a man on the edge. Of course the character would eventually disintegrate completely and, at the end of series 4, he would leave the Flying Squad forever; fittingly disappearing in the back of a black cab.

The second Sweeney film is altogether more violent than the first, its images bloodier and its humour darker. If the first film was the series attempting to come out into the light, the second was a retreat back into the shadows. The story of police corruption is combined with a narrative detailing the exploits of a group of ex-pat bank robbers who live in Malta but come back to 'blag' banks. Using money from the robberies, the band of thieves build a large villa complex in the sun where they live in what is a cross between a fiefdom and a commune. With a tragic inevitability the robbers are killed one by one whilst carrying out raids, leaving their home in the sun populated by women and children.

In the form of a collective will after their deaths, the robbers make what is perhaps the clearest statement on the dissatisfaction of most Britons in the turbulent decade of the 1970s:

> We the undersigned hereby leave all our worldly goods to the wives and children of all the said persons. We do this in the belief that England as a nation is finished. That its course is run and that the order of the day is to save what you can. We have built up by our own determination and, where necessary at the point of a gun, a structure on this island which will survive. We have passed this onto our wives and children asking that they look after it and expand it in the same spirit as it was built.

It is hard not to interpret this as a state-of-the-nation address for a film that was made in the middle of a turbulent decade.

1978 saw such films as Superman, The Deer Hunter, Halloween and Midnight Express being released and against these Sweeney 2 pales in comparison. However, as Leon Hunt states 'There's certainly a more interesting film struggling to get out'.[119] Like many of the films considered in this book, *Sweeney 2* offers us not only a glimpse of a Britain at a specific time and place but also highlights how the nation thought of itself. It is in equal measures humorous and bleak; the end scenes feature both the pessimistic tone of the thieves' will and a jubilant Regan dancing in the pub to a fiddle player surrounded by smiling faces and buxom barmaids. It is tempting perhaps to see these two images as alternative responses to the turbulent era that was Britain in the 1970s – some got drunk and some tried to forget, others left town altogether.

FOOTNOTES

96. Reiner, R., 'The Dialectics of Dixon: The Changing Image of the TV Cop', in Greer, C (ed.), *Crime and Media: A Reader*, London; Routledge, 2010, p.134.

97. Turner, A., *Crisis? What Crisis?: Britain in the 1970s*, London: Aurum Press, 2009, p.61.

98. Morton, J., *Supergrasses and Informers and Bent Coppers: A Survey of Police Corruption*, London: Time Warner Paperbacks, 2002, p.114.

99. Morton, 2002, p.144

100. Sandbrook, D., 2011, p.280.

101. Sydney Smith, S., *Beyond 'Dixon of Dock Green' Early British Police Series*, London: I.B. Tauris, 2002.

102. Knight, P., cited Sydney Smith, 2002, p.181.

103. King, G., *New Hollywood Cinema: An Introduction*, London: I.B. Tauris, 2002, p.14.

104. Murphy, 1992, p.232.

105. Murphy, 1991, p.232.

106. Turner, 2009, p.62.

107. Higson, A., 'Space, Place, Spectacle: Landscape and Townscape in the "Kitchen Sink" Film', in Higson, A. (ed.), *Dissolving Views: Key Writings on British Cinema*, London: Continuum, 1996.

108. Lumet, S., *Sidney Lumet: Interviews*, Oxford: University of Mississippi Press, 2006, p.142.

109. Cunningham, F., *Sidney Lumet: Film and Literary Vision*, Lexington: University of Kentucky, 2001, p.212.

110. Cunningham, 2001, p.212.

111. Cunningham, 2001, ibid.

112. Lumet, 2006, p.142.

113. Screen Education, 20, Autumn, 1976.

114. Buscombe, E., '"The Sweeney" – Better Than Nothing', in *Screen Education*, 1976, p.67.

115. Gilbert, P., *Shut It! The Inside of The Sweeney*, London: Aurum, 2010, p.126.

116. Hunt, L., *British Low Culture: From Safari Suits to Sexploitation*, London: Routledge, 1998, p.146.

117. Hall, S., C. Critcher, T. Jefferson, J. Clarke and B. Roberts, *Policing the Crisis: Mugging, the State and Law and Order*, London: Macmillan, 1978, p.195.

118. Gilbert, 2010, p.183.

119. Hunt, 1998, p.141.

CHAPTER FIVE: WORKING GIRLS

London to Brighton (2006)

It is no accident that the last volume of Henry Mayhew's London *Labour and the London Poor*, published in 1851 and tellingly entitled London's Underworld, begins with a description of the prostitutes who plied their trade around areas like Shoreditch and Whitechapel. Then, as now, prostitution was not only a form of criminality but regarded as a visible manifestation of moral degeneracy that was often seized upon by those who crusaded for the public conscience. Mayhew is uncharacteristically harsh on the women who sold their bodies in the streets of the Victorian capital; especially those who were ageing or stricken with alcoholism or disease as if their very presence was a reminder of the wages of sin and transgression. Mayhew is less judgemental of other categories of prostitutes such as those who resided in brothels or those who were kept as concubines by rich patrons. As would be the case with the various legal reports in the century that followed, for the Victorians the sex trade was made all the worse if it was carried out in the public view.

It was some of this sense that shaped contemporary reports of the murders attributed to Jack the Ripper in the late 1880s. The early newspaper industry was at once delighted to report the gory details of the slaughters and yet ironically reticent to fully address the occupations of those who were killed. As Judith Flanders outlines, the contemporary press used a variety of different euphemisms to sugar coat the pill of prostitution but did not feel the need to do the same with the descriptions of evisceration, partial decapitation and corpse mutilation:

> The newspapers, [she states] may have printed anatomical details more freely than before, but for the most part they remained circumspect about the occupations of these women.[120]

In a remarkable ethical *volte-face*, contemporary accounts of the Ripper murders describe the victims as living 'loose and miserable' lives and the murders themselves as being 'Heaven's scourge for prostitution'.[121] Prostitution, as many writers have suggested, for the Victorians stood at the intersection of a number of different social, psychological and medical discourses that would only be challenged in the latter half of the next century.[122]

The new journalism of the late nineteenth century, that was both formed by and reflected the lurid sensationalism of Jack the Ripper, also helped to concretise the popular image of the street walker. It is at this point that many of the clichés and stereotypes of the prostitute begin to circulate. This image, which was both fascinating and repellent, can be seen in the illustrations and descriptions of the contemporary press and clearly highlight the ambiguous relationship the surrounding society had to the sex industry – on the one hand condemning it, while on the other being inextricably drawn to it.

This chapter looks at how these kinds of discourses filtered through into popular British films. As Russell Campbell states, western cinema (British, American and French in particular) has always had a curious fascination for the image of the prostitute and the sex industry, often making it the centre of the film's narrative but also, not unlike Mayhew, using it as a signifier or a short cut to suggest a deeper social malaise.[123] This is not to say that representations of prostitutes in cinema are always unsympathetic; on the contrary, many films (especially those before and after the high points of cinematic censorship) attempt to challenge the accepted image as well explore the deeper reasons why women are forced to sell their bodies.

As we shall see here, the way in which prostitution is figured in popular British cinema can be broadly historicised and separated into distinct time periods that reflected the surrounding social morality. Representations of prostitution are also shaped by changes in the law and the way that it is policed, as papers like the *Wolfenden Report* of 1957 both reflected and altered prevailing public opinion. Like many areas of crime cinema, prostitution provides us with a fairly accurate barometer of how the British public views itself. If the cinematic gangster offers insights into the nature of masculinity and the heist movie gives insights into greed and economics, then the prostitute film sheds light on the changing face of sexual morality.

This chapter then is divided into three main periods – the 1950s, the 1980s and the 1990s – and traces how the working girl was presented in each of these. The picture that emerges from this exercise is one of slow change; from the paternalism of the 1950s, through the permissiveness of the 1960s, on to the politicisation of the 1980s. Representations of prostitution are also ineluctably tied to gender politics and the concomitant power relationships of socio-economics. Films about prostitution are almost always written, directed and produced by men but most often feature women; films that depict male prostitution such as Ron Peck's 1988 film *Empire State* are few and far between and contain radically different socio-politics as those that feature female sex-workers. This means that any study of cinematic prostitution must always consider the means of production, its context and its consumption. It must also do this with gender politics and ideology in mind.

The tension that emerges from a chronological consideration of prostitution in British cinema goes back to Mayhew and the Victorian public morality campaigners of the nineteenth century. It is the tension between liberalisation and increased legislation, tolerance and intolerance and sympathy and condemnation. This is most noticeable in the change between the 1950s and the 1980s, as the sexual liberation of the 1960s was combined with a rising sense of the personal as political, engendered by Queer theory and feminism, and a reluctance on the part of the Conservative government to legislate in the area of public morality.

Prostitution continues to be depicted in contemporary British cinema with films like *London to Brighton* (2006) and *Everything* (2004) inflecting their characters and narratives with a fin de-siècle anomie that we have seen in many of the other crime sub-genres. Again, this chapter will look at both canonical and non-canonical films that go right to the heart of the British psyche and its culture.

THE FLESH IS WEAK – THE INNOCENT, THE EVIL AND THE SIN IN THE DANCE HALL

As Phillip Gillett details, the dance hall, or palais de danse, is a reoccurring image in post-war British cinema.[124] Films like Charles Crichton's *Dance Hall* (1950), *Dancing with Crime*, *Appointment with Crime* and *Waterloo Road* (1945) all make use of dance halls in their narratives and all depict them as places of ambiguous morality. For a post-war country that was noticeably devoid of easy pleasures, the dance hall was the one place where, for the price of admission and a drink, the young and the restless could lose the restraints of austerity Britain.

The dance hall however, as Gillett suggests was 'Janus-faced'; it had the air of the exotic about it, the feint whiff of elicit pleasures, and with them the suggestion of unavoidable dangers. The dance hall is often depicted as being especially dangerous for young women who, attracted by the air of permissiveness and excitement, risk falling into the hands of unscrupulous men. The line between flirtation and prostitution becomes hard to discern in films like *Appointment with Crime*, as hostesses charge a shilling a dance and presumably can take this further if they wish. Many of the dance hall films flirt with the suggestion of prostitution but withdraw from overtly suggesting that continued post-war austerity could prompt women into selling themselves to the recently demobbed men who populated the halls.

The dance hall, then, like the prison and the racetrack, becomes what anthropologists might term a liminal space, a threshold between legality and criminality. Its dark corners and promise of pleasure singling it out as a place that was decidedly modern and yet also primitive, as Gillett states:

The dance hall was an urban phenomenon. In smaller population centres, dances were held in the more prosaic surroundings of church halls and similar multipurpose buildings. By comparison the dance hall operated six days a week, offered greater comfort and was likely to attract better bands. This could only enhance its mystique for girls unable to sample its pleasures.[125]

In *Dancing with Crime* Joy Goodall, played by Sheila Sim, takes a job as a dance hall hostess to investigate the illegal activities of Paul Baker (Barry K. Barnes) the local small time gangster. As she discusses her decision with her beau, Ted Peters (Richard Attenborough), the moral ambiguity of the job becomes manifest. Although not the kind of occupation for a good girl, it is clearly a step away from prostitution and Ted encourages his companion to take up the job.

Sim's wholesome image however is underlined by her dress and make-up that sets her apart from the other hostesses in the dance hall, whose position as purchasable commodity is less in doubt. Diana Dors, in an early uncredited role, provides us with the polar opposite to Sim's brand of sisterly sexuality. She is instantly more alluring, more on show, her speech veers from upper to lower class dialect and she seems more at home in the smoky atmosphere of the dance hall than the virginal Sim. Dors' casual sexuality immediately singles her out as a woman of fun, a good time girl.

The ambiguous position of the dance hall hostess is even more noticeable in *Appointment with Crime* where Carol Dane (Joyce Howard) becomes an unwitting accessory to murder as Leo Martin hires her for a dance to use as an alibi. The position of the hostesses is made immediately noticeable in this film, as they sit in a cordoned off seating area displaying themselves for eager gentlemen to offer them sixpence for a dance. Again, Carol Dane is clearly defined as a woman of questionable morality as she displays a world-weary nonchalance, her shiny silk dress making her seem every bit as part of the dance hall as the glitter ball or the gaudy ornateness of the architrave. Carol's alluring physicality is paired with a working class London accent that situates this dance hall at the lower end of the hierarchy, insinuating that it is little wonder that illegality goes on behind the façade of the music and the waltzes.

As Phillip Gillet observes, Carol explains that the other hostesses call her 'Chastity Ann' in an obvious reference to her unwillingness to cross the line between dancing and prostitution. Her specific brand of sexuality is for looking at and dancing with only. However for our purposes this only serves to highlight the fact that dance halls were a place where this line *could* be easily crossed; where working class women, especially those from families affected by the loss of a wage-earning male could earn money through selling the only thing they owned – their bodies. As was often the case, however, one transgression is depicted as leading inevitably to another and, by the end of *Appointment with Crime*, Carol is fully immersed in the London underworld, narrowly escaping being killed by Leo in the final frames.

Allied to the figure of the dance hall hostess is the lothario, an attractive, well dressed male (sometimes a singer, often a gangster) who lures girls into the seedy pit of the underworld, seducing and trapping them in equal measure. Not quite a pimp, these figures are a version of the spiv and it is they who are depicted as being the real stain on the nation's morality. In the days after the war, the lothario cuts a dashing local figure as he croons in front of the band or swaggers around the dance hall. Paul Baker in *Dancing with Crime*, Jim Connor in *The Green Cockatoo* and Toni Giani (John Derek) in *The Flesh is Weak* (1957) are all examples of the dangers of a handsome face and a supply of ready money; in the cinema of the post-war period we see a clear reaction against the kinds of flashy ostentation of the nightclub singer or host. John Hill traces how this figure (that he calls 'the playboy') provides a constant mirror image for that of the hard-working ex-soldier and family man; the lothario and the puritan hero – the two sides of masculinity in 1950s and 60s Britain.[126] Perhaps harking back to the images of Mary Kelly, Annie Chapman and the other Jack the Ripper victims, the women of the dance hall were often depicted as lost innocents in a harsh world; although clearly outside the bounds of public morality, they were also characterised as children rather than devils. It is the lothario who lures them into such immorality and it is he who is the real target of the film-maker's disapproval.

Don Chaffey's study of small time prostitution *The Flesh is Weak* continues this thematic trend but also imbues it with 1950s glamour. By 1957 the London underworld was in full swing, buoyed up by a slowly increasing national affluence and the influence of American popular culture. The dance hall gave way to the nightclub but it lost none of its air of exoticism and little of its seediness. Raymond Durgnat observes that films in this period often depicted sexuality as either problematic or criminally damaging, a position that he finds counterintuitive:

> …fifties X certificate sexology can almost be divided into two kinds: the devious and the glum. One might expect sex films to celebrate straight sexual ecstasies before going into the problems and perversions. The reverse happens. Eroticism, being regarded as something of a disease, is approached in its problem forms before its attractions dare to be stylised.[127]

Durgnat is uncharacteristically sentimental here if his surprise about British cinema of the 1950s dwelling on the darker side of sexuality is to be believed. Cinema, as we have suggested already has always had a long-standing fascination with the seedier aspects of eroticism and this was no different in the 1950s.

The Flesh is Weak declares its moral intentions from the very first shots. The film opens on Marissa Cooper (Milly Vitale) as she struggles through the crowds of a major British city. Noticeable against the background of dark shadows because of her light clothing and hair she carries a parcel and suitcase which singles her out as either a tourist or a runaway; immediately we note her air of innocence and amongst the smoke of the train station she looks like a lost child in a harsh, dark world. The soundtrack reminds us of the shadowy undertones of film noir and Chaffey's direction ensures that the noir-esque *mise-en-scène* is enhanced by low key lighting and head on framing. Marrissa is at once excited and afraid; she wanders the dimly lit streets and eventually walks up the steps to the Dorset Foundation Hostel for Young Women.

Chaffey cuts to a street scene on what we assume to be the following morning. We notice that the streets are busy now, the sunlight having robbed them of their mystique and their danger. Marissa, bleached blond hair now falling about her shoulders, is seen gazing into shop windows, crossing the market square, exploring the city to which she has runaway. These street scenes are clearly shot on location and members of the public stare both at Marissa and the camera as they walk by. However rather than destroying the illusion of cinema this only seems to add to her allure as she becomes locked in the gazes of the men on the street as well the camera. A more professional shoot with higher production values might well have produced a slicker product and removed the accidental fascination of the passers-by. Money for extras may have robbed Marissa of her admirers who, on reflection, are not staring at her but at the camera that she stands in front of. However, she is clearly someone to be looked at, a rare beauty on the drab streets of London.

What follows is a suggestive, if not symbolically blunt piece of dialectical montage. The camera alights on the face of a smartly dressed man; we can see his eyes are following Marissa but not casually as others are, he is interrogating her, assessing her. Clearly, he has singled her out from the crowd. She passes him and he continues to stare, looking her up and down, objectifying her not unlike a member of the cinema audience. We are unsure as to his exact intentions but (mainly due to the swelling music and the generic context) we gather they are unwholesome. As if the lasciviousness of his gaze were not enough, the camera pans down and settles on a drain by the curb. Feet walk past it and the title of the film is seen: *The Flesh is Weak*.

From its very beginning the director makes us aware of the moral position of the film. Marissa is clearly depicted as an innocent abroad and we, the audience, should prepare ourselves for a journey into the gutter. As Viv Chadder details, contemporary marketing for *The Flesh is Weak* stressed the verisimilitude of the narrative:

> Publicity material for *The Flesh is Weak* put a premium on exposing the 'truth' about London's vice kings. The screenwriter Leigh Vance supposedly frequented their haunts for accurate details and is given fictional representation in the film as Buxton, the middle-class philanthropist...[128]

The Flesh is Weak also reflects the contemporary legal position on prostitution and its attendant crimes. The major post-war statement on prostitution was the 1957 *Report of the Committee on Homosexual Offenses and Prostitution*, otherwise known as *The Wolfenden Report*. *Wolfenden* is, perhaps, better known for the impact it had on the decriminalisation of homosexuality but it also set the moral tone for Britain's stance on the sex trade for the next 50 years.

The main ideological position of *Wolfenden*, for both prostitution and homosexuality, was a belief in the separation of morality and politics. The mantra it repeated often was that 'the law is not concerned with private morals or with ethical sanctions' and consequently its recommendations were often non-interventionist in character.[129] However, Wolfenden did articulate many of the key concerns and prejudices surrounding prostitution in the post-war period, concerns that continue to be in the forefront of legal thinking even today. Whereas the selling of sex was seen as ultimately immoral and objectionable, it was also viewed as a matter for the private conscience and so allowed to exist unless it caused an annoyance to society at large. This of course included conspicuous loitering and soliciting.

In her essay, Chadder correctly asserts that the *Wolfenden Report* was noticeably light on the users of prostitution. Punters *are* discussed in it briefly but, by and large, it is assumed that they should not come under the jurisdiction of the law (this would change later when curb-crawling would be made illegal although it remains a contentious issue even today). This position is mirrored somewhat in *The Flesh is Weak*; in a relatively long exchange between Marissa and a client, the client is depicted as being unusually sensitive and understanding towards her obvious discomfort in offering herself to him. 'The only reason I came here was that my girlfriend left me last week', he explains, 'and I've had a few drinks. The chaps in the office told me the best cure was to pick up a…' He stops upon realising that Marissa is offended by the suggestion that she could be prostitute. As he turns to leave he declares 'I wanted the real thing, and you are not the real thing are you?' This turns out to be compliment and, although it results in Marissa's emotional break-down, it is also the instance at which she realises what has happened to her life and thus proves a turning point in the narrative.

Despite *Wolfenden*'s imbalance towards the clients of prostitutes, it is not as gender-biased as might first appear: some of its more condemnatory passages are reserved for the men who live off of immoral earnings, what the report calls '[the] ponce or [the] souteneur'. Despite outlining the difficulty of proving an offence, *Wolfenden* is unequivocal about the immorality of such an act:

> It may be the case that once the arrangement is established the 'ponce' makes more and more financial demands on the prostitute. It may also be the case that he is sometimes literally the bully. But in the main the association between prostitute and ponce is voluntary and operates to mutual advantage. To say this is not to condone exploitation; the 'ponce' or 'bully' has rightly been the subject of universal and unreserved reprobation, and we have already expressed the view that the law should deal with the exploitation of others.[130]

We can detect some of this distrust of the ponce in the character of Tony Giani, the man responsible for inducting Marissa into a life of prostitution in *The Flesh is Weak*. It is easy to see how governmental reports like *Wolfenden* might look upon a relationship such as Tony and Marissa's as mutually advantageous; Marissa falls in love with Tony and, through this, is tricked into walking the streets for him and his firm. However, a more nuanced reading might suggest instead that Tony cynically exploits Marissa's innocence and alienation and that he preys on young impressionable women in need of help. Marissa's romance is not one based in love but dependency and need; she is both lied to and deludes herself, gradually being drawn into a shadowy underworld that exploits her.

Both John Hill and Melanie Bell point to the figure of the outcast woman as providing a point of disruption in the social problem films of the 1950s and '60s. For Bell, the image of the prostitute in *The Flesh is Weak* and another film of the period *Passport to Shame* (1958) mirrors the assertions in *Wolfenden* that 'there must be some additional psychological element in the personality of the individual woman who becomes a prostitute'.[131] The concept that a prostitute was a breed apart from other women can be seen in the distinctions that are made in the films of this period. Part of the tension of *The Flesh is Weak* is in watching Marissa slowly falling headlong into the world of the street walker and part of her discomfort in the scene mentioned above is the fact that she is simply not made that way. She is, at heart, a good girl fallen on hard times.

As Bell also points out, the figure of the prostitute (i.e. the real prostitute, the one who is 'born to it') provides the audience with a form of visual pleasure that both drives and disrupts the narrative. In *Passport to Shame*, Diana Dors again plays the voluptuous prostitute who is both despised and longed for by the rest of society.[132] In this film the distinction between the good girl and her bad sister is made even more concrete as the brothel they both stay in has a door that leads from the respectable apartments (where the good girls live) into the brothel proper (where the bad girls dwell). Again we can see how this distinction between the good and bad girl relates to the wider social scene, with female sexuality being categorised and demarcated along moral lines.

The Flesh is Weak and *Passport to Shame* can both be considered social problem films; films that not only depict the issues and problems of society at a specific time but that also provide a discursive forum for film-makers to suggest answers. Ultimately however, both of these films are conservative in nature: the transgressive woman is brought to bear at the end of each film, rescued by either a well-meaning husband (*Passport to Shame*) or a bourgeoisie writer (*The Flesh is Weak*). This narrative conclusion is common in films depicting prostitutes. This is what Russell Campbell calls the prostitute film as love story where the fallen woman becomes rescued by a heroic man.[133] As will be the case with successive films like *Pretty Woman* (1990), the story we follow is of the saved woman, we are not interested in the fates of the other women, the women who remain in the shadows, those who are more fundamentally the 'prostitute-type'.

MONA LISA – PROSTITUTION IN THE 1980S

If the 1950s and early '60s presented an image of the prostitute that reflected the social philosophies of the *Wolfenden* report then the 1980s presented an image that reflected the changing social and economic climate. Spurred on by a variety of changes in the cultural zeitgeist, the 1980s proved to be a fecund period for the working girl on film and the decade, that will forever be linked with Thatcherism and a supposed return to Victorian moral values, produced a number of films that depicted prostitution in a sympathetic and ebullient light.

The British prostitute films of the 1980s do not constitute a cycle in the usual sense of the word. They are not linked in terms of theme, approach or ideological stance other than in their general empathy with the figure of the working girl. The films themselves cover a wide range of genres, from the crime inflected styling of *Mona Lisa* (1986) and *Tank Malling* (1989) to the social realism of *Prostitute* (1980), from the overt farce of *Personal Services* (1987) to the thriller-based narrative of *Half Moon Street* (1986). All in all there were around 15 mainstream, generally released feature films produced in the UK that specifically dealt with prostitution or have a prostitute as their main character. This does not include images of male prostitution (such as *Empire State*) or the many films where the sex trade is used as background scenery to a crime narrative. Neither does it include pornography (but does include documentary films like Nick Broomfield's *Chicken Ranch* (1983)).

One of the interesting (and perhaps telling) aspects of this corpus is that it encompasses many of the major female stars of the period. Although of course the willingness of female stars to play prostitutes has a long history and is certainly not specific to Britain in the 1980s, Sigourney Weaver, Helen Mirren, Cathy Tyson, Julie Walters and Amanda Donohoe all starred as working girls and plied their trade onscreen in a decade that is often seen as inherently masculine. In these films however, as we shall see, sex and crime become merely ways that gender and class can be discussed and re-negotiated, as the distinctions between street walkers and high class escorts, hookers and madams inflect the narratives and shape the moral frameworks that audiences were presented with.

The prostitute films of the 1980s allowed directors to examine a whole range of different themes and concerns, from race (*Mona Lisa*) to class (*Prostitute, Hussy* [1980]), from traditional notions of Britishness (*The Missionary* [1982]) to political intrigue and scandal (*Half Moon Street, Scandal* (1989)). One of the noticeable differences between the 1980s films and those of the 1950s is the moral stance that the various film-makers show towards their characters. No longer do we witness the kinds of discrimination that can be detected in films like *Passport to Shame* where prostitutes are seen as being somehow a breed apart from other women; if anything, many of the films of the '80s attempt to humanise and de-demonise the prostitute, asserting their ordinariness and exploring the fact that they are just like every other woman.

One of these films, *Prostitute*, directed by Tony Garnett and funded by a gift of £400,000 tells the tale of Sandra (Eleanor Forsythe), a working girl from Birmingham who travels down to London to pursue a more lucrative career. Shot on location in the Midlands, the film is notable for its frank depiction of the sex trade and for its exploration of the industry's ordinariness. Sandra has a husband and a child and sleeps with men to make ends meet in an area of high unemployment, social deprivation and lack of opportunity. The council estates and urban landscapes of Birmingham are shot in deliberately stark detail as the camera lingers on the prostitutes of its red light district. From its very opening shots, we can sense the sympathy that the filmmakers have towards their female characters.

Garnett, famous for his collaborations with Ken Loach, produced the iconic image of 1960s Social Realism *Cathy Come Home* (1966) and we can detect some of TV's 'Play for Today' style in *Prostitute*. As Russell Campbell, states the film also reflected changes in the way prostitution was seen by the public at large and how prostitutes were beginning to organise themselves:

> *Prostitute* came about in the context of a campaign being waged by PROS (Programme for Reform of the Law on Soliciting), for the decriminalisation of prostitution in Britain. Women working the street were constantly subject to arrest and subsequent fines or imprisonment, under the laws against soliciting and loitering.[134]

One of the most important narrative strains in Garnett's film concerns the efforts of Jean (Kim Lockett), a prostitute herself, who attempts to organise and unionise the girls on the street. Organisation becomes a defence against the dangers from both the punters and the police as the single, isolated prostitute is depicted as vulnerable and alone on the streets. In a period when the crimes of the Yorkshire Ripper were being publicised in the national media, collective action had more than a financial imperative and could literally mean life or death for the sex worker. This last point is emphasised when Sandra travels to London. After working for an exploitative madam, she ends up above a newsagent's shop, advertising her services on a card in the window. In a starkly shot scene, Sandra is abused and robbed by two police officers who force her to commit fellatio and demand payment. The viewer is left in no doubt that threats come from all sides as Sandra is forced to return home and resume walking the streets of Birmingham.

Prostitute then is firmly within a history of Social Realist film-making. Garnett's leftist political stance is clearly in evidence as the value of collective action and the importance of unionisation is foregrounded in a narrative that is also concerned with crime and the abusive nature of the police. Class also plays a major role in *Prostitute* as those on the lower end of the socio-economic scale are shown to be exploited and used by the upper and middle classes; in one particularly telling scene Sandra attends a party for upper class students who pay two young women to perform lesbian sex for them. The girls are clearly uncomfortable with the situation but are jeered on by drunken aristocratic young men. In contradistinction to the Thatcher ethos of the importance of the individual, Garnett's philosophy stresses the power of the collective in the face of industrial and social exploitation.

One of the most notable films to deal with prostitution in the 1980s was Neil Jordan's *Mona Lisa*, a film that has garnered a great deal of critical comment especially in the area of race and gender.[135] Unlike *Prostitute, Mona Lisa* subverts and challenges realist representation as it employs a *mise-en-scène* that skirts the dividing line between reality and fantasy. As Hallam and Marshment detail, realism in the cinema is based both on the verisimilitude of the visuals and on the plausibility of the narrative.[136] Realism has been employed throughout cinema's history as an alternative to the Classical Hollywood mode of narration and we can certainly see this at work in a text like *Prostitute* that uses faithfully rendered urban settings and eschews what Bordwell, Thompson and Staiger call 'compositional causality' in the construction of its storyline.[137] In contrast to a mainstream Hollywood film, *Prostitute* features an excess of narrative elements (we learn, for example, about other characters that do not feature in the main storyline) and its conclusion (much like life) is left open ended and ambiguous – we are not sure whether the film offers us a 'happy ending', a resolution, or merely runs out of time. These are all elements that characterise Garnett's film as being firmly in the tradition of British Social Realism (not to say global realism *per se*).

Mona Lisa, however, as I suggested above, cannot be viewed as existing within the same tradition, or at least not wholly. It should instead be seen in relation to Neil Jordan's folkloric fantasy *The Company of Wolves* (1984) and to his later crime film *The Crying Game* (1992). All three films reinvent fairy tale scenarios and have narratives that are concerned with transformation and performance. In *The Company of Wolves* Jordan (via Angela Carter) reinvents the tale of Red Riding Hood; in *The Crying Game*, the troubles in Northern Ireland (an archetypal realist backdrop) are used to explore the nature of transgenderism and gender performance; and, in *Mona Lisa*, we are made witness to a reversal of the usual Cinderella tale as the gangster George (Bob Hoskins) is transformed by his 'fairy godmother', Simone (Cathy Tyson).

Upon release from prison George secures a job as a driver for a high class call girl, Simone. Simone is Afro-Caribbean and her ethnicity is often derogatorily referred to throughout the film. George is depicted as an innocent in a new and changing London as he is catapulted into an underworld of vice and sin. Simone asks him to help her find Cathy (Kate Hardie), a young prostitute who has disappeared and who turns out to be her lover. Borrowing tropes from film noir, the narrative follows their search through both poles of the British class system until it ends in a bloody shoot out in a Brighton hotel where Simone kills her former pimp and gangland boss, Mortwell played by Michael Caine.

Mona Lisa reverses the usual pattern of the prostitute film wherein the lower class female is transformed by a rich and socially dominant male. George's class and prison sentence have made him uncouth and ungraceful; he looks awkward and ill-mannered amongst the high class hotels where Simone plies her trade. However part of his role is to act as her cover, so that she can avoid being stopped by the hotel security. In one scene Simone gives George money to buy clothes so that he might better fit in with the ornate surroundings of the London Ritz; however he squanders it on a flashy shirt, a shiny orange leather jacket and (of all things) a gold medallion. They argue, allowing Jordan to expose what is the film's real ideological intent: the exploration of class and race in a changing cultural climate. George (the white working class male) debases himself in front of Simone (the black sexually alluring woman) and eventually allows her to buy him a suit. As in many prostitute films, the ugly duckling turns in to a swan – but this time it is the man who is transformed and the woman the agent of transformation.

Throughout the film Simone is linked with a number of male fantasy images; she is, in turn, a madam, a tart, a submissive, a mistress, or (in George's eyes) a lady. None of the above however turns out to be true and, as Lola Young suggests, Simone's position is complicated even more because of her Afro-Caribbean ethnicity:

> The commodification of Simone's sexuality and its control by Mortwell – a white man – recalls the brutal exploitation of black women's bodies during slavery but it is Anderson, the black pimp, whose physical violence towards young white girls is that most often represented. Mortwell's control and commodification of Simone for sexual satisfaction should be recognised – to use bell hooks' phrase – as 'constituting an alternative playground', where those who are established in positions of dominance due to their gender or racial group or economic power can claim their power over subordinate groups. [138]

Throughout the film it is clear that George falls ever deeper in love with Simone. She is an obvious combination of the wife and daughter he has become estranged from while in prison. Together they form a two-sided Oedipal triangle, both acting as the protector and protected to the other. After the narrative is resolved, George is reunited with his real daughter and, together with his friend and confident Thomas (Robbie Coltrane) who has functioned as his substitute wife throughout the film, forms a makeshift family unit. In the final scenes of the film the threesome walk off into the sunset, seemingly happy and unified in their substitute family.

Mona Lisa presents us with a narrative that is noticeably inflected with influences from Hollywood genre films, most especially crime films and film noir. However it does not entirely depart from the realism that it is so obviously rooted in. Although many of the overarching narrative tropes could be seen in relation to 'compositional motivation' – i.e. characters do things because it furthers the story – there is also the kind of narrative excess that is an integral part of realist cinema. [139] Scenes between George and Thomas, for example, especially when Thomas shows George the consignment of plastic spaghetti he hopes to sell, have very little narrative purpose other than to explore their shared domesticity and to provide some comic relief in an otherwise dark narrative. Likewise small touches of tangential characterisation such as the scenes where George and Simone try on sunglasses on Brighton pier do nothing to further the narrative but do add insight into their characters and the relationship they have with each other – usually a technique more closely allied to realist cinema than mainstream Hollywood.

Nowhere does this mixture of genre and realism become more obvious than in the film's depictions of King's Cross railway station, a notorious site for prostitutes and their clients. Jordan fuses realism with a specific sense of the Dantesque as the *mise-en-scène* is inflected with low key lighting, smoke and long lingering shadows. The Jaguar that George drives acts like a ferry across the river Styx, allowing him and Simone a view of the condemned souls that lie on the other side. However, unlike Dante and Virgil, there is a tension that arises from Simone's background – she has escaped the life that she witnesses around her, but only just and therein lies the tension. Although she tries to remove herself she is inextricably pulled back into the inferno.

The city of London, in *Mona Lisa*, is both a hell and a shelter. It is also a place of extremes, where rich businessmen can buy young girls for a few pounds and where the innocent can be commodified and corrupted. British crime cinema has often explored the geographical demarcation between the East and West Ends – the gangsters and prostitutes of the East End mixing with the money and gentry of the West. Simone is at home in both places and so reflects a new kind of Londoner, one whose race and sexuality is open to question. George's journey throughout the film is not only across London but also into it, as he begins to scratch the surface of the sex industry and peel away the thin veneer of glamour that it has acquired.

Like most of the 1980s prostitute films, *Mona Lisa* does not shy away from the allure of the sex industry. Simone is not only depicted as being in control for much of the film but also provides the major object for the camera's gaze as she swathes herself in silk underwear and a luxurious cashmere coat. Later in the decade Sigourney Weaver would take this image to its logical conclusion in *Half Moon Street*, a narrative that details the story of a research fellow who decides to engage in prostitution to supplement her meagre earnings at the Anglo-Arab Institute in London. Based on the short novel, 'Dr Slaughter', by Paul Theroux, *Half Moon Street* reflects the decade's position on prostitution: that the surrounding morality is very much linked to class and social status. Dr Slaughter is saved from the kinds of ethical questions that litter *Mona Lisa* due to her elevated social class. It is difficult not to assume that Weaver's glamour adds to the moral positioning of the character also. Already a hugely bankable Hollywood name with two of the *Alien* films behind her, Dr Karen Slaughter does not even possess the moral ambiguities that we see with Simone – she sleeps with clients for money but very much on her terms; if she does not want to have sex, she merely declines their offer.

Although, as Russell Campbell correctly asserts, the suggestion that prostitution could be considered a viable employment option for the modern woman is ultimately found wanting in *Half Moon Street*, the camera does nothing but glamourise and fetishise her.[140] In one scene, Weaver's character begins to dress in the familiar uniform of the cinematic prostitute — stockings, short black dress, suspenders, and so on. However, upon catching a glimpse of herself in the mirror, she decides to change into a smart business suit, instead highlighting her agency and self-determination. She dresses for and as herself. This seems to suggest that film is making an ideological stance on the representation of women and sex-workers. However should we accept this statement at face value? If the character refuses to display herself for her clients, does the actress also? At various times throughout the film Weaver is shot in states of undress, in the shower, disrobing or in revealing underwear, undercutting the earlier image of empowerment and rendering it harmless. The clients are denied visual access to Dr Slaughter but the cinema audience is not. Like many prostitute films the narrative says one thing, the visuals another.

By the end of the film Dr. Slaughter is chastened by her experience and leaves the escort agency in what is perhaps a continuation of the 1950s assumption that prostitutes are born not made. What we do not see, however, is the same overt insistence of the inherent evil of prostitution that we witnessed in the films of the 1950s and '60s. Even *Mona Lisa*, a film that is noticeably critical of the sex trade, does not go so far as to suggest that sex for money is by its very nature wrong. At the heart of *Half Moon Street* is a simple 'innocence corrupted' narrative; however rather than being corrupted by the petty criminal or pimp, it is corrupted by big business, international espionage and government.

The prostitute films of the 1980s can be characterised by their unwillingness to condemn the image of the prostitute. In films like *Personal Services* and *The Missionary* this in fact extends into a ribald celebration of sexual excess. The prostitute here becomes something akin to the eighteenth century strumpet and is often contrasted with the repressed — and repressing — male. *Personal Services* is the semi-comic tale of brothel madam Cynthia Payne (Julie Walters). Directed by Terry Jones of the Monty Python team, the criticism of the film-makers is reserved for the authorities such as the police and legal system who are seen as staid, stuffy or hypocritical when held in comparison with the lusty ebullience of the women on the game. The same can be said of *The Missionary*, a historical narrative that follows the exploits of the Reverend Charles Fortescue (Michael Palin) who founds a missionary for fallen women in the East End of London and is seduced into a life of bawdiness and sexual freedom that provides an exciting counterbalance to his austere bourgeois existence.

None of these films with the exception of *Mona Lisa* deal with the contingent crimes that have become synonymous with prostitution — drug abuse, illegal trafficking and underage sex. However in the 1990s and 2000s all this would change as prostitution would become problematic again.

STELLA DOES TRICKS, LONDON TO BRIGHTON – THE PROBLEM OF THE PROSTITUTE

Two films that can be seen as being representative of post-1980s prostitute depiction are *Stella Does Tricks* (1996) and *London to Brighton*. Although released nearly a decade apart each articulates fears and anxieties about prostitution's links to a range of other crimes and social issues such as drugs, underage sex, abusive males and homelessness. Both films also exemplify a form of film-making that is markedly different from the models we saw in the 1980s. *Stella Does Tricks* for example was partly funded by the Scottish Lottery Fund and, as such, represents a homogenising of the production methods for small-scale British films that was not in evidence 1980s. By the mid- to late-1990s, National Lottery Funding had, along with FilmFour and BBC Films, become *the* major source of funding for British films. *London to Brighton* was also 'presented' by the UK Film Council. The free market philosophy of the Thatcher years which had so characterised the British film industry had coalesced into a two-tier system of Government funding and large-scale US backed production.

Produced on modest budgets for a mainly indigenous market, *Stella Does Tricks* and *London to Brighton* are far from the self-consciously Transatlantic-facing *Half Moon Street* or *The Missionary*. Their narratives display none of the bawdy comedy of *Personal Services*, much less the overtly political statement of *Prostitute*. They are melancholy stories displaying what Charlotte Brundson has called 'a thread of desperateness' in British film; something that will become more and more noticeable in the cinema of the post-millennial period.[141] If *Stella Does Tricks* has a politics, as Brundson also details, it is based in third wave feminism which challenges the essentialism of its second wave counterpart. Drawing on identity and gender politics, third wave feminists assert the multiplicity of the feminine experience and its links to the imaginary, promoting the self-generation and self-determination of women especially as they are linked to areas like sexuality, race and social class.

Both films show women struggling to remove themselves from the oppression of abusive pimps who also serve as surrogate father figures, often illustrated through acts that challenge their place on a moral high ground. The underlying subtext of both films is that women, especially abused women, need to employ any means at their disposal to free themselves. It is no accident that both texts have scenes of castration or genital mutilation in them, as the female characters attack that which both provides for and endangers them.

Both films also employ a realist mode of representation that is complicated by temporal fracture: in *Stella Does Tricks* via flashbacks, fantasy and memory and in *London to Brighton* through a non-linear diegesis that keeps vital information from the audience in order to build suspense. The result in both films is that we are knitted into the experience of the main female character and prostitute. The sex industry, however, in both films is used merely as background to the development of each character's journey, as they grow as women and as people. We can see instantly here that this paints a markedly different moral world to many of the films of the 1980s; the permissiveness in depictions of the sex industry that we saw in the previous decade has begun to be abandoned in the '90s.

Stella Does Tricks details the life of a young prostitute (Kelly Macdonald) who is abused and beaten by her older, father-like pimp, Mr Peters (James Bolan). In a series of flashbacks and memories, we learn of Stella's relationship to her drunken father and there is a strong suggestion that he too has abused her in a pigeon loft, a place that acts as a form of fantasy space which she ultimately burns down. Stella, after being gang raped, leaves Mr Peters and runs away with a young heroin addict, Eddie (Hans Matheson). Eddie and Stella journey to Glasgow where they wreak revenge on her father (Ewan Stewart) and Aunt (Joyce Henderson) in a series of pranks that escalate in their violence. The film ends, as Jim Leach states, ambiguously; Stella is seen taking an overdose of pills only to be depicted a few moments later in a fantasy sequence as a stand-up comic in a smoky nightclub. We are not sure if this coda is non-diegetic, represents some form of afterlife for Stella or is a last pill-induced fantasy. [142]

As Brundson states, the title *Stella Does Tricks* is open to a number of interpretations; Stella does indeed do (or rather turns) tricks in the American sense of the word – she is a prostitute – but she also carries out a series of mischievous acts that avenge abuses that have been carried out against her. [143] In this she is a trickster figure, the preternatural child of the folk tale who takes delight in making those who punish her suffer. Although shot in a vaguely realist way, we are never sure if we are witnesses to reality or to fantasy as Stella engages in a series of acts that are part-magic, part-criminal. That Stella uses fantasy and memory as a way out of her abusive environment is exemplified through the burning of the pigeon loft, an event that could be real or could just as easily be imagined.

One thing that is certain is that Stella struggles to escape from the Electra complex that grips her from her early childhood. Stella's father is both abuser and protector and encourages the young girl to drift off into a fantasy world of her own making; one that is inescapably coloured by his own barely realisable dreams of stardom as a comic. It is no coincidence that Stella ends up in the clutches of the seedy Mr Peters, a man who insists Stella masturbate him in public as they eat ice cream together in the park. The narrative of the film follows Stella's journey out of the shadows of her two father figures and away from their psychological influence.

Much of the *mise-en-scène* of the film is specifically designed to depict Stella as part woman, part young girl. As it opens we see her buying ice cream from a van, tasting some and then carrying it to the park where Mr. Peters sits. Her clothes give us mixed signals – her hair in bunches and her childish rucksack denote her as a young girl (as do the ice creams) but the length of her skirt suggests she is no innocent. After their meeting, Stella walks home through the market and immediately removes the bands from her hair; although obviously still young (the actress Kelly McDonald was twenty at the time of the film's release) she sheds some of the childishness that the bunches lend her. At various times throughout the film Stella is also pictured wearing oversized yellow high heels, a costume detail that, again, situates her between adulthood and childhood.

Stella is clearly at risk and yet, as Russell Campbell suggests, her story is universalised. She is not the only young girl taken in by Peters and the dedication at the end of the film – 'To all the girls we met' – clearly suggests that, for the film-makers at least, Stella's experience is not an isolated one. However, Stella's journey to the streets is clearly pathologised and through flashbacks we are made aware of the consequences of sexual and psychological abuse. The prostitute here, although feisty, is a victim of her past and moreover a victim of male sexual aggression. The tenets of the *Wolfenden Report* that suggested prostitutes are 'born not made' have been usurped by a psycho-pathological discourse that suggests abuse can lead to further abuses and a vaguely feminist discourse that suggests a patriarchal society creates its own victims and its own avenging angels.

One of the noticeable aspects of *Stella Does Tricks* is the way in which the punters are depicted. Like *Mona Lisa*, clients are variously shown as pathetic, desperate and ugly, as their bloated male bodies are contrasted with Stella's youthful physicality. In one scene Stella fantasies taking one of her clients home to meet her father and Aunt. He cowers in a pair of oversized underpants as she introduces him as if he were her boyfriend. It is the client who is the figure of disgust and embarrassment here, his body that causes the revulsion in the audience and his morality that is called into question, not that of the prostitute. The director, Coky Giedroyc, is careful never to eroticise the sexual activity between Stella and her punters; it is always seen as seedy, furtive and unappealing. Although the camera follows the young prostitute she is very rarely objectified in the way that became so noticeable in the 1980s.

The same visual sense underlines Paul Andrew Williams' *London to Brighton*, winner of the Best Film award at the British Independent Film Awards and a Grand Jury prize at the Sundance festival. *London to Brighton* was partly funded by the New Cinema Fund, a body affiliated to the National Lottery and UK Film Council. The New Cinema Fund, as Andrew Higson asserts, was charged with funding 'riskier and more experimental low-budget work' such as *The Magdelen Sisters* (2002), *Bullet Boy* and *This is England* (2006). The New Cinema fund saw part of its mandate as encouraging new talent and promoting equality and inclusion. Films as diverse as *Adulthood* and *Touching the Void* (2003) benefitted from this avenue of finance.[144]

London to Brighton exemplifies a form of British realist cinema, emerging out of the late 1990s and early 2000s that foregrounded performance and character-driven narratives. Rather than a return to the social realism of the 1960s, films like *London to Brighton*, *Dead Man's Shoes* (2004), *Bullet Boy* and *Harry Brown* are infused with aspects of genre cinema from Hollywood and 'Indiewood'. Rather than sticking to the usual bounds of narrative and visual naturalism, such films can be distinguished also from so-called 'Brit Grit' texts of the '90s like *Nil By Mouth*, *Ladybird, Ladybird* (1994) and *TwentyFourSeven* (1997). These new millennial films are more aesthetically hybrid than either of the two previous waves; they feature fractured narratives, non-linear time, mixed semiotics and a generic instability that often means they can display a number of different traits in the same film. [145]

London to Brighton is part realist text, part crime film, part road movie as it tells the story of Kelly (Lorraine Stanley), a prostitute who grooms a young homeless girl, Joanne (Georgia Groome), for her pimp, Derek (Johnny Harris). Derek in turn has been charged with finding an underage girl for a local gang boss, Duncan Allen (Alexander Morton). The films opens with Kelly looking severely beaten on the train to Brighton, it becomes obvious that she and Joanne are running from someone and, as the narrative plays out, we learn in flashback that Kelly has stabbed Allen and left him for dead on his bathroom floor after he has attempted to sexually abuse her. The film is the story of Kelly and Joanne's journey from London to Brighton and of Derek's pursuit. It ends with Joanne being reunited with her maternal grandmother and Kelly returning to a life of prostitution in London.

If *Stella Does Tricks* skirted the line between the adult and the child prostitute *London to Brighton* crosses it completely. Joanne is twelve and her descent into a world of prostitution, crime and murder is seen as the inevitable outcome of her life on the streets. Hunger and desperation makes her vulnerable to those who would prey on the weak and the helpless. Unlike her closest cinematic counterpart, Iris in Martin Scorsese's *Taxi Driver*, Joanne is never sexualised or eroticised for the camera; even when she is made up for her client towards the end of the film, it is a clownish mask that barely disguises her childish features. The relationship she has to Kelly is one of mother and daughter as Kelly endangers herself trying to save her surrogate daughter from the life she has known.

As in *Stella Does Tricks*, London is seen as a place of sleaze and easy money. This is contrasted with lingering poetical shots of the Brighton seafront which, although deserted, have a strange melancholic beauty to them. In one notable sequence, Joanne wanders the arcades of Brighton's pier whilst Kelly prostitutes herself so that they might afford a train ticket to Devon to visit Joanne's grandmother. Williams edits the two experiences together to form a montage that offers direct access into the two girls' relationship. The youthful joy of Joanne's desire to spend money and win a toy from a gaudy arcade machine is matched with what Kelly has had to do to earn the money and, as in *Brighton Rock* and *Mona Lisa*, Brighton is depicted as a town of both liberation and seediness.

The relationship between Kelly and Joanne is exemplified in the scene where they meet Derek in the café. This happens about 25 minutes into the film, however due to the manipulation of diegetic time, it actually occurs at the beginning the trio's relationship. After an establishing shot of a café, we are taken inside and immediately presented with a close-up of Joanne greedily eating. The visual language here is more reflective of the frugality of television than cinema; the shots are tightly framed, the depth of field is shallow and the action is closely miked, making us feel part of the action rather than detached voyeurs. We are then presented with what is a standard shot/reverse-shot sequence that unites the two figures in time and space. Kelly begins to question Joanne about her life on the streets and we see the first glimmers of the burgeoning mother-daughter relationship that will provide the moral heart of the film.

Their conversation is interrupted by Derek walking into the café and sitting down beside them. He kisses Kelly in a way that suggests affection rather than the pimp-prostitute relationship we know them to have. A cut to Joanne's face suggests to us that such displays of affection might be for her benefit. The scene is made tense due to two main things: firstly, because we, the audience, know that Derek and Kelly are really grooming Joanne for sexual purposes (although we do not know exactly what); and, secondly, as we have already been party to the outcome of this meeting at the beginning of the film, we know that something will go horribly wrong. The seemingly comforting familial scene in the café will turn, and indeed has already turned for us the viewer, into a violent bloody nightmare. Williams uses the temporal fracture of the narrative to create tension in the audience both through what we know and what we do *not* know.

London to Brighton can be thought of in terms of the Russian Formalist concepts of fabula and sjuzhet. Fabula, as David Bordwell states, describes the elements of the narrative that are constructed or inferred by the audience, the sjuzhet how this is presented to them or, as Bordwell puts it 'the architectonics of the film's presentation of the fabula'.[146] This distinction has particular resonance in a film such as *London to Brighton* that incorporates elements of the crime film but is stylistically Social Realist. The fabula invites us to construct events and infer narrative connections; isolating some information as important, others as not so. However, the narrative time of *London to Brighton* is fractured, events are mixed up, presented out of context and out of chronological order. The sjuzhet both complicates and facilitates our relationship to the fabula, on the one hand giving us the information that we need to construct the fabula and on the other frustrating or confusing us.

We can see that the relative narrative processes of *Stella Does Tricks* and *London to Brighton* exemplify this last point well. In the earlier film Stella's past is evoked through memory and flashback to add to our understanding of the story. The sjuzhet, in other words, contributes to the clarity of our understanding. In *London to Brighton*, the sjuzhet works against successful construction of the fabula until its resolution at the end of the film. Only then do we know the whole story, only then can we successfully (or at least satisfactorily) join up the elements of the story into a workable narrative. It is this element that separates the two films and their relative genres – *London to Brighton* as a crime film, *Stella Does Tricks* as a *bildungsroman*. We can see here also how use of the terms fabula and sjuzhet also allow us to understand the relationship between narrative and style.

Both *Stella Does Tricks* and *London to Brighton* articulate contemporary fears about children's involvement in the sex industry. This inevitably affects both the visual style and the moral position of both texts. Both films strenuously avoid eroticising the act of prostitution in the way that earlier texts arguably have done, and both depict women escaping from what are abusive and patently Oedipal relationships.

The depiction of prostitution has, as was stated earlier, a long history in British cinema, often reflecting the larger debates around criminality gender and sexuality. The degree to which prostitution is a victimless crime has often been central to the discourses surrounding it and a major element of the laws feeding into it. Aside from a small number of films prostitution is depicted as being a mainly female issue and thus also sheds light on how female sexuality is situated within a still largely patriarchal system. As we have seen however, film-makers are not always condemnatory towards the working girl and often depict her as a free spirit who refuses to be tamed. The prostitute as a figure, has often then been doubly excluded from society – first in relation to gender and, secondly, in relation to morality. Prostitution has always been a primarily female crime and as such it crosses more than just legal boundaries. Work carried out in the area of prostitution by feminist sociologists and historians in the 1960s and '70s no doubt paved the way for the more permissive attitudes of the 1980s films, however; as is suggested by the later post-'80s films, public morality never stands still.

FOOTNOTES

120. Flanders, J. The Invention of Murder: How the Victorians Revelled in Death and Detection and Created Modern Crime, London: Harper Press, 2011, p.431.

121. London Evening News, 1 October 1888.

122. Walkowitz, J., Prostitution and Victorian Society: Women, Class and the State, Cambridge: Cambridge University Press, 1982; Fisher, T., Prostitution and the Victorians, Charlottesville: University of Virginia, 1997.

123. Campbell, 2006, p.28.

124. Gillet, 2003, p.136.

125. Gillet, 2003, ibid.

126. Hill, 1986, p.72.

127. Durgnat, 1970, p.194.

128. Chadder, 1998, p.76.

129. Wolfenden, 1960, p.133.

130. Wolfenden, 1960, p.162.

131. Wolfenden, 1960, p.131.

132. Bell, 2004, p.141.

133. Campbell, 2006, pp.319–341.

134. Campbell, 2006, p.306.

135. Young, L., Fear of the Dark: 'Race', Gender and Sexuality in the Cinema, London: Routledge, 1996; Brundsen, 2007; Hill, 1998 etc.

136. Hallam, J. and M. Marshment, Realism and Popular Cinema, Manchester: Manchester University Press, 2000, p.20.

137. Bordwell, D, J. Staiger and K. Thompson, *The Classical Hollywood Cinema: Film Style and Mode of Production to 1960*, London: Routledge, 2006, p.14.

138. Young, 1996, p.169.

139. Bordwell, Staiger and Thompson, 2006, p. 19; Hallam and Marshment, 2000, p. 17.

140. Campbell, 2006, p.229.

141. Brundson, C., 'Not Having it All: Women and Film in the 1990s' in Murphy, R (ed.), *British Cinema of the 90s*, London: BFI Publishing, 1999, p.168.

142. Leach, 2004, p.140.

143. Brundson, 1999, p.168.

144. Higson, A., *Film England: Culturally English Film-making Since the 1990s*, London; I.B.Tauris, 2010, p.19.

145. See for example Lay, S., *British Social Realism: From Documentary to Brit Grit*, London: Wallflower, 2002.

146. Bordwell, D., *Narration in the Fiction Film*, London: Routledge, 1985, p.49–50.

CHAPTER SIX: SERIAL KILLERS

Tony - London Serial Killer (2010)

The term 'serial killer' had its true genesis in the 1970s. It was the same decade that spawned the early slasher film – *Halloween* (1978), *The Texas Chain Saw Massacre* (1974), *The Last House on the Left* (1972), etc. – and the first flowerings of postmodern culture. As we shall look at here, the serial killer narrative goes hand in hand with a range of different discourses not immediately connected with crime or deviance. Notions such as consumerism, narrative theory and the rise of capitalist modes of production can all be read through or against this type of film.[147] Serial killer narratives cut across generic boundaries, sometimes appearing in the police procedural, sometimes in the psychological thriller, sometimes in the biographical film and sometimes in horror. Like the gangster or prostitute film, serial killer cinema is defined largely by the characters that populate it; therefore any distinct generic definitions are hard to assert.

The place of the serial killer in contemporary culture has been studied by both sociologists and criminologists who often stress the connections that exist between their crimes and the media. Robert Ressler, the former FBI agent who coined the term 'serial killer' in the 1970s, explains that he took it from the many serial films that he witnessed as a young boy.[148] The weekly serial would end leaving you wanting more, leaving you unsatisfied and looking for the next encounter. It would satiate you only briefly before driving you on to want another experience. This is also the basic compulsion at the heart of the serial killer. Not just a human being (usually a man) who kills but one who does so because they are driven to do it time and time again, as Richard Dyer explains:

> Serial killers kill serially: one murder after another, each a variation and continuation of those before, each an episode in a serial. Then the police and the media identify apparently disconnected murders as connected, and the logic of the serial unfolds:

the discovery of further corpses, the next instalments in the killing, the investigation, the culprit's apprehension, trial and even their life in prison.[149]

Dyer goes on to say that this seriality is expanded out to the history of serial murder itself; successive killers are seen as forming a link in a chain, or an episode in a series of murderous acts that can be connected up. Beginning perhaps with Jack the Ripper and ending with Hannibal Lector, the history of serial killers reads more like a genealogy, with perversity and cunning being handed down from father to symbolic son; a form of dark heredity or a direct lineage of influence. The serial killer film can also be seen in this way; prone to sequels and re-imaginings, movies like *The Silence of the Lambs*, *Se7en* and *Saw* (2004) have spawned their own copycats, aping the modus operandi of former killers and the style and semiotics of former texts.

It is the flexibility of the serial killer narrative that makes it difficult to discern generically. In the seminal work *Shots in the Mirror – Crime Films and Society*, Nicole Rafter suggests that we should view serial killer cinema as being allied to what she calls 'slasher movies' and 'psycho movies'.[150] For Rafter, slasher movies can be exemplified by their onus on the visceral enjoyment of the crimes themselves. Rarely focusing on the morality of the deaths, the slasher film (e.g. *Friday the 13th* [1980], *Halloween*, arguably *A Nightmare on Elm Street* [1984]) offers its audience the thrills of vicarious enjoyment over narrative and character. In this, it is more akin to the ghost train than the crime film.

The psycho film, however, offers a more nuanced experience, one that explores the nature of madness and thus attempts to present a more rounded vision of crime and criminality, as Rafter states:

> Psycho films, unlike slasher and serial killer movies, are not a recent development but have appeared since the first talkies. Thus, they now exist in considerable numbers, giving us a large group of films to analyse. The most revealing way to classify them is by types of protagonists and the impulse that lie behind their evil deeds.[151]

Psycho films allow us to experience the madness of the killer and, as in Hitchcock's 1960 film *Psycho*, often offer us consoling explanations as to how the criminal differs from the rest of society. Our faith in the sanity, and essential goodness of humanity is often restored through recourse to the comforting logic of narrative resolution or (in more recent times) psychiatry.

For Rafter, the serial killer film is 'like a slasher film for adults'.[152] We are as concerned with the detection of the murderer here as either the act (as in the slasher film) or the psychopathology (as in the psycho film). The serial killer film, according to Rafter, posits a killer who is devoid of humanity, a cold-blooded murderer, a personification of evil who contrasts with the consoling good of the pursuer (for example, Agent Starling and Hannibal Lecter in *The Silence of the Lambs*, David Mills and John Doe in *Se7en*, MJ and Daryll Lee Cullum in *Copycat* (1995) etc.). Unlike the psycho film, serial killer cinema cares not for the reasons behind the killing but instead presents us with a more voyeuristic, gratuitous portrait of homicide – this is perhaps why they often feature unrealistic and (quite literally) formulaic narratives that rely heavily on an audience's suspension of disbelief. The contrived storylines of *Se7en* or *Copycat* for example serve more as exercises in narrative inventiveness than studies of criminality. The serial killer in these texts tends to be beyond human, a killing machine that serves as a gothic dark heart to a modern, consumerist society.

However illuminating, Rafter's classification must be approached with caution: Her citing of the British film *10 Rillington Place* (1971) as an example of a 'psycho' rather than a 'serial killer' film – despite the fact that it details the life of John Christie, who murdered 8 women between 1943 and 1953 – highlights the slippage that exists between the two definitions and begs us to question their validity. In this chapter, then, I will not be employing Rafter's taxonomy other than as a basic starting point for analysis.

Robert Cettl's encyclopaedic *Serial Killer Cinema* also highlights the problems of distinct definition in this area. Cettl *does* include *10 Rillington Place* in the category of the serial killer film as well as almost 500 others ranging from one extreme – *Henry: Portrait of a Serial Killer* (1986) – to another – Woody Allen's *Shadows and Fog* (1991). However, again, the definition of what exactly constitutes a serial killer film is both wide-ranging and unsatisfying. The introduction to Cettl's book traces the genealogy of the sub-genre film back to the earliest cinematic texts – is not Robert Wiene's *The Cabinet of Dr. Caligari* (1920) an early example of a serial killer film, he asks? Although the character of Cesare is a pawn of Caligari and, as Cettl points out, his killing driven by hypnosis rather than madness, he is still a serial killer in the modern mode and forms part of the genealogy of repeated homicide. This is a fair point; however, in opposition to Rafter, the definition of 'serial killer' cinema here seems overly loose. There is killing in Wiene's film but this is very rarely taken as its main generic constituent; we are more concerned with its stylistic tropes, its pop-psychology and its mythopoetics than its murders. Do we gain anything by asserting that films like *The Cabinet of Dr. Caligari* can be fitted into a historical narrative of crime cinema at all? Can we assert that they exist as examples of specific crime narratives? This chapter suggests that we have to be more nuanced in our readings of these texts and that we need to place them in their socio-historical context; tracing not only how they form a diachronic evolutionary line but how they absorb specific fears and folk devils relevant to their time. In a more concrete analysis Cettl traces the influence of the German murderer Peter Kürten, 'the Vampire of Dusseldorf', on German Expressionist texts like *M* and *Nosferatu* (1922). A contemporary press that was hungry for sensation ensured that Kürten's crimes (including child murder and cannibalism) quickly entered the realm of public consciousness and manifested themselves in a variety of different, otherwise disparate cinematic texts. Like later killers such as Jeffrey Dahmer and Ted Bundy, Peter Kürten would provide the real-life blueprint for some of the period's most terrifying cinematic figures and become reflective of a nation's nightmares.

At their heart, as Sarah Casey Benyahia details, serial killer films delight in the pleasures of narrative.[153] The seriality of the act itself mirrors the structures and mechanisms of narrative flow; as the killer goes from victim to victim so the audience is projected from plot point to plot point and act to act. Towards the end of their career, many murderers long for an inevitable 'closure', just as an audience member awaits the resolution of the narrative and the end credits. The serial killer film is pure storytelling, delighting in plot construction and encouraging (temporary) identification with evil. Whereas slasher films ask us to identify with the victim, to shudder at the sight of the blade and to scream along with the vulnerable, the serial killer film often tricks us into siding with the maniac. If we care about narrative (and of course we do) then we are made complicit in the act of murder itself.

In its foregrounding of narrative over realist representation, the serial killer film signals its own textual presence. In this way it is also anti-mimetic and thus often challenges the usual modes of Hollywood narrative that strive for ever immersive, ever realistic representation. Serial killer cinema distances its audience from the spectacle by highlighting the narrative procedure that it employs and exposing the text's internal working. However even these statements must be used cautiously as the serial killer film very often also encompasses the biopic and the Social Realist text. Films like *Monster* (2003), *Gacy* (2003), *Dahmer* (2002), *Citizen X* (1995) and so on all draw on realist techniques and narrative modes to depict murder and murderers. This is particularly the case with depictions of British killers that tend to be allied to the social problem film or biography rather than the horror genre – we see this, for example with TV dramas like *See No Evil* (2006) and *Appropriate Adult* (2011), which detail the lives of the Moors Murderers and Fred West respectively.

Whereas most national cinemas have their variants of the serial killer film, Hollywood produces them in abundance. As Cettl outlines, this may have a great deal to do with their socio-historical context but might also relate to the ideological standpoint of Hollywood itself that canonically privileges the individual over the collective.[154] The serial killer is the individual *par excellence*; separated from the rest of society, they work alone (or at most in pairs) and their only goal is self-satisfaction, whether that is financial, psychological or sexual. As Jarvis outlines, the serial killer is also the ideal consumer, he both collects and destroys, wanting more and more, all the while accumulating waste.[155]

The sequential narrative flow of the serial killer film, with its tropes of overcoming evil and the restoration of a peaceful equilibrium, also reflects Hollywood ideology. At the end of a film like *Citizen X*, that details the shocking story of Andrei Chikatillo, the Russian serial killer thought to have brutally murdered and violated 50 women and children, we are presented with a consoling scene of the criminal being executed at the hands of the state. The detective-hero of the film is shown driving his young family away from the prison in a gesture that signifies he has reached a level of financial and personal success and the audience is presented with a scene of peaceful resolution and evil has been defeated. The pain of murder or the mourning of the victims' families are never addressed or allowed to spoil the peace of the narrative conclusion. Time and time again we see this in serial killer cinema, a narrative trope which is in itself heavily imbued with the ideology of Hollywood that values triumph over adversity in the all-important happy ending.

As we shall see, British cinema has been noticeably reticent about depicting its serial killers. Aside from Jack the Ripper, who has appeared in many films since the 1920s, British killers are not nearly as ubiquitous as their Hollywood counterparts and where they are depicted they are often allied more to realism than horror. This chapter will look at three films where serial killing is the main thrust of the narrative. However it will not consider films that are more usually allied to the horror genre; recent British films like *Severance* (2006), *The Cottage* (2008) and *Mum and Dad* (2008) are concerned with killing but they draw more heavily from contemporary horror staples like *Saw* and *Hostel* (2005) than the crime film and so belong in another survey. Like all areas of the crime film, British serial killer cinema is inextricably linked to Hollywood; however, it also strives to distance itself, drawing on quintessentially British histories, images and texts.

SAUCY JACK – THE CONSTRUCTION OF A MYTH

In his essay 'Decline of the English Murder', George Orwell bemoans the passing of a Golden Age of British homicide. Coming between 1850 and 1925, the high point of British killing boasted such luminaries as Dr. Crippen, Neil Cream, Joseph Smith (the Brides in the Bath murderer) and Mrs Maybrick.[156] Like many things, Orwell blames this decline on the influence of America and of Hollywood. Post-war murder, he bemoans, has not the sophistication or the gentility of its late Victorian or Edwardian counterparts; it is too violent, too angry, too homicidal.

Interestingly however, there is one set of murders that Orwell leaves out of this list and which he describes as being 'in a class by itself' – Jack the Ripper. The Whitechapel murders simply do not fit into the image of the repressed middle class poisoner of Orwell's classic period; the sheer ferocity of the killings prevent him from talking so glibly about this specific set of homicides. However Jack the Ripper is perhaps the dark shadow that lurks behind all other serial killers, both in real life and in the cinema.

As Darren Oldridge argues, the Ripper murders were always inextricably bound up with the media and the press that reported them.[157] As we saw in Chapter Five in relation to prostitution, the new journalism that grew up in the late nineteenth century revelled both in the lurid sexuality of the East End of London and the visceral nature of the Whitechapel murders. One of the outcomes of this was that the murderer himself was soon elevated to the status of myth. Jack the Ripper was, in the eyes of the contemporary press, part maniac, part ghost and part vampire as he stalked the backstreets of Whitechapel murdering women and instantly disappearing back into the shadows. As Oldridge details:

> The idea of a single killer… reflected the anxieties about the 'degraded' state of East London. Fears that parts of the capital were descending into 'savagery' accorded with the concept of a maniac driven by bloodlust…This thinking was explicit in the *East London Observer*, which deduced that a 'fiend' was responsible for [Polly] Nichol's killing because robbery was not a plausible motive.[158]

This stress on the preternatural elements of the case would not only single out the Ripper killings as different from many of the other pre-war murder cases; it would also bleed into the nation's consciousness, providing the basis for countless mythical retellings and re-imaginings throughout the twentieth century. Contemporary accounts of the murders have more than their fair share of Gothicism, something which has been drawn upon in later retellings. Even as they were happening, the Jack the Ripper murders were mythologised by the popular press beyond the bounds of their grisly reality, providing an early example of how the media shapes and colours our experience of crime.

One of the first films to be inspired by the Jack the Ripper killings was Alfred Hitchcock's *The Lodger* (1927), itself based on the Marie Belloc Lowndes novel of the same name. Subtitled 'A Story of the London Fog' it was clearly designed to articulate the myth rather than the reality of the Ripper's crimes. *The Lodger* is generally considered to be the director's first recognisably Hitchcockian film and presents the viewer with an unrestrained mixture of suspense, German Expressionism, Catholic iconography and silent era melodrama. Starring the contemporary heart throb Ivor Novello, it tells the story of a nameless lodger who takes a room in a house in London's East End where a serial killer, dubbed The Avenger, stalks the streets. The daughter of the household, Daisy Bunting (listed only as June in the titles), falls for the lodger and Hitchcock not so subtly suggests that she might be in constant danger from this good looking but intense stranger. Aside from this, Daisy is also courted by Joe, the thick-set local detective (Malcolm Keen) who has co-incidentally just been assigned to the case.

As the narrative unfolds, Hitchcock builds suspense by withholding the vital information that the lodger is, in fact, the brother of the first Avenger victim. The incriminating evidence found in his room by Joe (maps of the murder sites, an image of the murdered girl, etc.) are tools of pursuit not of murder. Eventually the real killer is caught and the lodger and Daisy are married.

The Lodger, although clearly a youthful work, contains a number of elements that will not only feature in Hitchcock's future films but that reoccur with notable regularity throughout serial killer cinema. Firstly, as already hinted at, *The Lodger* depicts the killer as myth rather than reality. Although never seen in the film itself, The Avenger has a clearly defined set of mythological and supra-human traits that allow him always to avoid detection – he blends into the crowd, he can never be identified, he can kill at will and so on. This image will be recycled in future years with figures such as Hannibal Lector who constantly evades the police and can slip through the tightest of dragnets.

Secondly, there is what Claude Chabrol and Eric Rohmer called the 'transference of guilt', whereby an innocent party is punished for the sins of another; in this case the lodger is pursued and beaten by a crowd thinking that he is The Avenger. Transference of guilt will play a major role in much of Hitchcock's future work and would shape his wider philosophical vision.[159]

Lastly, we see in *The Lodger* a misogynistic streak that twins feminine transgression with murder and punishment. Hitchcock, through The Avenger, punishes young women for their easy sexuality and their flashy display. Again this is a trope that we can see played out time and time again in his work, from the infamous punishment meted out to Tippi Hedren in *The Birds* (1963), to the strangulations of *Frenzy*, his return to English murder narratives in 1972.

William Rothman's *Hitchcock: The Murderous Gaze* contains an in-depth consideration of *The Lodger*, and more especially its place as the progenitor of cinematic Modernism, an art form that is both self-reflective and self-referential, drawing on its own traditions and images for inspiration.[160] As we shall explore here, *The Lodger* is as much a reflection of the influence of German Expressionism on Hitchcock as the Jack the Ripper myth and the characters within it taken as much from the castles of Transylvania as the streets of Whitechapel.

Hitchcock travelled to Germany in 1924 as part of a deal struck with the German studio UFA by producer Michael Balcon. As McGilligan details, Hitchcock would work closely with German directors and cameramen during this period, absorbing Expressionism in both its moral and visual forms, something that inevitably found its way into *The Lodger*.[161] Years later in classics such as *Psycho* and *North by Northwest* (1959) we can still detect the visual trickery and inventiveness that was the hallmark of directors like Fritz Lang and F.W. Murnau.

William Rothman opens his analysis with a description of the film's prologue:

> *The Lodger* opens with a view of a woman screaming; then the scene fades to black. We are not shown what precedes the scream or what immediately follows it, but in a moment we will understand that this shot is a fragment of a scene of murder.[162]

The scream is something that will be used several times throughout the film and will punctuate the high points of terror in the narrative. For a silent film this is unusual; without sound, screams lose much of their impact and yet they still carry semiotic meaning. As Rothman states, the point of view in these opening shots fuses the gaze of the camera with the gaze of the murderer, making the viewer complicit in the act of homicide, but also ensuring that we are never party to the face and thus identity of the killer. Like the Ripper, he exists merely in shadow.

Hitchcock then cuts to a low level shot of the dead girl intercut with the face of a terrified onlooker again screaming. The action here has been elided, the grisly business of murder has been passed over in favour of depictions of the terror it causes in others. We are spared the gory details of how the girl died but we are made fully aware of how her presence disturbs the public that flocks around the corpse with open eyes and mouths. There is no blood here, no last gasps of breath, no pain – just shock. This squeamishness towards the corporeal nature of death will become a noticeable trait in cinema concerned with the Jack the Ripper killings, as such films as *A Study in Terror* (1965), *Man in the Attic* (1953), *Murder by Decree* (1979) and *Time After Time* (1979) will all fail to embrace the bloody and visceral nature of the murders in the way that the nineteenth century press did.

In terms of audience experience, this opening montage provides us with a blueprint that will be followed throughout the rest of film. There will be other murders but we will never be party to who is committing them or how they are being carried out. As murderous acts they are neither brutal nor bloody and remind us not of the messy descriptions of new journalism but the more rarefied and beautiful seductions and vanquishes of the vampire. Just as Dracula disappears through the open window so The Avenger melts into the night; just as vampiric victims are cleanly drained of blood, so The Avenger kills cleanly and (at least as far as the camera's gaze is concerned) bloodlessly. Again, here Hitchcock betrays his debt to the German Expressionist directors of the 1920s, Novello is often depicted as being tormented by some inner turmoil, some existential yearning. As Napper and Williams outline this was not only a feature of Hitchcock's direction but a part of the actor's star appeal. Novello's features were at once 'safe' and 'bland', allowing meaning to be projected on them by either camera or audience.[163]

In anticipation of films like *Zodiac* (2007) and *Natural Born Killers* (1994) Hitchcock offers an early montage that demonstrates the power of the press in the construction of a serial killer. We are presented with an image of a furtive reporter feverishly taking down notes, a gossipy crowd watching on, a woman being interviewed and a story being telephoned into the news office. We then see the machinery of the newspaper churning out stories, feeding an eager public, stoking the fire, creating a myth. The crowd that has gathered at the murder site are whipped into a frenzy of paranoia and anxiety as they begin to suspect each other of being the killer.

As Hitchcock himself revealed to François Truffaut, these opening scenes describe the ease with which modern communication systems can transmit their messages:

> Through all the different means of communication, the information [of the murders] begins to spread, and finally the evening papers are out on the street. Now we show the effect on various people. Fair haired girls are terrified. The brunettes are laughing. Reactions in the beauty parlours or of people on their way home. Some blondes steal dark curls and put them under their hat.[164]

As early as 1927, then, Hitchcock was exploring the relationship between the media and the serial killer.

This sense of paranoia and fear underlines the rest of the narrative and provides the suspense that is played out against Daisy's relationship with the lodger. Novello's somewhat theatrical but fragile performance imbues the character with an air of tragedy that stands in marked contrast to Malcolm Keen's more masculine Joe, the hardened police officer. The lodger is an outsider, an alien and we are told ambiguously that he is 'not keen on girls'; however none of this stops Daisy falling for his feminine air of detachment despite the fears of her parents. The link between serial murder and ambiguous sexuality will crop up time and time again in crime cinema. Deviant behaviour, for the movies at least, goes hand in hand with deviant sexuality.

As Michael Walker states, *The Lodger* is one of the best examples of transference of guilt in Hitchcock's canon; a concept and term originally posited by Rohmer and Chabrol in their book *Hitchcock: the First Forty-Four Films*.[165] Punishing an innocent party for the sins of another is a common and persistent theme in Hitchcock's work; we see it in *Strangers on a Train* (1951), for example, between Bruno and Guy, but also in *Frenzy* between Dick Blaney and Bob Rusk, in *Murder!* (1930), in *Spellbound* (1945) and in many others. However, in *The Lodger* this trope is extended: not only does the lodger become punished for the sins of The Avenger (i.e. he is pursued by the crowd and symbolically sacrificed) but he also takes on some of the guilt attached to his sister's death. Novello's pained and emotive facial expressions underline the character's angst at his failure to protect his sister and, we could assert, his need to look after Daisy (another curly haired blonde) is as much a reflection of this as his love for her specifically.

The lodger, then, suffers for the sins of another, both at the hands of the crowd and through his own conscience. In two memorable moments, Hitchcock makes this explicit: as Novello is pictured firstly with the shadow of the window frame making a cross on his face and, secondly, as he hangs Jesus-like from the railings before being torn at by the crowd after being pursued through the streets. After the real Avenger is caught, the lodger is assuaged of guilt and allowed to take up a healthy life, but first he has been made to suffer.

One question remains, however, and it relates to the enigmatic name of the serial killer – The Avenger. Like Jack the Ripper before him and like many after (most notably the Zodiac killer from San Francisco who taunted the press with drawings, symbols and ciphers to his own identity) The Avenger is part murderer, part marketer, as he selects for himself not only a highly memorable name but a suitably apt logo – a triangle. Like many cinematic killers The Avenger also has a highly original modus operandi; he only kills young blonde women with shiny golden curls and, as he explained to Truffaut, Hitchcock went to great pains to highlight this point:

We opened with the head of a blonde girl who is screaming. I remember the way I photographed it. I took a sheet of glass, placed the girl's head on the glass and spread her hair around until it filled the frame. Then we lit the glass from behind so that one would be struck by her light hair.[166]

No one familiar with the rest of Hitchcock's career will fail to notice the similarities between the director and The Avenger; both murderer and filmmaker targeted young, pretty blonde women, putting them in danger and punishing them for their attractiveness. The Avenger did it with the knife, the director with the camera. Both actions can be read as misogynistic, a working through of personal obsession and personal repression. The Avenger avenges moral laxity, a signifier of which for him (and for countless of those who will follow him) is the female form. It is no coincidence that Hitchcock depicts his potential victims as being not only blondes but also showgirls; the resonances of Jack the Ripper are not difficult to spot.

Hitchcock would return to serial murder many times throughout his career but the blueprint was set early on with The Lodger. Here he explored the narrative tropes and stylistic flourishes that he would put to use in landmarks such as Frenzy, Strangers on a Train and Shadow of a Doubt (1943). As an exploration of serial murder however The Lodger is problematic due in part to the homicidal act not being its main focus; instead it concentrates on the margins of crime, the outskirts, its interest lying in how murder and murderers are mythologised; how the press creates mass panic and how the crowd desperately seeks someone to blame for the sins that are its own. Throughout the twentieth century we would see instances of this time and time again, as figures like Ian Brady, Dennis Nilsen or Peter Sutcliffe would be vilified by eager crowds baying for blood. The Lodger never concentrates on The Avenger because the killer was very rarely where Hitchcock's interest lay. Instead he was fascinated by the innocent man who was sucked into the nightmare through no fault of his own – the patsy forced to shoulder the guilt of another's sins.

10 RILLINGTON PLACE – SERIAL KILLER REALISM

Like many of the films we have looked at in this book, Richard Fleischer's 10 Rillington Place has been largely passed over by film critics and historians, a fact that is perhaps surprising given the calibre of its cast and director. Although the film's claims to a British pedigree are clearly debatable – being produced by a large Hollywood studio and directed by an American – in its settings, style, cast and narrative it is recognisably culturally British. This last point is exemplified by its inclusion in both Alexander Walker's National Heroes, the quintessential history of British cinema in the 1970s and Denis Gifford's British Film Catalogue, perhaps the ultimate source for cinema in the UK. As we shall determine here, the story that it tells resonates with many of the most pressing socio-political debates of the post-war period, and as well as being a biopic of one of the century's most notorious murderers, it is also a statement on the death penalty and the legalisation of abortion.

The lack of attention it has received may have something to do with the realist aesthetic that heavily informs it; both in its script and in its visual language, *10 Rillington Place* aims for a realism that is seldom seen in serial killer cinema and that owes more to the British New Wave and the social problem film than the crime movie. Told in chronological order (although not always sticking strictly to the chronology of the facts) it not only details the story of Christie and the eight murders he committed in the eponymous house in Notting Hill but also of Timothy Evans, the innocent Welshman who was hanged (but posthumously pardoned) for the murder of his wife, Beryl, and his daughter, Geraldine. Visually, the *mise-en-scène* owes something to Edgar Anstey and Arthur Elton's 1933 documentary *Housing Problems* that detailed the overcrowding and shocking conditions of London's East End. One of the tacit political points of Fleischer's film is that the overcrowded slum inevitably harbours evil, not only providing the means but also the impetus for murder.

The film's cinematographer, Denys Coop, had previously worked on notable New Wave films such as *Billy Liar* (1963), *This Sporting Life* (1963) and *A Kind of Loving* (1962), and these would inevitably inform the basic visual language of *10 Rillington Place*. It is claustrophobic, dingy and the decay of post-war London hangs heavily in the air as we are made acutely aware of the privations of 1950s Britain. The house itself owes more than a little to the English Gothic tradition that posits a connection between psychology and environment; we can place 10 Rillington Place, the building, in the same category as the Bates Motel or the Castle of Otranto as they become objective correlations to the madness that lurks within the minds of those that live in them. Filmed in Rillington Place itself, before its demolition in 1974, number 10 is characterised as a cage that breeds discontent, misery, perversion and murder.

Alexander Walker suggests another reason for the film being overlooked:

> For all the lurid expectancy its multiple murders aroused, *10 Rillington Place* looked like a humane society's pamphlet compared to the moral void opened up within weeks of its appearance by two other British-made movies. [167]

The oppressive realism of Fleischer's film was eclipsed, states Walker, by *Get Carter* and *Villain*; films that, as we have already seen, fused sexuality and violence in a way that suggested new moral and ethical territory. Whereas Fleischer's previous serial killer film *The Boston Strangler* (1968) would attempt a hybrid of crime narrative and avant-garde visual techniques, *10 Rillington Place* is harsh and stark, the horror of Christie's actions never softened or glamorised by camerawork, performance or star status. However, despite detailing everything from necrophilia to infanticide, we are very rarely made party to gratuitous scenes of violence towards the women. Instead the director shoots the murders from their point of view and we are placed in the position of one of Christie's victims, forced to be a witness to his murderous gaze as his chokes the last breaths out of our bodies. Hitchcock would employ this technique a year later in *Frenzy*, a film that owes a lot to Fleischer's. However, again, this is a debt that has never really been explored.

An opening title assures us that what we are about to witness is based on factual information, something that underscores and underlines the text's relationship to realism and to truth:

> This is a true story. Whenever possible the dialogue has been based on official documents.

Such realism extends into the construction of the dialogue itself which closely mirrors the stutters and imperfections of everyday speech. Characters fail to finish sentences, stumble over their words and struggle to express themselves clearly in a script that self-consciously shuns the usual slickness of the Hollywood mode. Christie's dialogue especially is peppered with pauses, stalls and nervous utterances that root the film firmly in a realist tradition. In the scene in which the Evans (John Hurt and Judy Geeson) family first meet the Christies (Richard Attenborough and Pat Heywood) their speech is stilted and forced. As they stand on the doorstep of 10 Rillington Place, Timothy and his wife speak over each other in a way that is at once familiar and strange. Used as we are to the highly polished dialogue of the Hollywood crime film, it seems unusual to have such clumsiness in the speech act, but this only adds to the oppressiveness of the film and to the burgeoning horror that develops between the two couples. This horror is all the more terrifying for the recognisable reality that the director creates.

Unlike *The Lodger*, there is little mythologising in *10 Rillington Place* although we can detect a touch of German Expressionism in the character of Christie who seems sometimes to appear out of the shadows like Nosferatu or Dracula. Again, in a technique that Hitchcock would employ in *Frenzy*, Fleischer makes use of close miking for many of the more intense scenes. As I have explored elsewhere, this not only brings the viewer closer to the action but also encourages us to draw on our own experience of bodily proximity to understand the emotions and physical experience of the victims.[168] As Christie ties the rope around one of his victims' neck and begins to pull we can not only hear his breathing but we can sense it on or skin, we can feel his breath on our cheek, hear the creak of the rope close to our ears and sense the smell of fear. We become inextricably linked to the act of murder in all its visceral meaning, existing in a form of shared cinematic space between the screen and ourselves. This sense of physical unease is heightened by the set design and the cramped conditions in the house, as characters struggle to maintain personal boundaries as they navigate around the confined environment.

We could suggest that Fleischer here employs a form of hyper-realism, where the closely miked soundtrack and the close-up become the main tools of expression. This enables him to transcend the usual techniques of realist cinema that rely on medium and two-shots to assert the connection between character and space. At specific points in the narrative, most particularly during the murders, the director eschews the detached naturalism of canonical realism by utilising techniques from horror and suspense as we are drawn into the space inhabited by the characters, especially the victims. This makes the film a much richer text stylistically than might first appear and one that is perhaps more inventive than either *Get Carter* or *Villain*. It also suggests that the film is much more than just a biopic of Christie and Evans, as it explores the relationship of the cinema viewer to the screen.

As Christian Fuchs details:

> Richard Fleischer, who did not only intend to study the anatomy of a case of murder but also wanted to condemn the deplorable death of Tim Evans, stages his film as a claustrophobic, intimate play. Narrowness, anxiety, blank walls behind which atrocious secrets lie. The events outside the house hardly matter. [169]

Fuchs points to a vital aspect of the film's design here: that Rillington Place is not only setting and *mise-en-scène*, it is a character in itself. We only catch brief glimpses of the outside world in the film but when we do, such as the scenes in which Timothy Evans returns to Wales after the death of his wife, they will have a dreamy quality to them as if they are moments of heaven away from the hell of London and its cramped terraced houses. Again, the interior shots of the house remind us of the documentaries of the 1930s that are in sharp contrast to the green of the Welsh valleys.

It is interesting to compare the moral standpoint of *10 Rillington Place* with that of *The Boston Strangler* made by Flesicher only three years earlier. On the surface *The Boston Strangler* has a more progressive aesthetic; it is notable for the innovative methods through which the mind of Albert DeSalvo was explored and employs a series of masks and sub-frames that offer the viewer a multiple perspective on the events. As Harper Cossar details:

> In *The Boston Strangler*, Fleischer generates and heightens suspense via the multipaneling technique as the police, the victim, and the killer are shown simultaneously within the same image occupying different segments of the widescreen frame. The suspense and terror are ratcheted up because, as the police are looking for the killer, the viewer is watching the killer torture his victims simultaneously. [170]

Through its visuals *The Boston Strangler* explores the nature of the subjective experience, quite literally asserting the plurality of criminal acts. Albert De Salvo (played by Tony Curtis) is seen, for example in one section, consoling his young daughter as they watch the funeral of John F. Kennedy but then we witness him venturing out to a nearby apartment to rape, abuse and murder a middle aged woman. It is DeSalvo's schizophrenia that Fleischer is interested in, using cinematic techniques to explore the relationship between normality and madness, murderousness and domesticity. It is interesting to note that the other famous use of the split screen technique in this period was Michael

Wadleigh's documentary *Woodstock* (1970), a film that has also been seen as presenting a plurality of discourses.[17]

At the end of *The Boston Strangler*, Fleischer begins to expand out from the depiction of the crimes and cross over into moral education as DeSalvo is turned into his own victim. Through a series of intense interviews with investigators, he slowly begins to remember his own actions, a situation that both disturbs and shocks him. Albert DeSalvo is shown coming face to face with the Boston Strangler and society's inability to function correctly (to isolate and treat such people) is seen as a major element of the crimes. The director leaves the audience in no doubt as to the moral lessons that can be gleaned from the film, as a title card explains:

> This film has ended, but the responsibility of society for the early recognition and treatment of the violent among us has yet to begin.

This is perhaps a surprisingly liberal stance for a mainstream Hollywood film to take especially in an era that would also spawn films like *Dirty Harry* and *Death Wish*, texts that would appear to tacitly condone vigilantism against violent criminals. *The Boston Strangler* is noticeable for the sympathy that is shown towards De Salvo who is constantly depicted as a tortured soul who has fallen through the cracks of an ever fractured and uncaring society. In the battle for his mind, it is the compassion of law professional John Bottomly (played by the ineffably decent Henry Fonda) that wins through and allows De Salvo to break down his own psychological barriers.

This is a markedly different vision of homicide than that presented by *10 Rillington Place* where Christie is culpable not only for the murders themselves but for the framing of Timothy Evans. In fact, as Fuchs hints at, this latter crime is depicted as his most heinous; it not only adds one more victim to the rising death toll but also attacks the very basis of the criminal justice system itself. The death penalty for murder was abolished in Britain in 1965, the Evans case being a major factor in its abolition, so we might suggest that Fleischer's cinematic message was directed more towards the United States than the UK.

The other social problem that we can detect in *10 Rillington Place* is that of abortion, and society's handling of it. Fleischer leaves his audience in no doubt that restrictive abortion laws drove often desperate young women into the hands of individuals like Christie. Some of the most tender scenes in the film occur as Beryl Evans prepares for the abortion that she believes is about to happen. Judy Geeson, known at the time for her roles in *To Sir With Love* (1967), *Prudence and the Pill* (1968) and *Here We Go Round the Mulberry Bush* (1968), was, like Julie Christie, a symbol of the new British female. Her public persona linked inextricably to 'swinging London', the contraceptive pill and the glamour of youth. To see her helpless at the hands of a middle-aged killer like Christie resonated with the spirit of the time, the same spirit that runs through *Performance* and *Get Carter*. The 1970s had arrived and the 1960s had ineluctably passed.

However much *10 Rillington Place* looks back to the 1950s then it is also inevitably rooted in its time. It was made on the cusp of what has been seen as the great dark period of British cinema production, the 1970s. Soon after its release, Hollywood studios like Columbia would all but pull out of funding British films and would concentrate on small scale American independent projects from directors like Arthur Penn, Martin Scorsese and Mike Nicholls. Within a few short years, such films as *10 Rillington Place* would be usurped by *On the Buses* spin-offs (1971, 1973, 1974), *Confessions of a Window Cleaner* and the increasingly lewd tail end of the *Carry On*s.

It is difficult to discern why *10 Rillington Place* has been so noticeably passed over by historians and critics of British film. It is mentioned only once in Richard Attenborough's memoirs, *Entirely Up to You Darling* and is not mentioned at all in many of the most important surveys on British cinema to date.[172] Importantly, as I have tried to suggest here, *10 Rillington Place*, can be seen as a bridge, or transitionary text, between the social problem film of the 1950s and the more overt violence of the 1970s. It is a film that draws on a number of different generic elements (Gothicism, horror, crime film) but does so with such a deftness of touch that means we might merely mistake it for a biopic, the type of which have become popular on mainstream television. As this chapter has argued, however, Fleischer's film is a much richer text than has previously been considered and one that draws on a number of specifically British images and traditions; traditions that encompass the employment of specific actors and actresses for deliberate effect (audiences would have been aware of Attenborough's Pinkie Brown, for example, or Geeson's image as the nation's sweetheart). As with *The Boston Strangler*, Richard Fleischer not only produced a detailed study of the mind of a murder, he also delivered a film with real social relevance, one that is disturbing but nonetheless rooted in distinct socio-political discourses.

HENRY, TONY AND PETER – THE ORDINARY LIFE OF THE SERIAL KILLER

There are four serial killer films whose influence extends beyond all others. We have already mentioned *Dirty Harry*, *Se7en* and *The Silence of the Lambs* but the last, *Henry: Portrait of a Serial Killer* (1986) is perhaps the most pervasive. As Shaun Kimber details, *Henry* not only forged new ground in the depiction of on-screen violence, it also created a blueprint for low budget cinematic production that valued performance and character above narrative and spectacle.[173] Although produced in 1986, John McNaughton's film was not officially released in the UK until 1991 where it achieved instant notoriety amongst audiences and critics alike. Its mixture of stark intensity and a refusal to offer any distinct moral stance on the actions of the characters meant that it became a foundational text for independent film-making, especially those concerned with crime and murder.

This last section looks at how *Henry: Portrait of a Serial Killer* has influenced recent British film-making, most notably in the form of Gerard Johnson's 2010 film *Tony: London Serial Killer* and Skip Kite's study of the Yorkshire Ripper, *Peter: Portrait of a Serial Killer* (2011). All three of these films raise interesting questions about the nature of cinematic truth and the depiction of reality; with *Tony* especially highlighting the degree to which British film-makers can draw influence from America whilst at the same time produce work that is totally British in its character. All three films blur the line between documentary and fiction and present constructed narratives based firmly on real life events.

As Hallam and Marshment outline, much of the controversy surrounding *Henry* upon its release can be attributed to its employment of a starkly realist aesthetic.[174] Released in the UK in the same year as *The Silence of the Lambs*, McNaughton's film has none of Jonathan Demme's high concept Gothicism, there is no sharp division between good and evil, no pantomime figures like Hannibal Lector or Jame Gumb. Based on real life murderer Henry Lee Lucas (played by Michael Rooker), *Henry: Portrait of a Serial Killer* briefly follows a murderous career as it spirals out of control and as the central character moves from one homicide to the next. In terms of narrative construction it exemplifies precisely Richard Dyer's point about the seriality of plot; eschewing any discernible narrative arc we are merely propelled from one murder to the next seemingly without motivation. As Henry himself says about killing, 'they are always the same [but always] different'. The storytelling in *Henry* is episodic and it has no distinct narrative resolution; the real life Lucas was arrested in 1983, three years before the making of the film, however its own ending is open-ended and ambiguous as to the fate of the central character.

It was the film's refusal to comment on the morality of its characters that proved divisive to critics on its release, as Hallam and Marshment state:

> The reviewers are divided; does the film align the viewer uncritically with the psychopath because there is no aesthetic distancing from him as the central character of narrative agency? Can such an alignment offer a moral critique of Henry's character or concern with his situation? Or does the film seek to persuade viewers to consider the morality of their own position as a voyeur, to question the nature of voyeuristic pleasure?[175]

The classic realist text attempts a discourse of objectivity that stands outside the moral boundaries of its subject matter. Like documentary movements such as cinéma vérité and Direct Cinema, such films open themselves up to the criticism that they exploit their participants or their images, especially if they are violent or explicit. As Hallam and Marshment also outline, realist texts claim no responsibility for presenting their characters as likable; the audience simply spends time with the film's subjects viewing their lives as if they were a slice of reality.[176] This position is of course greatly complicated when the reality you are presenting is that of a serial killer; the question becomes: to what extent should the film explain, condemn or otherwise debate the motives of the killer themselves? What is the underlying morality of these films? And furthermore what moral or ethical judgements have to be made when watching them?

Like *10 Rillington Place*, *Henry* does offer some clues as to the reasons for the killer's actions; however, unlike *The Boston Strangler*, these are implied rather than explicit. In a scene between Henry and Becky (the girl he briefly lives with), for example, the former details the abuse he suffered at the hands of his alcoholic mother adding a familiar motivational back story to what is a brutal and shocking series of tableaus. What the film does not do is incorporate these elements into a narrative; there are no moments of consoling exposition that reassure the audience of the central character's specific monstrosity or that delineate him as being a psycho-social Other. Compare the end of *Henry* to that other exemplar of cinematic excess, Norman Bates. At the end of *Psycho*, and through some fairly heavy-handed psychological explanation, the audience is reassured that Norman is unlike them; he is recognisably different, insane, living in an alternative reality. In *Henry*, however, audiences have to come to this conclusion for themselves and, if they never do, they are left with the uncomfortable feeling that murder could be a possibility for anyone. The sheer normality of the character of Henry (when he isn't killing) is one of the film's most disturbing elements and maybe one of the reasons why audiences reacted so strongly to it.

The moral positioning of *Henry* is made all the more uncomfortable through meta-cinematic discourse. Some of the more disturbing (and controversial) moments in the narrative occur as Henry and Otis (his killing partner played by Tom Towles) videotape themselves killing a family in their suburban home. The attack is frenzied and cynical, designed not only to satiate their lust for violence but also for humiliation. Later on Henry and Otis watch the tape together, seated on the sofa in a grisly pastiche of a familiar domestic scene. The relationship between the desire of the lead characters to (re)witness their own violent behaviour and the film's audience is both clear and unsettling. The audience's tendency towards voyeurism is mirrored in the morally repugnant Otis (who is much less sympathetic than Henry and is also the one for whom the video holds the most attraction) and the line between him and us is slowly challenged.

Shaun Kimber explains how the stylistic realism of the grainy VHS image can also be seen to tap into depictions of violence as it is linked to realism:

> The violence in this scene is framed by an operative modality that emphasizes seriousness and proximity to the real world and employs 'turn off' and 'authentic' representations of violence… Strong violence is characterised by depth of meaning, serves a narrative purpose and encourages emotional and moral responses in the spectator.[177]

The violence of *Henry: Portrait of a Serial Killer* has none of the distancing effects of slasher films like *Halloween* or *Saw*. Unlike *The Lodger* and, to a lesser extent, *10 Rillington Place* the language that is being drawn from is not Gothicism (that is, consoling and familiar) but the more problematic documentary and realism, genres that we usually associate with truth and seriousness. It is this that disturbs us most.

Gerard Johnson's film *Tony: London Serial Killer*, as the title suggests, can be seen in the same light as McNaughton's. It utilises many of the same stylistic devices, it is loosely based on the real-life serial killer Dennis Nilsen and the story is portrayed in a stark realist mode that evokes many of the moral arguments that we have already been considering. Through constant reference to 1980s action films, Tony even contains similar meta-cinematic elements as it plays with the notions of voyeurism and the proliferation of violence through Hollywood and the media.

Tony, however, not only draws from *Henry: Portrait of a Serial Killer* but from a whole variety of quintessentially British filmic texts that both characterise it as culturally different and ensures that it avoids being merely an 'English translation' of the earlier film.

The story of the archetypal loner, *Tony* depicts a brief period in the life of a serial killer (Peter Ferdinando) who kills without guilt and seemingly without logic, murdering and dismembering some victims but letting others go unharmed. The images are both dark and visceral as we are made witness not only to the killing but its grisly aftermath, all shot with the low budget realism that characterised its American forebear. *Tony*, however, is perhaps an even starker film, its use of realism even sparser than McNaughton's; whereas *Henry* employed cinematic techniques such as non-diegetic sound and flashbacks to create tension (especially in the opening montage) Johnson's film follows Tony in real time, only once relying on non-diegetic dialogue to suggest a repressed past (we hear scenes from Tony's childhood played, as if being remembered on the soundtrack).

Tony has a particularly poetical vision of London which is depicted as being at once beautiful and alienating. Shot on 16mm film, David Higgs' cinematography captures a city that is full of promise and danger in equal measure. The central character is photographed against the backdrop of the harsh Brutalist architecture of Poplar and he is free to murder within its anonymous, faceless buildings. Johnson constantly frames his action with establishing shots of Robin Hood Gardens, an infamous estate in the East End of London, and we are asked to draw our own conclusions about the effect such architecture has on the minds of its inhabitants. Rather than Hollywood, Johnson here draws his visual aesthetic from British serials like *Shameless* and documentaries such as LWT's *Summer on the Estate* (1991).

If Henry managed to avoid detection by keeping on the move, Tony manages to do the same through the sheer anonymity of the modern metropolis; he is the quintessential man in the crowd who goes unnoticed and undisturbed. London is as important a character in the film as Tony, and the two become complicit in the crimes as the city not only provides the victims but the means of their disposal (like Nilsen, Tony dismembers them and deposits them around London in blue plastic bags).

In its depiction of London as a place of duality and anonymity, *Tony* also draws on films like Ron Peck's *Nighthawks* (1978), the story of a young gay schoolteacher who spends his evenings looking for sex in clubs and bars. Peck's film has some of the seriality of serial killer cinema but the promise of the next kill has been replaced by the promise of the next sexual conquest. However both films also explore life on the margins of society and thus are equally concerned, at their heart, with outsiders and the excluded. In an important scene from Johnson's film, Tony is surprised by the kindness of one of his neighbours (Vicky Murdoch). She knocks on the door of his flat and asks for a plaster; after they have talked for a while the neighbour, Dawn, invites Tony to a Sunday dinner and we are made witness to a brief moment of calm and warmth in what is an otherwise bleak story. Such moments serve not only to humanise the characters but to allow audiences a point of identification. We are invited to speculate as to our place within the narrative; where do we stand in relation to Tony? How do we relate to him, if we can at all? This scene ends with a lyrical moment in which the dialogue is faded out and we are left with Matt Johnson's sonorous soundtrack playing over the images. The words the characters speak are unimportant now, all that matters is the brief moment of calm between the killings. For Tony and for us it is a silence between the violence.

Like *Henry*, *Tony* eschews narrative resolution and instead is allowed to simply play out its story offering no moral answers or conclusions. The last scenes of the film are what the director calls 'a love song to London' as a Steadicam shot follows Tony through the streets of the West End where clubs and nightclubs are emptying. The lights of Piccadilly provide us with a strangely uplifting end to a film that has, for the most part, been claustrophobic and intense, and we are reminded of works like Michael Winterbottom's *Wonderland* (1999) where London itself becomes a swirl of colours, sounds and sights. Like Tony we are lost in the enormous beauty of the city as it exhilarates us but also threatens to swallow us up. As Richard Dyer states:

> Serial killing is often taken to be the crime of our age. It is held to be facilitated by the anonymity of mass societies, and the ease of rapidity of modern transport, to be bred from the dissolution of the affective bonds of community and lifelong families…[178]

Tony's crimes are born out of his isolation and he remains undetected because the bonds of contemporary society have been shattered by an alienation that is endemic to modernity, a situation that is reified in the compartmentalised nature of its architecture. The implicit suggestion that lies beneath Johnson's film is that we might all be living next door to a Tony, or that each one of us might meet him on the street and not know it until it is too late. Like many serial killer films this is taken to be endemic within the (post) modern condition; the architecture of Robin Hood Gardens is both awe-inspiring and shocking as we see brief glimpses of the lives that are lived inside the tiny flats. Time has weathered the once gleaming concrete and the futurist dream of 'cities in the sky' has given way to a bland and mountainous rock-face of anonymity.

The interior *mise-en-scène* of *Tony* is also drawn from Social Realism rather than horror. The small flat that he lives in mirrors the *mise-en-scène* of the classical realist text that, as Hallam and Marshment outline is 'characterised by a redundancy of detail that convinces us that these could be the real environments of real people'.[179] In the DVD director's commentary to the film, Gerard Johnson states that actor Peter Ferdinando lived in the flat for some days before filming started in order to ensure parity between character and environment. In this, we can not only detect the influence of classical realism but canonical British directors like Mike Leigh and Ken Loach who privilege improvisation and collaboration over rigid script construction and the traditional three-act structure of the Hollywood paradigm. *Tony* refuses the immersive elements of the Hollywood serial killer film and draws on a much more home grown aesthetic.

The relationship between crime drama and the documentary film can be seen as being even more in evidence in Skip Kite's *Peter: Portrait of a Serial Killer*, which fuses actual documentary footage concerning the case of the Yorkshire Ripper with theatrical duologues between Sutcliffe and members of the prison service. Like the other two texts, the film's title evokes a quest and a concern for discernible truth – the term 'portrait' suggesting some form of exploration or exposition that might throw light on the actions of a criminal. What we get in all three films, however, is more akin to a Cubist portrait where we are presented only with facets or shards of the truth, something that is inevitably frustrating. Never are we able to build a discernibly true picture, never are we able to fully distinguish truth from fiction. This is perhaps endemic within the form and even more so within the concept of the serial killer itself.

Henry: Portrait of a Serial Killer is often seen as providing the blueprint for a whole variety of different films about murderers: *Gacy, Monster, Dahmer, H6: Diary of a Serial Killer* (2005) and so on all attest to its influence. However, by and large, these contain none of the textual depth of the original and very little of the self-reflective commentary. Compared to Hollywood, British cinema has very few high concept serial killer films in the vein of *Se7en* or *The Silence of the Lambs*. Narratives like *Messiah*, *Prime Suspect* and even the recent series *Red Riding* (2009), in part set against the Yorkshire Ripper killings, are more suited to the longer form of television drama than cinema. The serial killer films Britain does produce are inevitably inflected by outside influence – in the case of *The Lodger* it was German Expressionism, *10 Rillington Place* Fleischer's experience with *The Boston Strangler* and with *Tony* and *Peter* it was *Henry: Portrait of a Serial Killer*. Ultimately, however, these films also attempt a form of stylistic hybridity that fuses elements of Hollywood film-making with a British sense of place and space. As we have seen, this is not unusual in British crime cinema.

The relationship to reality and to realism is crucial in examining serial killer cinema not only because this is by far the dominant mode but because serial killers are themselves largely works of fiction. From Jack the Ripper to Henry Lee Lucas, the careers of murderers have been part truth, part fiction and the public at large have been eager to consume them.

FOOTNOTES

147. Jarvis, B., 'Monsters Inc.: Serial Killers and Consumer Culture', in Greer, 2010; Dyer, R., 'Kill and Kill Again', in Arroyo, J (ed.), *Action/ Spectacle Cinema: A Sight and Sound Reader*, London: BFI Publishing, 2000; Benyahia, 2010.

148. Ressler, R and T. Shachtman, *Whoever Fights Monsters*, London: Simon and Schuster, 1992, p.35.

149. Dyer, 1997, p.145.

150. Rafter, 2006, pp.87-108.

151. Rafter, 2006, p.95.

152. Rafter, 2006, p.91.

153. Benyahia, 2011, p.62.

154. Cettl, 2007, p.22

155. Jarvis, 2010, p.532.

156. Orwell, G., 'Decline of the English Murder', in *Essays*, London: Everyman, 1946/2002.

157. Oldridge, D., 'Casting the Terror: The Press and the Early Whitechapel Murders', in Warwick, A. and M. Willis (eds), *Jack the Ripper: Media, Culture, History*, Manchester: Manchester University Press, 2007

158. Oldridge, 2007, pp.52-53.

159. Chabrol, C and E Rohmer, *Hitchcock: The First Forty Films*, New York: Frederick Unger, 1982, p.92.

160. Rothman, W., *The Murderous Gaze*, Cambridge: Harvard University Press, 1982.

161. McGilligan, P., *Alfred Hitchcock: A Life in Darkness and Light*, New York: John Wiley and Sons, 2004.

162. Rothman, 1982, p.8.

163. Napper, L. and M. Williams, 'The Curious Appeal of Ivor Novello', in Babington, B. (ed), *British Stars and Stardom From Alma Taylor to Sean Connery*, Manchester: Manchester University Press, 2001, p.45.

164. Hitchcock, A. and F. Truffaut, *Hitchcock: A Definitive Study of Alfred Hitchcock*, New York: Simon Schuster, 1986, p.45.

165. Walker, M., *Hitchcock's Motifs*, Amsterdam: University Amsterdam Press, 2005, p.211.

166. Hitchcock and Truffaut, 1986, p.44.

167. Walker, 1985, p.24.

168. Elliott, P. *Hitchcock and the Cinema of Sensations: Embodied Film Theory and Cinematic Reception*, London: I.B. Tauris, 2012.

169. Fuchs, C., *Bad Blood: An Illustrated Guide to Psycho Cinema*, London: Creation Books, 2002, p.62.

170. Cossar, H., *Letterboxed: The Evolution of Widescreen Cinema*, Lexington: University of Kentucky, 2011, p.205.

171. See for example the discussion in Saunders. D., *Direct Cinema: Observational Documentary and the Politics of the Sixties*, London: Wallflower Press, 2007, pp.99-125.

172. Attenborough, R., *Entirely Up To You Darling*, London: Arrow, 2009; Sargeant, A., *British Cinema: A Critical History*, London; BFI Publishing, 2005; Street, S., *British National Cinema*, 2nd, London: Routledge, 2009; Newland, 2010 etc.

173. Kimber, S., *Henry: Portrait of a Serial Killer*, London: Routledge, 2011, p.11.

174. Hallam and Marshment, 2000, p.237.

175. Hallam and Marshment, 2000, p.240.

176. Hallam and Marshment, 2000, p.234.

177. Kimber, 2011, pp. 102-103.

178. Dyer, 2000, p.146.

179. Hallam and Marshment, 2000, p.80.

CHAPTER SEVEN: JUVENILE DELINQUENCY

Made in Britain (1982)

The phrase 'juvenile delinquent' has been used to describe criminal children since the mid-nineteenth century; it was employed in particular by Mary Carpenter in her study *Juvenile Delinquents: Their Condition and Treatment* first published in 1853.[180] Interestingly, many of the debates that are played out in Carpenter's study can still be seen to be in evidence almost 100 years later in one of the first British delinquency films, Lewis Gilbert's *Cosh Boy*. Both *Cosh Boy* and Carpenter's text debate the nature of delinquency and its relationship to class, to education, to parental values and ultimately to society at large. As this chapter shall detail, then, although an endlessly prescient and emotive area, the subject of the juvenile delinquent represents both continuity and change for British society and cinema – on the one hand offering an ever present folk devil and barometer for social mores and, on the other, lending a constantly evolving image that forever allies itself to other problems. It also offers special insight into how successive generations view themselves and their successors.

Before the mid-nineteenth century, criminal children tended to be treated in a similar manner to that of adults. Therefore, as John Munice details, it was not unusual for the under-13s to be executed by hanging for crimes such as larceny, fraud and burglary and for children to be regularly transported to the colonies for petty theft and street crimes such as pickpocketing.[181] As Muncie also records, children found guilty of a crime were often also liable to be sentenced to terms in the adult penal system; in 1853, for example, almost 12,000 inmates of Great British prisons were between the ages of 10 and 20 and it was not until 1908 that this was outlawed entirely.

The juvenile delinquent came of age in the early parts of the twentieth century when changes in the education system, especially the raising of the school leaving age to 14 in 1918 (*The Fisher Education Act*), also created the category of the adolescent. *The Fisher Act* cemented what had been a growing interest in compulsory secondary education and widened the gap between the child and the working adult; gradually the adolescent emerged in the interstice between parental ownership and the work place and its dark cousin, the delinquent, soon became a prominent cultural image.

Interest in the category of the juvenile delinquent was concretised in the 1920s and '30s when it fell under the same sociological mandate as adult criminal behaviour in what became modern criminology. As Rutter and Giller outline, delinquency has been theorised in a number of different ways, many of which conform to the usual rubrics of contemporary criminological theory (strain theory, labelling theory, biological theories, positivist theories and so on).[182] The major debates however can be seen (at least in relation to the cinema) to revolve around the notions of 'voluntarism and determinism' or those which stress the role of the psychology of the individual in youth and crime and those which stress the effect of environment and upbringing. [183]

It is this debate that enables both John Hill and Marcia Landy to characterise the delinquent film as a social problem text and to assert its place in a cycle that deals with other issues such as prostitution (*Women of Twilight*), racism (*Sapphire*) and homosexuality (*Victim*).[184] Occasionally, as in the B movie *Wind of Change* (1961) or Roy Ward Baker's *Flame in the Streets* (1961) an audience is presented with a plurality of discourses that will attempt to tackle numerous social problems at once offering a number of outcomes and a variety of narratives, although admittedly these films are noticeably rare and, very often, one concern tends to dominate the others. Ideologically, the social problem film represents a working through of different, and oftentimes, opposing discourses and solutions to 'the problem'; characters are self-consciously inscribed into the conflict, sometimes existing as little more than positions in a political debate. These films, however, do highlight popular culture's role as a forum for debating the tensions inherent within society and for representing sometimes deep rooted anxieties that are missed by traditional high culture and art.

The juvenile delinquency film is especially noticeable for its treatment of place and time. Deeply connected to its social milieu, the young of a society are often seen as its most vulnerable citizens, particularly susceptible to moral and cultural decay. The juvenile delinquent film, then, is also always a film about environment, about morality and about the purity of indigenous culture. Since the 1950s this has inherently involved debates about the dangers of foreign media, usually American. We see such fears played out in relation to Rock and Roll in films like *Violent Playground*, *Serious Charge* and *Wind of Change* but also in relation to rap and gang culture with more recent films like *Kidulthood*, *Sket* (2011) and *Ill Manors* (2012).

British cinema has always lagged behind Hollywood in its fascination for delinquent youth. The reasons for this are intimately connected to the differing processes of cinema production and consumption in the two cultures. As Timothy Shary outlines, since the 1950s Hollywood experienced a gradual 'juvenilisation' of its product designed increasingly to appeal to a young demographic with expendable income and few financial commitments.[185] Mainstream films like *Rebel Without a Cause* (1955) and *The Wild One* (1953) and B movies like *Juvenile Jungle* (1958) and *Rumble on the Docks* (1956) not only provided an image of out-of-control teens for an ever-expanding adult audience but their unerring undercurrent of dissatisfaction and ill-ease inevitably appealed to an adolescent market.

In contrast, British cinema began slowly in this area. As Marcia Landy details, the first manifestation of the juvenile delinquent in British films could be thought to be characters such as Pinkie Brown in *Brighton Rock* or Ted Peters in *Dancing with Crime*, both played by the youthful and fresh-faced Richard Attenborough.[186] However, these characters, despite their youth and immaturity, were teenagers in name only; they were youngsters playing at being adults and, more to the point, existing within an adult criminal world. It would not be until the 1950s and '60s that the British juvenile delinquent made a full appearance on film and then it would always be under the watchful eyes of a responsible adult.

Possibly the most influential of these juvenile imports was Richard Brooks' 1955 film *The Blackboard Jungle*. Probably more for its inclusion of Bill Haley and His Comets' 'Rock Around the Clock' than any narrative or social message, *The Blackboard Jungle* not only inspired a host of British copies but also laid the foundations for teenage insurrection in the real world, as one Teddy Boy from 1955 details:

> What happened next changed my life. The overpowering and unforgettable sound of Rock and Roll hit me between the ears. After twelve bars the words 'One, two, three o'clock, four o'clock rock' came belting into the cinema. *Blackboard Jungle* had begun and Bill Hailey and His Comets had indelibly stamped my soul… I sat there in the Red Hall stunned at the behaviour of *Blackboard Jungle* delinquents, my suede shoes tapping to the compulsive soundtrack.[187]

COSH BOY – CHILDREN OF THE RUBBLE AND THE POSTWAR WAR TEENAGER

Before the electrifying rhythms of Bill Haley and His Comets burst into the public consciousness, being a British teenager was a less exciting prospect, as Tony Judt details:

> Until this time, young people had not even existed as a distinct group of consumers. Indeed 'young people' had not existed at all. In traditional families and communities, children remained children until they left school and went to work, at which point they were young adults. The new, intermediate category of 'teenager' in which a generation was defined not by its status but by its age – neither child nor adult – had no precedent.[188]

While there is a general truth to this, a survey of British cinema before 1955 reveals that the teenager began to slowly emerge much earlier, from the dust and the rubble of Britain's big cities after the war. Troublesome and angst-ridden, these proto-teens were born out of the problems of conflict and would be beset with issues such as absent fathers, broken families, a collapsed economy and a country that never quite knew what to do with them. Left to their own devices during wartime, peace brought a patrician authority that was difficult to deal with for many children and they existed in a form of socio-cultural wasteland until rock and roll would give their lives meaning.

The two films that concretised the image of the early post-war British delinquent were Montgomery Tully's *Boys in Brown* (1949) and Lewis Gilbert's *Cosh Boy*, both films that dealt firmly with young people and criminality. As Adrian Horn argues, it is wrong to suggest that the British teenager (and, thus, delinquent) miraculously appeared fully formed from nowhere in the 1950s; they had a much longer development that stretched back to before the war. However, *Boys in Brown* and *Cosh Boy* depict what are clearly discernible shifts in thinking regarding the nature of juveniles and how they fitted into adult society.[189] Each film depicts a society coming to terms with itself after the war, as crime and criminality is linked to a whole range of causal factors, from the absence of fathers, to environment, to the corrosive effects of Americanisation. However, whereas *Boys in Brown* depicts its teenagers as young versions of adults, even to the extent of casting a 29-year-old Jimmy Handley as an inmate of Borstal, *Cosh Boy*'s delinquents are recognisably juvenile both in their behaviour and their mode of dress. In a narrative trope that will be repeated time and time again in juvenile delinquent cinema, the thrust of *Cosh Boy* is the danger that occurs when young people engage in 'adult' behaviour, be it criminal or sexual. Without the guiding hand of the adult, so the theory goes, the teen can very easily descend into delinquency.

This developmental arch also appears in the *Mass Observation Study* into juvenile delinquency published in 1949 by H.D. Wilcock.[190] The study, part of a larger attempt to capture all aspects of British culture, is noticeable for its patrician tone and schizophrenically veers between welfare and punishment; a dichotomy that will constantly characterise films (and British social policy) in this area for the next 50 years. Although there is a chapter on the 'highbrow delinquent' that promises to 'best penetrate Borstal through the subjective stresses of a boy who dramatises his journey thus', most of the cases that come under the gaze of the study's microscope are from the lower end of the social and educational scale and their relationship to authority is one firmly based in a rigid hierarchy.[191]

It is worth noting, as does John Muncie, that British criminology (like its cinema) was largely uninterested in the area of juvenile delinquency before 1950.[192] In the US, understanding of teenage criminality had developed through a series of stages that each focused on a specific causal explanation. Theory developed by the Chicago school in the 1920s and '30s had stressed the importance of environment and immigration in shaping criminal behaviour in teens; the 1940s and '50s brought concerns over the role of the popular media and by the end of the decade we have the first flowerings of subcultural theory and the role of other illegal behaviours like drug use. We can detect all of these in Hollywood films of the periods.

The British picture is somewhat less distinct. Films like *Cosh Boy* and, later, *Violent Playground* and *Serious Charge*, present a plurality of causes that, commensurate with their position as social problem films, were designed to engender debate rather than offer explanations. This makes their characters and narrative resolutions less finely drawn than their Hollywood counterparts, as film-makers battled with the contradictions that existed between the presence of teenage delinquency and an overriding faith in the character of youth. In both *Boys in Brown* and *Cosh Boy*, this tension is resolved, as it would be so often, with recourse to notions of exceptional criminality and its links to madness and innate evil. In both films, the font of criminal behaviour lies ultimately in the weak psychology of individual characters. The consoling outcome of both of these films is that, *but* for a few bad apples, delinquency is a phase that can be grown (or be beaten) out of.

Boys in Brown was one of the first depictions of Borstal in British cinema. By 1949 Borstals had been existence for over 40 years; however they had already gained a reputation for breeding discontent and aggression rather than rehabilitation, a situation that would continue into the 1970s and '80s. As Wilson and O'Sullivan state, the post-war period signalled an optimistic stance towards the institution of prison and, moreover, its ability to reform and re-educate as well as punish:

> In the post-war welfare state era it became less acceptable to see prison as an entirely closed institution. The war itself had seen an emergence of documentary film-making and the idea of film as a form of education had taken hold. The post-war period was characterised by concerns about crime and delinquency and its treatment and prevention. The films of this era clearly reflect these concerns with film itself being part of prevention and treatment.[193]

We can certainly view *Boys in Brown* within this mould. Telling the story of a group of eight boys who escape from a Borstal, its tone is less discursive than later films and more didactic, with Jack Warner's fatherly presence as the Governor bringing fairness and orderliness to a group of rebellious young criminal boys. Richard Attenborough plays the lead character, Jackie Knowles, a well-meaning lad who is sent to borstal after being informed upon by a criminal partner. Much of the film is dedicated to anthropologically examining life inside, however the narrative tension is ratcheted up after Jackie attacks a warder whilst the group attempt an escape, eventually however all are captured. The authorities in this instance display a paternalism that resonated with post-war reconstruction, as if the New Jerusalem of Clement Atlee had reached over the walls and extended into the Borstal grounds. The last lines of the film underline its entire philosophy, as the Borstal Governor surveys the exercise yard full of inmates he muses on the nature of the penal system to one of his staff:

Governor: There you are, Johnson. [He states] The wheat and the chaff.

Johnson: Yes sir, but the thing is which is which?

Governor: No, Johnson; the thing is to find out what is the chaff and why.

This liberal vision of the penal system would not last but neither was it as straightforward as it might seem in the film itself. The closing scenes depict the narrative resolution of Jackie Knowles but the more divisive and problematic behaviour of the others in the group remains in the background. Whereas Attenborough's character becomes contrite and apologetic by the film's conclusion, most of the gang who try to escape with him remain defiant in the face of authority, refusing to communicate or even look the Governor in the eyes as they are being admonished. For his compliance with authority Knowles gets the girl and his violence is understood as merely a phase he will grow out of. With kindness and understanding from the Governor and the love of a sweetheart, Jackie Knowles might just have a future, but the film is less sure about the fates of those who refuse to comply with the wishes of the authorities. They, the chaff, are left to their own devices or are thrown back into a system that does not know how to deal with them.

Cosh Boy expresses its intentions from the very first shots. It opens on what is obviously an inner city pub. In the background we hear the sound of an accordion and the unmistakable tones of an East End woman as she walks home drunk. Both sounds evoke a bawdy pre-war London that seem curiously out of place in the period in which the film is set, the early 1950s; in fact, without the two teenagers in the centre of frame, both of whom are dressed in recognisably youthful clothes, we might imagine that we are in the late nineteenth century and that this were a Jack the Ripper narrative. As the old woman makes her way over a piece of derelict wasteland, the two young men approach her, try to steal her bag and, when she resists, they deal her a single blow with a cosh and she falls down screaming. The two youths run off to the sound of a police whistle and dog barking and the film has begun.

The setting of these opening shots is crucial in understanding how *Cosh Boy* situates juvenile delinquency within post-war Britain. The two young men, Roy Walsh (James Kenney) and Alfie Collins (Ian Whittaker), disappear into the darkness and the voids of the urban landscape, their crimes hidden by the city and by the gaps and fissures that were left by the Luftwaffe and its doodlebugs. *Cosh Boy's* first statement is that the casualties of war do not dry up with the declaration of peace but instead resonate and have lasting effects on the generations that follow. This trope is continued throughout the film as we are made well aware of the fact that Roy's increasingly immoral behaviour can be directly attributable to the lack of any discernible paternal figure in his home, his father having died on active service.

Cosh Boy's opening scenes are reminiscent of Hollywood gangster films like *Dillinger* (1945) and *Gun Crazy* (1950), as Roy and Alfie run through the crowded streets of

London to the abandoned house where they hide out in times of trouble. However, as a criminal duo, they are noticeably youthful, perhaps even child-like and they are caught by the police very soon after committing their crime. To make matters worse, as he is told that he is being taken to the police station, Alfie says in a plaintive tone 'But my Mum says I have to be home by ten!', a remark that not only undercuts the seriousness of the narrative but undermines forever his credentials as an aspiring London gangster.

What we see in *Cosh Boy*, that we do not see in *Boys in Brown*, is a picture of true juvenile delinquency as distinct from adult criminal behaviour enacted by minors. The violence meted out by Roy and Alfie is unmistakably youthful in its aims and its execution; it is opportunistic, brutal and un-thought through. In a foreshadowing of the problem films of the 1960s, Roy also leans towards sexual aggression, making Alfie's sister pregnant and denying responsibility when she tries to commit suicide. His errant actions are, however, seen as exceptional as he gradually descends into a form of teenage psychosis that will be more familiar to audiences of American delinquency films.

As Anthony Aldgate and James Robertson detail, *Cosh Boy* was the first British film to receive the newly created X certificate, its infamy heightened by the recent case of Derek Bentley, Christopher Craig and the shooting of PC Sydney Miles.[194] Derek Bentley, a 19-year-old with a mental age of ten, was convicted and hanged for the murder of Miles after he had allegedly shouted 'Let him have it' to Craig, a statement that was interpreted by the jury as an incitement to kill. Craig, who was underage at the time, was sentenced for murder and was released from prison in 1963. The closeness of the film's release to the trial and outcome of the case resulted in it being banned from many cinemas throughout the country and in producer Daniel Angel making several cuts and bookending the narrative with the kind of pseudo-sociological moral jargon that characterised post-Hays Code gangster films like *Scarface*.

Although the behaviour of Roy Walsh is not noticeably different from the more defiant characters in *Boys in Brown* what is different is the reaction of the authority figures. Whereas *Boys in Brown* advocated a liberal approach to punishment and penal servitude the message of *Cosh Boy* is unequivocal: punishment must be swift, violent and, if possible, physical. After a spate of juvenile delinquency that involves mugging, assault, robbery and sexual proclivity, Roy Walsh is disciplined through an old fashioned beating by his future stepfather (Robert Ayres), who also serves as a symbol of the paternal state. The beating not only serves as punishment but also exposes Roy's inherent psychological fractures as he is reduced to the position of a snivelling child, denied the consoling arms of his mother. The assumption however is that the beating has done its job and, given time, Roy will realise that it had been done for his benefit.

The film's conclusion must be seen in ideological terms and can be viewed against the contemporary socio-political landscape. Despite the fears of contemporary reviewers, *Cosh Boy* is ultimately a highly conservative film that views delinquency as an issue that can be countered by stern parenting; it also then legitimates and underlines the value of the family (and its traditional roles) to post-war Britain.

Both *Boys and Brown* and *Cosh Boy* represent early attempts by British film-makers to work through contemporary fears about the place of young people in a society whose social fabric had been fractured by war. In a touching scene in *Cosh Boy*, for example, Roy's grandmother and mother discuss the death of his father. The grandmother sympathises with her daughter but states 'You only lost one, I lost all four'. The variation in the methods of dealing with delinquency in the films reflects this desperation to rebuild the nation and the sadness that such rebuilding needed to be done at all. For both films the answer to delinquency is the restitution of the nuclear family – in *Boys in Brown* through Jackie Knowles' marriage and in *Cosh Boy*, Roy's mother's marriage to his stepfather. Again, this reflects the socio-political ethos of the time that, as David Kynaston suggested, was firmly based on an increasing onus on domestication.[195] Compared to successive films and a more violent conception of delinquency, *Cosh Boy's* depiction of out of control youth may seem quaint and naïve however, as contemporary reaction to it showed, it was a landmark film in British crime cinema.

VIOLENT PLAYGROUND – THOSE INFECTIOUS RHYTHMS

The 1960s has a unique place in Western cultural history. It is often viewed as the period that spawned the teenager, when subcultures were born and when popular entertainment reached stellar proportions. Whereas of course there is some truth to this, as most cultural commentators will state, the seeds of the 1960s were well and truly sown in the decade before and nowhere is this more noticeable than in the cinema. The films of the late 1950s, especially those depicting youth and juvenile delinquency, highlight the fact that the cultural turn that occurred in the '60s was in fact more evolution than revolution, as moral attitudes softened and liberalism became more widespread. In *A Mirror for England* Raymond Durgnat makes the prescient point that the greater affluence of the 1950s resulted in an expansion of the middle classes and with this came a greater respect for law and order.[196] Viewing many of the films of the period we might suggest that this also resulted in a greater tolerance towards delinquency and juvenile behaviour, as the punitive harshness of the immediate post-war period cooled and coalesced into a more laissez faire attitude.

Dominic Sandbrook highlights the large number of juvenile delinquency films that were produced during the late 1950 in what he describes as 'an atmosphere of panic' that 'in keeping with the general suspicion of affluence and consumerism among artists and writers, linked the disaffected violence of the young to the degenerate, lazy prosperity of the age'.[197] Whilst this is undoubtedly true, we should also highlight the constant debate that runs throughout these films about how to deal with the 'problem' of youth and how to accommodate this powerful new force within society. Although, as we shall see below, there was certainly an anxiety about the rise of youth culture on the part of the older generation, there was also the underlying sense that the battle was already lost and that the soundtrack of the future was more likely to consist of rock and roll than the military two-step.

One of the noticeable elements in delinquency films during the '50s and '60s was the importance of the youth centre. In films like *Cosh Boy*, *Violent Playground* and *Serious Charge*, the youth centre is seen as a place of socialisation and gentrification where, through strenuous sports and leisure activities, problematic behaviour can be curtailed and dealt with. Its role was both a metonym and an extension of the paternalism of the state and it encouraged involvement and cooperation that filled up spare time, expending excess energy in a moderated environment that would otherwise be spent in more unsavoury activity. Of course, it was also a symbol of the establishment, something to rebel against and to tear down, figuratively and often actually.

The youth centre provides an important focal point in Basil Dearden's *Violent Playground* (1958), a film that can be seen as being in the centre of a number of different social, political and cultural discourses. As John Hill states:

> Inspired by the Liverpool Juvenile Officers Scheme... the organising principle of the film is once again reform. But... the film displays an uneasiness about how far the process of reform can go. Indeed, in the case of the film's central character, Johnny, the scheme proves a failure and once more the ostensive liberalism of the reform position gives way to a logic of punishment and repression.[198]

Violent Playground is the third in what is often considered to be Basil Dearden's teenage trilogy.[199] Beginning with *The Blue Lamp* and continuing with *I Believe in You* (1952) these three films represent a gradual evolution in Dearden's style and liberal socio-political vision. They also present a snapshot of the rise of the teenager, from the proto-Teddy Boy of *The Blue Lamp*'s Tom Riley (played by a youthful Dirk Bogarde), through the well-meaning misfit of *I Believe in You* (Charlie Hooker) to the fully fledged teenage tearaway of *Violent Playground*. The last two films in the trilogy especially present narratives that depict members of the older generation learning from and adjusting to members of the younger, as Dearden explicitly challenges the accepted moral superiority of age and experience over youth.

Violent Playground details the life of Truman, a hardboiled CID officer played by Stanley Baker who is transferred to the Juvenile Delinquency section of the Liverpool Constabulary. More used to arson and armed robbery than petty thievery and delinquency, Truman is initially resistant to his new role and is teased by colleagues and belittled by the worthlessness of the crimes he is charged with investigating. The initial debates of the film revolve around the value of early intervention by the police in the lives of potential criminals; after wearily reading the form sheet of a juvenile that includes 'larceny from shop – two bottles of lemonade', Truman has to be reminded by a colleague that 'they all begin somewhere' and that criminals are formed from 'someone who pinched a bottle of milk when they were a kid, next time it's a bicycle, then bigger things'. The tone is at once paternal but there is a discernible difference between the authorities here and those in *Cosh Boy*: here there is a tacit assumption that corporal punishment is not enough to deal with the delinquent young; something more socially embedded is needed.

Investigating a series of thefts from local shops, Truman is charged with dealing with two underage scamps, Mary (Brona Boland) and Patrick Murphy (Fergal Boland), and takes them back to their home in the heart of a Liverpudlian tenement housing block. There he meets their morally upstanding sister, Cathie (Anne Heywood), and their rebellious older brother, Johnny (David McCallum). It is now that *Violent Playground* enters different generic territory and resembles a detective story or whodunit. Truman's transfer to the juvenile unit coincides with a series of unexplained arson attacks on local buildings and as the narrative plays out we gradually come to realise that it is Johnny who is to blame. Johnny's delinquency soon turns into out and out criminality as he attempts to destroy the Grand Hotel and eventually holds up in a local school with a gun and a class of hostage children. At the conclusion to the film, Johnny is arrested and taken away, his humiliation serving as a warning to the delinquents who surround and look up to him. In the process of arresting and punishing Johnny, Truman learns a vital lesson about the nature of justice and his place in the community.

It is the conclusion to the film that has drawn the greatest critical attention. John Hill suggested that it is caught between 'voluntarism and determinism'; Raymond Durgnat criticised its central moral assumption that 'all bullies are cowards'; and, as Steve Chibnall states, many contemporary reviewers saw in it nothing but 'sham liberalism' and an 'exploitation melodrama in the clothing of documentary realism'.[200] However, these are perhaps overly harsh declarations of a film that - like much of Dearden's work – attempted to reconcile post-war attitudes with a more progressive ideology. Like *Sapphire* a year later or *Victim* a year after that, *Violent Playground* represents Basil Dearden's attempt at creating in-roads into a more liberal social philosophy. Critics like Hill and Durgnat overlook the fact that the film's conclusion is as much concerned with Mary and Patrick (Jonny's siblings) as with Johnny himself. Like Michael Curtiz's *Angels With Dirty Faces* (1938), the arrest of Jonny is not an act of 'punishment and repression' over reform but is in fact concerned with the education of the younger characters who view Johnny as a hero and role model.[201] Commensurate with prevalent subcultural theories of delinquency, Johnny and his gang provide each other with the social standing that is denied them by mainstream society. Void of legitimate role models, they see in Johnny a form of folk hero, an almost superhuman presence. In the scene in which they try to infiltrate the Grand Hotel for example, one of the gang tellingly says 'You watch, Johnny will get in anywhere', an indication that they view him as being beyond the usual constraints of the law. His arrest and humiliation strips him of this and the younger members of the gang are (presumably) saved a similar fate.

Alongside these subcultural theories of delinquency are *Violent Playground*'s statements on the pejorative effects of foreign culture, especially the pounding sexually charged rhythms of rock and roll. As stated earlier, *The Blackboard Jungle* had begun this debate in 1955 when its use of 'Rock Around the Clock' was linked to a rise in teenage violence; but by 1958 it was seen as an altogether more insidious influence. In one noticeable scene in Dearden's film Johnny is shown dancing to a rock and roll record in a friend's flat. Occurring about half way through, the scene provides a turning point in the narrative for both Truman and the audience who begin to see Johnny as not only a delinquent but also suffering from the kind of juvenile psychosis present in *Cosh Boy*'s Roy Walsh. After Truman and Johnny enter the flats together, we are made immediately aware of the gap that exists between the two age groups. Truman's tie and hat characterise him as being part of the pre-war generation and he looks awkwardly out of place as he follows the younger through the concrete jungle.

We hear the sound of the rock and roll music before we see what is going on in the room, but we can immediately note the effect it has on Johnny who stares through the window mesmerised by the dancers inside. The lyrics to the tune resonate with the sexy, spiked atmosphere of the juvenile delinquent:

> I'm a gonna play rough, rough, rough
>
> I'm a gonna get tough, tough, tough
>
> I'm gonna play rough and tough and she's my baby.

However it is the incessant rhythms that seem to transfix the teenagers. What occurs next is a depiction of the orgiastic excesses that such music can apparently send teenagers into, as Johnny is enticed into dancing with the others. He flails his arms about and shakes his head in a way that suggests the sort of Dionysian abandonment more usually associated with religious ceremony. As Truman looks on, the teenage boys preen and admire each other in a closeness that suggests nascent homosexuality can also be an outcome of the decadence to which the young are prone. In a particularly striking sequence, Johnny and Truman are linked by a series of shot/reverse-shots as the former displays himself to the latter in a manner that borders on exhibitionism. After their eyes meet, Johnny prostrates himself on the floor, thrusting and shaking himself to the music. If Johnny were a female we might be witnessing a scene of seduction, a dance of the seven veils; but this is less *Romeo and Juliet* and more *West Side Story* as the boys of the gang turn dance into warfare – their zombie-like eyes staring at Truman as they gradually close in.

The message behind this scene is simple: popular culture (especially American) can infect British youth turning them into mindless clones, eager only for the next record or, in more recent times, for the next video game. As Adrian Horn suggests, the craze for jukeboxes in post-war Britain meant that American popular music could be widely disseminated to young people despite the concerns and protestations of the BBC that strictly limited the amount of jazz and rock and roll it played on its radio stations.[202] By 1958, however, rock and roll had gone mainstream and artists such as Bill Haley, Elvis Presley and Little Richard regularly topped the hit single charts. Later on in the century we would see the same kinds of fears displayed in relation to punk music, heavy metal and rap, as those who enjoyed musical liberation in their own youth became suspicious about it in their adulthood. Dearden's camera clearly adopts the gaze of the older Truman and it seems to mirror both his fascination and his horror. Like Truman, the audience is asked to understand the troubled teen but also to distance ourselves from him.

Towards the end of the '50s, the image of the delinquent youth which was, after all, an import from America, would be partially supplanted by a more positive image of the home-grown teenager. As Andrew Spicer asserts, the late 1950s and early 1960s saw the rise of a particular brand of teenage idol that would not seek to widen the generation gap but to bridge it.[203] Beginning with Tommy Steele's *The Tommy Steele Story* (1957), continuing into *The Duke Wore Jeans* (1958) and finding a form of apogee in Cliff Richard's *The Young Ones* (1961) and *Summer Holiday* (1963) this new brand of cinematic teenager would be aimed at young people and parents alike, appealing to a wider audience and healing the wounds of the early rock and rollers, as Spicer details:

> [Cliff Richard] represented a further stage in the manufacture of the anodyne teenage star: 'Before him, all pop singers sounded like what they were, solidly working class. Cliff introduced something new, a bland ramble, completely classless.'[204]

The film that provides us with the transition between these two cultural periods (the 1950s delinquent teen with the more anodyne teen of the '60s) is Clive Donner's *Some People* (1962). *Some People* tells the story of four juvenile delinquents from Bristol who are persuaded to form a rock and roll band by middle class choir master, Mr Smith – played by Kenneth More, himself a symbol of the old guard of pre-war Britain in films such as *Scott of the Antarctic* (1948), *Genevieve* (1953) and *Reach for the Sky* (1956). In a pre-Beatles era, *Some People* highlighted the intergenerational nature of rock and roll that, if correctly framed and packaged, could be appreciated by all ages and all members of the family. *Some People* also depicted the rise of schemes such as the Duke of Edinburgh Award that attempted to stem the tide of delinquency by channelling the energy of youth into pursuits like boat-building, orienteering and community service. It is a film that unashamedly depicts the embourgeoisement of the young working class during the early 1960s and prefigures the kinds of narratives that would constitute the basis of the 'Swinging London' texts. It is a safe vision of a youth desperately trying to please the older generation as well as carve a separate identity for themselves in a changing cultural scene.

Eventually of course, delinquency would give way to the high jinks of The Beatles' *A Hard Day's Night* (1964) and images of British youth would be exported all around the world and serve as poster children for 'Swinging London'. The delinquent would continue but it would be framed in less urban settings, often appearing, like Colin Smith in *The Loneliness of the Long Distance Runner* or Frank Machin in *This Sporting Life*, as marginal outsiders not only separate from the older generation but from the majority of the younger too. The philosophy behind these films would be existential rather than sociological and their young characters symbolic of a more deep rooted malaise. We would also see a shift in sympathies. Whereas it is clearly the eyes of a confused and exasperated authority we are looking through in *Violent Playground* and *Cosh Boy*, it is the outsiders and delinquents who possess the gaze in cinema of the '60s British New Wave.

SCUM, MADE IN BRITAIN AND SCRUBBERS – ANGRY, POOR AND YOUNG

The 1960s was a period of liberalisation generally towards juvenile delinquency. The much vaunted *Children and Young Persons Act* of 1969 proposed that systems of care and reform replace those of criminal punishment and that punitive institutions be supplanted by educational establishments and community homes.[205] The image of the wayward teenager would be tempered culturally by a surfeit of more positive images that would not only alter how young people were seen but would eventually come to symbolise the new and exciting Britain to emerge in the '60s. British popular culture was the most obvious outlet for this new faith in the value and beauty of the young and cinema especially would become younger and younger as both its stars and its audiences would be increasingly drawn from the under-25 age group.

This flirtation with the young however would not last, and by the middle of the 1970s the youth of Britain would again be viewed, by the authorities at least, as a force that needed to be controlled, regulated and, if all else failed, punished. As Rutter and Giller detail, by 1978 custodial sentences for those between fourteen and sixteen rose to 7,000, a rise of almost 4,000 from eight years earlier.[206] This figure would increase until it reached an all-time high in 1981 with almost 8,000 underage inmates. Not only were more young people being locked up, the nature of that imprisonment was also changing and becoming noticeably harsher. The philosophy of 'welfarism' that would underline social policy in the late 1960s would give way to what the 1979 *Conservative Party Manifesto* referred to as the 'short, sharp shock [treatment] for young criminals' in a modern, tougher regime. The 1979 Manifesto also made reference to curtailing the behaviour of 'hooligans' and 'thugs' and made explicit the links between 'senior' and 'junior' criminals.[207]

However we should be wary of assuming that this process of toughening-up can be laid entirely at the feet of the in-coming Thatcher government. Hall, et al's 1978 text *Policing the Crisis* already talks about the 'the moment of the mugger' and the 'descent to dissensus' a year before Thatcher's win in 1979.[208] By the end of the decade, it was obvious that the era of Detective Truman's fatherly understanding was fading fast and that a more authoritarian stance on crime was beginning to emerge.

This new vision of a broken and lost generation would also find its way into popular culture and fashion, as subcultures that were formed in the 1960s burst into the public consciousness and became, as Dick Hebdige details, a mirror for the plurality of social identities.[209] Punks, skinheads, rastas, a mod revival and a Teddy Boy revival would all contribute to a decade where the young fought for representation and significance from society at large as well as amongst themselves. Subcultures would also be inextricably linked to delinquency and problematic behaviour. Race riots such as those in Handsworth and Brixton would imbue major British cities with an undercurrent of social tension that would crackle across the media. Specific economic measures, such as the creation of the YTS (Youth Training Scheme) would not only alienate large portions of the young population, it would inevitably lead to crime and social listlessness, as unemployment and poverty would be tied to youth and the future of Britain. We see this played out not only in crime films but in social realist texts of the period like Mike Leigh's *Meantime* (1984), The Clash's film *Rude Boy* (1980) and more avant-garde films such as Derek Jarman's *Jubilee* (1978)

In John Hill's classic text *Sex, Class and Realism* he devotes an entire chapter to the work of Basil Dearden, so important was he to the evolution of British socio-political cinema. If Hill's study had extended into the 1980s we might suggest that it would more than likely contain a chapter on Alan Clarke, a director whose work has become synonymous with British Social Realism and visions of the underbelly of Thatcher's millions. This last section, then aims to continue Hill's auteurist conception of realism and look at two major works by Clarke both of which deal with juvenile delinquency in the late '70s and early '80s and moreover how it was dealt with by the authorities. This section will then move on to consider the role of gender in constructions of the juvenile by considering Mai Zetterling's 1983 film *Scrubbers*, a prison narrative set in a young girls' remand home but that employs Brechtian dramatic tools to alert the audience to a more radical agenda. All three films articulate the very real suggestion that it is the young who bear the full force of socio-economic tensions in society and that narratives of youth often expose the fractures that are inherent in the rest of the social system.

Alan Clarke's *Scum* had a chequered history. Originally made for the BBC's *Play for Today* strand in 1977, it was banned by Director-General Billy Cotton and not aired until 1991, by which time it had not only been remade for the cinema but had also achieved the kind of reputation that is usually reserved for an elite form of British film-making. Like *Get Carter* and *The Italian Job*, *Scum* has passed into British male folklore and its central character, Carlin (Ray Winstone), has been canonised by male culture in the same way as Jack Carter and Jack Regan.

Both the TV and cinema versions detail the lives of a group of Borstal inmates, many of whom have been imprisoned for relatively petty crimes (Carlin states that he was imprisoned for '30 bob's worth' of junk; another prisoner, Archer, for fraud and so on). After being sent to the Borstal, Carlin quickly asserts his dominance over the other inmates and takes over as 'the daddy' through displays of violence and criminal cunning. Carlin's character is a complex mixture of intelligence and violence as he plays the system and the guards as well as beating his rivals into a bloody submission. After the suicide of one of the inmates, Carlin encourages a riot amongst the prisoners and is duly quashed by the authorities.

Scum is another testimony to the links that exist in Britain between television and film. Close examination of both the cinematic and televisual films highlights revealing differences between them and exemplify their relative place in the cultural hierarchy. The 1977 version (the television film) is visually tighter and more complex in terms of character and narrative than the 1979 feature film which has the time to dwell, perhaps overly-gratuitously, on the violence and the sex. In the TV version, for example, Carlin asks another inmate to be his 'missus'; after reassuring him that he is no 'poof', he makes what is a stilted and awkward seduction towards the boy – however it is a surprising seduction nonetheless and one that humanises and deepens his character. This homosexual narrative thread however is dropped completely in the film version that chooses instead to paint Carlin as a much more defiant anti-hero in the tradition of prison movies like *The Criminal* (1960). Carlin's character is, as a result of this, less rounded and it is this, perhaps, that has formed the basis of the film's cult status. The omission of Carlin's flirtation with institutional homosexuality is a testament to the kinds of experimentation that television can indulge in, especially the licence fee-funded BBC, where writers and directors were not tied to market forces (and the 'Play for Today' strand was arguably the height of this philosophy). Of course, the irony here is that it still remained unaired.

Although a prison film, *Scum* is also concerned primarily with juvenile delinquency. One of the many socio-political points made by it is that the crimes inflicted against the inmates *inside* the Borstal are more violent and more damaging than those committed by the prisoners on society. The imbalance in the penal system provides much of the ideological subtext, as inmates are constantly beaten, intimidated and humiliated by the wardens and the authorities in general. As Dave Rolinson discusses, *Scum* also served to reflect the political zeitgeist of the late 1970s.[210] The tension and violence inside the Borstal mirrors many of the social and economic problems of Britain in that decade – we see race riots, intergenerational tension, economic pressures and endemic problems with the authorities. The prison here becomes a metaphor for society and, again, the young are seen as the most vulnerable and the most at risk.

As Rolinson also states, this metonymic relationship between the Borstal and the outside world is mirrored in the film's cinematography:

> Throughout *Scum* social structures are mirrored in the geometry of the framing. Some of these relate to the play's class subtexts, the way 'the system… divides and rules the working class'. [211]

There are two notable ways in which this is carried out: the first is through the use of shot/reverse-shot and the second through the frequent use of the two-shot, where two whole figures can be viewed simultaneously on screen. Clarke uses the combination of these two well-established elements of film grammar to suggest the interpersonal relationships between the inmates and the staff, a relationship that, as Rolinson states, is both based *on* and reflective *of*, the larger antagonisms of the British class system. A clear example of this occurs in a scene half way through the film when Carlin goes to visit Goodyear, the housemaster. In narrative terms this scene is important not only because it concretises Carlin's position as the dominant inmate in the Borstal but because it also underlines his power over the authorities. Goodyear insists that it is *he* who has ownership of the wing, that it is *he* who wields the power; however, both through framing and through performance, the audience knows differently. We understand the implicit information in Carlin's look, the distain in his eyes and the loaded meaning that is contained within the silences that pepper the exchange.

In the original TV play, this scene is conducted in low level light, both characters (Goodyear and Carlin) are seated, and the *mise-en-scène* is more domestic than institutional. In the film version this scene is markedly different: the room is now brightly lit and the camera is mobile, slowly moving around the central figures as Clarke intercuts shot/reverse-shots to emphasise the relationship between them. The major difference between the two versions, however, is that, in the film, Carlin is now standing and the eye line matches reflects their differences in height. Goodyear is now looked down upon and Carlin looked up to, a physical manifestation of the gradual change in their statuses, something that is also conveyed in their interaction – Carlin is defiant and arrogant, Goodyear, compliant and retiring. This is the very point in the film where Carlin changes from being just another con to 'the daddy', over both the other inmates and the screws. As Rolinson suggests, the subtext here is mirrored by the film's framing.

Another major difference between the versions is the extended exterior shots in the film. Filmed in the winter of 1979, the cinematic release reflected the difficult weather conditions as well as the extreme zeitgeist, as Sean Chapman highlights:

> The atmosphere that *Scum* was shot in was tangible, it comes off the screen in waves – this bleak, blue English winter light. Compounded by the fact that the way we shot it was brutally simplistic.[212]

Visually, the external scenes of *Scum*, with its depictions of figures in the harsh snowy landscape of a British winter bring to mind nineteenth paintings like Van Gogh's *Prisoners Exercising, After Dore* (1890) or the bleak descriptions of the poor in realist novels by Dickens or Emile Zola. The film version dwells on these significances more than the original TV play and thus invites comparisons with a longer standing tradition of prison narratives.

The TV play however, due to the age of the actors, is more recognisably concerned with juvenile delinquency and the place of young people in a hard, Victorian system. Characters like Davis and Woods in the 1977 version are recognisably youthful and their presence in the tough atmosphere of the Borstal is all the more challenging for this. As Ray Winstone outlines, this is an aspect that is missing in the remake:

I really liked the original, because we were younger, there was something about that that made it seem more violent, more terrifying. We were vulnerable kids being abused by men and then abusing each other – in every way, violently, sexually, the lot, in a fucking Victorian building. We were kids in the feature film but in two years we grew up, we weren't so vulnerable anymore.[213]

Clarke's realist aesthetic in both versions is underlined by a distinctly traditional set of cinematographic tools; editing serves to create the spatio-temporal world of the characters and the framing and shot selection highlights the relationship between them and their environment. The ideological message of the film is clear: institutions such as Borstals dehumanise those who are within them and, ipso facto, those who support their existence. No one in Scum escapes the violence that is endemic within the system and no one is left unharmed by the overriding waste of life and potential that Borstal represents.

Alan Clarke's next film about juvenile delinquency, Made in Britain (1982), would concretise this point all the more. The story of a young delinquent skinhead, Trevor (Tim Roth), it combined Social Realism with a technical innovation that would bring the audience ever closer to the mind of the young offender. Unlike Scum, which dealt with group psychology, Made in Britain returned to the narrative perspective of the 1960s British New Wave and privileged the experiences of an individual caught within a world that held little for him. Like the heroes of the New Wave, Trevor was also intelligent and self-knowing, able to express himself to authority figures who seem slow and inarticulate in comparison.

There was a sharp decline in the numbers of custodial sentences for juvenile delinquency during most of the 1980s. From an all-time high in the late 1970s, the numbers fell to just over two thousand in 1989. As Newburn details, this situation had more to do with changes in the way young offenders were treated (and the demographics of the population) than any lessening in the numbers of incidences that occurred.[214] From 1981 onwards, young people were less likely to be given a custodial sentence and more likely to be inculcated into a system of multiagency care, involving social workers, hostels, care homes and police supervision. In other words, the heavily institutionalised situation outlined in Scum, where large numbers of young offenders found themselves imprisoned in borstals, was changing and a more community-based system of care and supervision prevailed.

It is this that we can recognise as providing the backdrop for Made in Britain, the narrative of which depicts the central character's interaction with an aggressive and authoritarian system. The ideological shift between Scum and Made in Britain is reflective of the rise of what Michel Foucault termed 'the carceral system' a process that extends the observational panopticism of the prison system into the society at large.[215] As Foucault details, prisons and borstals are not needed in a system that is inherently punitive and observational:

We are in the society of the teacher-judge, the doctor-judge, the educator-judge, the social worker-judge; it is on them that the universal reign of the normative is based; and each individual, wherever he may find himself, subjects to it his body, his gestures, his behaviour, his aptitudes, his achievements.[216]

Such thinking illuminates *Made in Britain*, a film after all that depicts an individual with a dangerous excess of physical and emotional energy. As Rolinson details, the teleplay concerns itself with 'movement and its restriction by authority' as Trevor prowls around the streets of London like a young tiger, scowling, menacing and full of undirected anger.[217] As we have seen, such figures are dangerous to the status quo and their unpredictability presents huge problems for authorities; their uncontrollable energy threatens to burst open the bounds of polite, regulated society and in this there is a line of hereditary between Trevor and Carlin, Carlin and Johnny and Johnny and Ray. The major crime all four commit is not theft, violence or TDA (Taking and Driving Away) but refusing to accede to the adult conception of propriety; the juvenile delinquent represents an excess of energy that is difficult to contain and impossible to predict.

Trevor's refusal to exist within the bounds of polite society extends, as Foucault might have asserted, into the bodily and the corporeal. In the climatic scenes of the film, especially those shot in the Blackwall tunnel, Trevor again becomes allied to the heroes of the French and British New Waves whose only desire is to escape the confines of a constrictive system. Like Colin Smith or Antoine Doinel in Truffaut's *The 400 Blows* Trevor runs but has no place to go and in order to highlight his sheer physicality his shirt is removed revealing a body that is white, skinny and studded with tattoos.

The physicality of the central character is underlined by Clarke's use of the Steadicam. As Stephen Frears details, the use of the Steadicam was inspired by viewing the rushes of Frears' own 1982 work, *Walter*.[218] Recently invented, the Steadicam allowed directors to follow a single character in a way that the more traditional handheld camera did not; it also lessened the need for complex editing processes, allowing for greater shot length. Use of the Steadicam allowed Clarke to further efface the line between audience and character as the spectator could follow Trevor wherever he chose to go. Space was no longer created merely by editing but also by camera movement and a shot's length could be extended without jeopardising visual acuity. The camera could follow Trevor down stairs, through doors, into cars and through tunnels at will; the effect is a greater connection between what we see and how we feel about the characters as we more easily inhabit their consciousness for the duration of the film. Clarke's last film, *Elephant* (1989), which details a series of Sectarian killings in Northern Ireland, made extensive use of the Steadicam and would, in turn, inspire Gus Van Sant's film of the same name (2003).

The relationship between movement (or more precisely its curtailment) and authority is exemplified in the central scene of *Made in Britain*, one that lasts almost twenty minutes and that has become one of the most intense moments in juvenile delinquency cinema. Set in the basement room of the care home, the scene details the interaction between Trevor and three of the men who are charged with his 'care'. The original concept behind this scene, as David Leland, the scriptwriter, recalls was to have a fixed camera in a room into which Trevor would talk and whose frame he would intermittently walk through.[219] However, through Clarke's insistence, this was changed to a carefully choreographed mixture of shot/reverse shots and Steadicam filming, a combination that heightens the tension and brings us closer to the gradually rising emotions of those within the room.

The central section of this scene involves a *tour de force* of acting on the part of Geoffrey Hutchings who plays the superintendent charged with dealing with Trevor's disruptive behaviour. As the latter stands and watches, the superintendent delivers a monologue about Trevor's past and his place in a circular system of deprivation and crime. His lack of attendance at school, the superintendent suggests, has caused Trevor difficulties in finding a job, which in turn leads to poverty and resentment; this leads to crime, prison and a downward spiral of opportunity. Clarke's camera work here not only captures the superintendent's lecture but also Trevor's incredulous reactions to it as he finally meets his intellectual match in a man he cannot help but respect.

The message of this scene is not dissimilar from those we have already looked at in this chapter. It is close to the paternal statements in *Boys in Brown* or the street-wise advice given in *Violent Playground*; however, by the 1980s, the rhetoric seems hollow and unbalanced. Although the superintendent suggests that Trevor has sole responsibility for his position, Clarke and Leland are not so sure and we are made fully aware of the inevitability of the position of the delinquent stuck within a cyclical system of crime and punishment, unable to get out, labelled as worthless before he starts.

We can recognise here a shift between *Scum* and *Made in Britain* in Clarke's depiction of juvenile delinquency. Whereas *Scum* is political in its concerns, *Made in Britain* is more existential, the questions it asks not emanating from the group but from the individual. Carlin triumphs over the system in his own way, but Trevor does not. In the final scenes of the film, Trevor is beaten by a policeman and his face is locked in a freeze frame that recalls the end shots of *The 400 Blows*. If Antoine Doinel can be viewed as being representative of post-war France, staring into the future with a mixture of anxiety and innocence, then Trevor represents the beaten and frustrated face of 1980s British youth, unsure about their place in a world that is rapidly changing and losing its identity. As the title of the piece suggests, however, this position is one that is purely homemade.

In a similar vein, Mai Zetterling's 1983 film *Scrubbers* deals with juvenile delinquency as it relates to girls and to the female Borstal. Scripted by *Scum*'s Roy Minton and funded by George Harrison's HandMade films, *Scrubbers* has been largely overlooked by critics and theorists and often written about only in relation to the earlier text. Inexplicably, for example, David Wilson and Sean O'Sullivan's *Images of Incarceration: Representations of Prison in Film and Television Drama* makes no mention of *Scrubbers* at all despite a lengthy discussion of *Made in Britain* (a film which, after all, is not set in, and does not strictly feature, a prison.) The same can be said of Chibnall and Murphy's *British Crime Cinema* and Bruce Crowther's *Captured on Film: The Prison Movie* both of which deal with masculine prison texts like *The Criminal* and *Scum*.[220] However, as Karlene Faith states, *Scrubbers* was a 'landmark' film that fused realism with a Brechtian dramaturgy that highlights the privations of Borstal without recourse to the tropes of confined masculinity that so permeate other texts.[221]

The film opens with the now familiar scene of two Borstal inmates on the run. Immediately the audience's gaze is twinned with the younger of the two, Carol (Amanda York), as she and Annetta (Chrissie Cotterill) hitch a lift from a lorry driver, steal his vehicle, are recaptured and end up back inside. We learn that Carol has deliberately engineered her capture so that she might be with her former lover, Doreen and that Annetta is desperate to see her daughter, held in a children's home. We follow Carol's journey through Borstal as well as exploring the lives, anxieties and tragedies of the other women she meets. Unlike Carlin and Trevor however, Carol is the innocent thrown into the hell and, in this, the narrative of *Scrubbers* is imbued with a more observational tone. Like Carol, we become the victim rather than the aggressor and the main narrative thrust is one of survival rather than domination. It soon becomes clear, for example, that there are no distinct hierarchies in this girl's Borstal, no ladder up which it is possible to climb.

The tone of Zetterling's film also distances itself from *Scum*, a film it is often, perhaps unfairly, unfavourably compared to. If *Scum* and *Made in Britain* detailed the contemporary scene, *Scrubbers* is more universal and thus timeless in its statements; ribald songs and meta-reflective poems litter the narrative and serve to comment upon and highlight the emotional lives of the characters. Humour is also used to distinguish the characters as they interact, laugh and support each other more than their masculine filmic counterparts. All of which serves to imbue Zetterling's film with an aesthetic and poetical sense that verges on the Victorian; the characters in *Scrubbers* are not the violent criminals of *Scum* or even *Made in Britain*, they are the urchins of Dickens or the sentimentalised street walkers of the Jack the Ripper narratives, smiling and singing through the hell of their existence. *Scrubbers* could have been filmed at any time and its inmates are not the proto-criminals of many juvenile delinquent films; they are scared, locked-up girls.

This is not to say that *Scrubbers* elides the violence of the prison or juvenile film. There *is* violence here, especially in the closing shots of Annetta beating Carol because she believes she has informed on her. However the effect of the violence is lessened by the use of slow motion that turns the beating into something more balletic. This also occurs earlier in the film when Eddie (Carol's lover) rapes an inmate with a broom handle; here, instead of showing the violence, Zetterling cuts to a shot of a TV showing *The Long Good Friday* as if to highlight the links between violence and masculinity in film. We are made well aware of the bullying and humiliation that exists in the girl's Borstal but the camera stops short when it comes to depicting the actuality of violence, another manifestation of Zetterling's direction that self-consciously avoids the trappings of the prison and/or juvenile delinquent movie.

Whereas in *Scum* the themes are domination and survival, in *Scrubbers* it is love and restitution. Its most representative and poetic scenes are those detailing the night time ritual of the inmates calling to each other through the bars of the windows. Each declares their love for the other and, using an elaborate system of strings and baskets, they send messages and gifts to each other's cells. The atmosphere is more supportive than their male counterparts and the homosexuality more overt and unashamed. If Carlin was apologetic about his homosexuality in the TV version of *Scum* then the girls of *Scrubbers* see it as an inevitable part of institutional life; they dance together, walk arm in arm together and sleep together. Even the central antagonism of the narrative (that between Carol and Annetta) is resolved in the last moments when the former escapes so that she might find a telephone number that will aid the latter retain her child. It is difficult to imagine such reciprocity and mutuality occurring in the hyper-masculine environment of *Scum*.

Scrubbers is unusual in that it deals with female delinquency; however recent films like *Sket*, *4321* (2010) and *Kidulthood* continue this motif, exploring the behaviours and tensions within girl gangs and interrogating the nature of young female criminality. Traditionally delinquency has been seen as primarily a male problem – in 2011 there were only 104 under-18 females in custody compared to 1,787 males, and by far the most widespread crimes for both genders were Violence Against the Person and Theft and Handling, suggesting that not much has changed since *Cosh Boy*.[222] As we saw in earlier chapters the fear of the young delinquent is inextricably linked to the fear of the gang; we also see this played out in cinema since the 1940s where Pinkie Brown's psychotic youthfulness is framed by discourses of gang culture and the world of the adult criminal.

As we have seen here, the juvenile delinquent is both a constant and a changing image: on the one hand providing a specific mirror to the anxieties and concerns of a society and, on the other, existing as an image that is constantly relied upon and re-invented. The terms of the debate also change very little; delinquency is often linked with the pejorative effects of a foreign culture, whether that be rock and roll or rap music, and young people are also often seen as the weakest element of society, both vulnerable and intractably dangerous. Space here prohibits how delinquency has been linked to subcultures in films like *Quadrophenia* (1979), *Away Days* (2009) or the various punk movies of the 1970s. All of these films deal essentially with delinquency but do so in a way that avoids the trappings of the crime film. Delinquents, it is often assumed, grow out of their criminality and therefore films like these are as much about youthful energy and passion as criminal behaviour. A film like *Made in Britain*, of course, blurs the borderline between these two things, possibly an indication of why it has had a lasting effect on audiences.

As with many of the films that have been covered in this book, the films here fall into two categories: those that have been (over)analysed and written about and those that have been overlooked entirely. Of the films concerned with young offenders, *Violent Playground* and *Scum* are perhaps the most notable and do appear in a number of important studies. However, texts like *Cosh Boy*, *Some People*, *Made in Britain* and *Scrubbers* are given only scant consideration if they are mentioned at all. Partly, we might guess that this is due to the assumption that these British texts are merely remakes, or versions of more successful, more vibrant Hollywood originals. Ultimately however, like their adult counterparts, the juvenile delinquents of British cinema are a rich part of its history and culture and deserve to be considered in their own right.

Since the millennium, the juvenile delinquency film has made a resurgence in mainstream British cinema. High profile movies such as *Kidulthood* and *Eden Lake* and low budget independent films like *F*, *Summer Scars* (2007), *Heartless* (2009) and *Cherry Tree Lane* (2010) have mixed depictions of violent and criminal youth with social commentary, genre hybridity and psychosocial anxiety in what have become known to some critics as 'hoodie horrors'.[223] It is overwhelmingly argued that these films articulate both the fears and the prejudices of the middle classes towards the working classes; fears that arise from media images, news stories and representations of an underclass that is perceived as being both a drain on and a threat to a post-Thatcherite society. Referring to their relationship to the horror genre, Johnnie Walker states:

> Certain films have placed 'underclass' youth as the source of the narrative's horror, in a direct echo of contemporary media generalities surrounding gang crime, the hoodie/chav (terms used synonymously about British youth) phenomena and, most recently, the English riots.[224]

Although featuring recognisably similar characters and certainly drawing on pools of similar fears, most of the films mentioned in the previous paragraph mobilise social anxiety in subtly different ways: *Heartless* and *F* are supernatural tales where faceless teenagers become akin to demons and folk devils, *Cherry Tree Lane* and *Kidulthood* are realist in their aesthetics and relate much more to the social problem film of the 1950s and '60s and *Summer Scars* (a film that was released during the New British Cinema festival at the Institute of Contemporary Arts in 2009) draws on regional British settings and references American films like *Stand By Me* (1986) and *The Blair Witch Project* (1999). It is tempting to group all of these films together as reflecting notions of 'Broken Britain' and its children; however they all represent differing perspectives on how and why this might be the case and therefore present different elements to be analysed.

Perhaps the most famous of all the recent crop of juvenile delinquent films is James Watkins' *Eden Lake*, the story of a middle class couple (Jenny, played by Kelly Reilly, and Steve, Michael Fassbinder) who are terrorised by a gang of working class youths in a picturesque forest in the middle of England. As Walker suggests, *Eden Lake* (like *Harry Brown*) soon became representative of a social as well as a cinematic type as its reactionary characterisation of working class teenagers and their parents drew both approbation and criticism from cultural commentators. Peter Bradshaw, for example, saw the film as a being 'believable in a way that does not depend on the neurotic attention to sensational newspaper stories', whereas Owen Jones stated that 'it may not come as a surprise that the *Daily Mail* treated *Eden Lake* as though it were some sort of drama-documentary, quavering that it was "all too real" and urging every politician to watch it'.[225]

It is no surprise that Jones discusses *Eden Lake* in a chapter entitled 'Class in the Stocks' because, despite Bradshaw's insistence that it is concerned primarily with a fear of the young, it is clearly class that provides the major socio-political anxieties of the narrative. Like the social problem films of the past, the sins of the children are traced firmly back to the parents as the working class adults in the story are painted as being every bit as violent and out of control as their offspring. As Owen Jones states:

> When I asked the director, James Watkins, for an interview, I was told that he was 'very flattered...but he doesn't want to impose any authorial interpretations on *Eden Lake*, preferring instead the widely divergent reactions to the film'. But it is difficult to imagine any other interpretation than that of the *Sun*'s movie critic who condemned Watkins' 'nasty suggestion that all working class people are thugs'.[226]

There *are* in fact other interpretations to the film, one of which is exemplified by John Fitzgerald who (although acknowledging the ideological basis of it) sees *Eden Lake* as tapping into more generic structures and conventions:

> *Eden Lake* is, after all a piece of genre cinema, playing to long-established responses in the audience. Perhaps what is so unsettling is that the film forces a spectator reaction that may well tap into his or her own consciousness, whether shaped by a *Daily Mail* headline or an unpleasant encounter with an angry stranger.[227]

Neither Jones' nor Fitzgerald's interpretation address the film as a productive text; one that creates its meaning rather than merely reflects either an existing extra-textual reality or a series of generic codes and conventions. *Eden Lake*'s depictions of juvenile delinquents are framed by a camera style and a *mise-en-scène* that reflects contemporary horror. However its characterisations are drawn from the social problem film, suggesting a real-world referent that has distinct social and political value. As Walker details, the director's decision to cast Thomas Turgoose (who had enjoyed several high profile successes in realist films like Shane Meadows' *This is England* and *Somers Town*) in the role of Cooper, a member of the murderous group, underlined the extent that *Eden Lake* merged realism with horror subtly manipulating the audience's relationship to the text and thus also to the ethical issues it throws up. Fitzgerald's suggestion that the film's main antagonist Brett (Jack O'Connell) 'is as much a monster as Freddy from *A Nightmare on Elm Street* (1984), and even less explicable' might well be true in terms of the film's appropriation of horror conventions but largely ignores the impact such a character might have on an audience not versed in genre cinema. This genre hybridity blurs the line between nightmare and reality and adds to the ideological confusion that met the film's release.

The crime film, as we have explored throughout this book, relativises and negotiates moral positioning, offering audiences texts that are, on the whole, polysemic and heterogeneous. We are asked, for example, to sympathise with the criminal, to understand the killer or to aspire to be the gangster. Even in a film like *Villain*, that features a violent and homicidal gang leader, we are afforded the space to read characters against the grain, to sympathise with someone like Vic Dakin, even if it is only because we feel sorry for him. *Eden Lake* very rarely allows for this fluid audience position and, as such, is much more akin to the horror than the crime genre. The opening of *Eden Lake* exemplifies this point: as sonorous music begins to play the blood-red titles are slowly faded in, intercut with brief glimpses of images that will feature later on – highly colour-saturated moments of Jenny screaming, a bloodied wound and a still lake at twilight flash before the screen and are punctuated by a scream on the soundtrack. If the title sequence of a film prepares the audience for the experience that is about to come in this way, then we are rooted firmly in the domain of terror and the horrific. The sense of unease, however, is quickly undercut by the initial shots, as Jenny is pictured in a classroom teaching a class of well-behaved cherubic children as a swelling orchestral score plays underneath. In what will be a constant narrative trope throughout the film, Jenny's responsible middle class parenting and teaching style is contrasted with the hellish outcome of a less rarefied upbringing, close-ups of children's faces also serving to remind us that even the teenagers we will meet in the woods were innocents once. The horror to which she is subjected to later on in the film is made all the more terrifying because, in these opening moments, she is depicted as being the ultimate in nurturing motherhood; she is alert and caring and the honeyed, golden colour palette of the images reflects this. We can compare this to the use of colour later on as the film takes on some of the green and blue tinge of contemporary horror (see also the discussion of colour in relation to *Harry Brown* in chapter two). Subtly, almost imperceptibly Watkins takes us from the familiar and the comforting to the strange and horrific.

Julian Richards' *Summer Scars* is closer to the morality of the crime film than *Eden Lake*. It tells the story of a group of teens who steal a moped and joyride through a wood in South Wales, eventually running into a mysterious drifter Peter (Kevin Howarth) who befriends them but, gradually, begins to bully each one. The tone of the film is tense and anxious as the petty delinquency of the teenagers is held in contrast to the far more dangerous and worrying violence of Peter, a grown man. At one stage, Peter forces one of the teenagers to expose himself to the group and we are reminded of their young age and vulnerability in the presence of the older and stronger man. Here, as in earlier films like *Cosh Boy* and *Brighton Rock*, the violence of children is compared to that of adults and it is the latter that is seen as more divisive and ultimately more destructive. At the film's conclusion, Peter is shot by one of the gang who, tellingly, steals a gun from his father's bedroom. However rather than galvanising the group through bravura, the incident leaves them chastened and clinging to each other for support. The gang have come of age, but only by adopting the violence of the older generation. Peter's constant reference to his time in the army suggests that he is also a victim of a bigger, more socially engrained violence, that discards loners like himself once they have fulfilled their purpose.

Although beginning with an image of juvenile delinquency, *Summer Scars* avoids the contemporary cliché of assuming young people to be endemically evil or criminal. Both in their dedication to each other and in their personal morality (at one point the only girl of the group, Leanne [Amy Harvey] offers to expose herself to protect the others) the young people here are seen to be morally superior to the only adult in the film. This is also one of the very few films of this type that adopts the gaze of the working class young person, allowing the audience a point of view that is neither condemnatory nor judgemental.

The fear of the young is nothing new, neither is its depiction in cinema. The juvenile delinquent has always been an image of fascination and fear to the older generation who are, obviously, also those who fund cinema production. What is noticeable, however, is the trend in genre hybridity that mixes horror with the social problem, creating a folk devil that is at once recognisable and other worldly. Films like *Eden Lake* and *Harry Brown* do more than reflect contemporary fears about the young; they produce them, creating modern nightmares that leave very little space for ethical negotiation or resistance and that turn society's children into monsters and demons.

FOOTNOTES

180. Carpenter, M, *Juvenile Delinquents: Their Condition and Treatment*, New Jersey: Princeton University, 1853.

181. Muncie, J., *The Trouble with Kids Today: Youth and Crime in Post-war Britain*, London: Hutchinson, 1984, p.33.

182. Rutter, M. and H. Giller, *Juvenile Delinquency: Trends and Perspectives*, London: Penguin, 1984, pp.242-265.

183. Hill, 1986, p.82.

184. Hill, 1986; Landy, M. 1991 etc.

185. Shray, T., *Teen Movies: American Youth on Screen*, New York: Columbia University, 2006, p.1-2.

186. Landy, 1991, p.442.

187. Scala, M., *Diary of a Teddy Boy: A Memoir of the Long Sixties*, London: Mim Scala, 2009, p.17.

188. Judt, T., *Post-war: A History of Europe Since 1945*, New York: Random House, 2010, p.347.

189. Horn, A., *Juke Box Britain: Americanisation and Youth Culture 1945-60*, Manchester; Manchester University Press, 2009, p.90.

190. Willcock, H.D., *Report on Juvenile Delinquency*, London: Falcon Press, 1949.

191. Willcock, 1949, p.98.

192. Muncie, 1984, p.47.

193. Wilson, D. and S., O' Sullivan, *Images of Incarceration: Representations of Prison in Film and Television*, London: Waterside Press, 2004, p.38.

194. Aldgate, A. and J. Robertson, *Censorship in Theatre and Cinema*, Edinburgh: Edinburgh University Press, 2005, p.85.

195. Kynaston, D., *Family Britain, 1951-57*, London: Bloomsbury, 2009.

196. Durgnat, 1970, p.136.

197. Sandbrook, D., *Never Had it So Good, A History of Britain From Suez to the Beatles*, London: Abacus, 2005, p. 446.

198. Hill, 1986, p.79.

199. See Chibnall, S., 'The Teenage Trilogy: The Blue Lamp, I Believe in You and Violent Playground', in Burton, A, T. O' Sullivan and P. Wells (eds), *Liberal Directions: Basil Dearden and Post-war British Film Culture*, Trowbridge; Flicks Books, 1997.

200. Chibnall, 1997, p.148.

201. Hill, 1986, p.79.

202. Horn, 2009, p.66.

203. Spicer, 2000, p.98.

204. Spicer, 2000, p.99.

205. Newburn, T., 'Young People, Crime and Youth Justice', in Maguire, Morgan and Reiner, 2002, p.550.

206. Rutter and Giller, 1983, p.75.

207. The Conservative Party Manifesto, 1979 in Craig, F.W.S., 1990, British General Election Manifestos 1959 – 1987, London: Parliamentary Research Services, pp.267-283.

208. Hall et al, 1978, p.293; Hall et al, 1978, p.238.

209. Hebdige, 1979.

210. Rollinson, D. *Alan Clarke*, Manchester: Manchester University Press, 2005, p.79.

211. Rollinson, 2005, p.78.

212. Cited in Kelly, R., *Alan Clarke*, London: Faber and Faber, 1998, p.120.

213. Cited in in Kelly, 1998, pp.124-125.

214. Newburn, 2002, p.553.

215. Foucault, M. *Discipline and Punish*, London: Penguin, 1991, p.304.

216. Foucault, 1991, p.304.

217. Rollinson, 2005, p.103.

218. Cited Kelly, 1998, p.142.

219. Cited Kelly, 1998, ibid.

220. Crowther, B., *Captured on Film: The Prison Movie*, London; B.T. Batsford, 1989.

221. Faith, K., *Unruly Women: The Politics of Confinement and Resistance*, London: Seven Stories Press, 2011.

222. Source: Civitas, 2011

223. Maher, K. "The kids are all frights" in *The Times*, 26 June 2008; Walker, J. "A Wilderness of Horrors? British Horror Cinema in the New Millennium" in *Journal of British Cinema and Television*, Vol. 9, Number, 3, 2012, p. 447.

224. Walker, 2012, p.447.

225. Bradshaw, P. 'Eden Lake', *The Guardian*, 12 September 2008; Jones, O., *Chavs: The Demonization of the Working Class*, London: Verso, 2011, p.131.

226. Jones, 2011, p.131.

227. Fitzgerald, J. *Studying British Cinema: 1999–2009*, Leighton Buzzard: Auteur, 2010, p.221.

BIBLIOGRAPHY

Aldgate, A. and J. Robertson, *Censorship in Theatre and Cinema*, Edinburgh: Edinburgh University Press, 2005

Attenborough, R., *Entirely Up To You Darling*, London: Arrow, 2009

Bell, M., *Femininity in the Frame: Women and 1950s British Popular Culture*, London; I.B. Tauris, 2010

Benyahia, S. C., *Crime*, London: Routledge, 2012

Bordwell, D., J. Staiger and K. Thompson, *The Classical Hollywood Cinema: Film Style and Mode of Production to 1960*, London: Routledge, 2006

Bordwell, D., *Narration in the Fiction Film*, London: Routledge, 1985

Brown, M., *Performance*, London: Bloomsbury, 2000

Brundson, C., 'Not Having it All: Women and Film in the 1990s' in Murphy, R (ed.), *British Cinema of the 90s*, London: BFI Publishing, 1999

Brundson, C., *London in Cinema: the Cinematic City of London Since 1945*, London: BFI Publishing, 2007

Buscombe, E., '"The Sweeney" – Better Than Nothing', in *Screen Education*, 1976

Carpenter, M., *Juvenile Delinquents: Their Condition and Treatment*, New Jersey: Princeton University, 1853

Cettl, R., *Serial Killer Cinema: An Illustrated Guide*, Jefferson and London: McFarland and Company, 2007

Chabrol, C. and E. Rohmer, *Hitchcock: The First Forty Films*, New York: Frederick Unger, 1982

Chadder, V., 'The Higher Hell: Women and the Post-War British Crime Film' in Chibnall and Murphy, 1999

Chibnall, S. and R. Murphy (eds), *British Crime Cinema*, London: Routledge, 1999

Chibnall, S., 'The Italian Job', in Ward Baker, R. and B. McFarlane (eds), *The Cinema of Britain and Ireland*, New York: Columbia University Press, 2005

Chibnall, S., 'Travels in Ladland: the British Gangster Film Cycle, 1998-2001', in Murphy, R. (ed.), *The British Cinema Book*, London: BFI Publishing, 2001

Chibnall, S., *Brighton Rock*, London: I.B. Tauris, 2004

Chibnall, S., *Get Carter*, London: I.B. Tauris, 2003

Chibnall, S., 'The Teenage Trilogy: The Blue Lamp, I Believe in You and Violent Playground', in Burton, A, T. O' Sullivan and P. Wells (eds), *Liberal Directions: Basil Dearden and Post-war British Film Culture*, Trowbridge; Flicks Books, 1997

Chion, M., *Audio-Screen: Sound on Screen*, New York: Columbia University Press, 1990

Clarens, C., *Crime Movies: An Illustrated Guide*, London: Secker and Warburg, 1980

Cohen, S., *Folk Devils and Moral Panics*, London: Routledge, 2011

Conservative Party Manifesto, 1979

Cossar, H., *Letterboxed: The Evolution of Widescreen Cinema*, Lexington: University of Kentucky, 2011

Crowther, B., *Captured on Film: The Prison Movie*, London; B.T. Batsford, 1989

Cunningham, F., *Sidney Lumet: Film and Literary Vision*, Lexington: University of Kentucky, 2001

Dave, P., *Visions of England: Class and Culture in Contemporary Cinema*, London: Berg, 2006

Dickens, C., *Oliver Twist*, London: Penguin, 2007

Dickens, C., *Sketches by Boz*, Oxford: Oxford University Press, 1837/2007

Durgnat, R., 'Some Lines of Inquiry into Post-war British Cinema', in Murphy, R. (ed.), *The British Cinema Book*, 3rd

Edition, London: Palgrave Macmillan/BFI, 2009

Durgnat, R., *A Mirror for England: British Movies from Austerity to Affluence*, London: Faber and Faber, 1970

Dyer, R., 'Kill and Kill Again', in Arroyo, J (ed.), *Action/ Spectacle Cinema: A Sight and Sound Reader*, London: BFI Publishing, 2000

Elliott, P., *Hitchcock and the Cinema of Sensations: Embodied Film Theory and Cinematic Reception*, London: I.B. Tauris, 2012

Faith, K., *Unruly Women: The Politics of Confinement and Resistance*, London: Seven Stories Press, 2011

Field, M., *The Making of The Italian Job*, London: Batsford, 2001

Fisher, T., *Prostitution and the Victorians*, Charlottesville: University of Virginia, 1997

Fitzgerald, J., *Studying British Cinema: 1999–2009*, Leighton Buzzard: Auteur, 2010

Flanders, J., *The Invention of Murder: How the Victorians Revelled in Death and Detection and Created Modern Crime*, London: Harper Press, 2011

Foley, M., 'The Blair Presidency: Tony Blair and the Politics of Public Leadership', in Chadwick, A and R. Heffernan (eds), *The New Labour Reader*, Cambridge: Polity Press, 2003

Forshaw, B., *British Crime Film: Subverting the Social Order*, London: Palgrave, 2012

Foucault, M., *Discipline and Punish*, London: Penguin, 1991

Fuchs, C., *Bad Blood: An Illustrated Guide to Psycho Cinema*, London: Creation Books, 2002

Gilbert, P., *Shut It! The Inside of The Sweeney*, London: Aurum, 2010

Gillett, P., *The British Working Class in Postwar Film*, Manchester: Manchester University Press, 2003

Gormely, P., *The New Brutality Film: Race and Affect in Contemporary American Cinema*, London: Intellect, 2005

Hall, S., "Notes on Deconstructing the Popular", in Storey, J (ed), *Cultural Theory and Popular Culture: A Reader*, New York: Prentice Hall, 1998

Hall, S., C. Critcher, T. Jefferson, J. Clarke and B. Roberts, *Policing the Crisis: Mugging, the State and Law and Order*, London: Macmillan, 1978

Hallam, J. and M. Marshment, *Realism and Popular Cinema*, Manchester: Manchester University Press, 2000

Hebdige, D., *Subculture: The Meaning of Style*, London: Routledge, 1988

Higson, A., 'Space, Place, Spectacle: Landscape and Townscape in the "Kitchen Sink" Film', in Higson, A. (ed.), *Dissolving Views: Key Writings on British Cinema*, London: Continuum, 1996

Higson, A., *Film England: Culturally English Film-making Since the 1990s*, London; I.B. Tauris, 2010

Hill, J., *British Cinema in the 1980s*, London: Clarendeon Press, 1999

Hill, J., *Sex, Class and Realism: British Cinema 1956-1963*, London: BFI Publishing, 1986

Hitchcock, A. and F. Truffaut, *Hitchcock: A Definitive Study of Alfred Hitchcock*, New York: Simon Schuster, 1986

Horn, A., *Juke Box Britain: Americanisation and Youth Culture 1945-60*, Manchester; Manchester University Press, 2009

Hunt, L., *British Low Culture: From Safari Suits to Sexploitation*, London: Routledge, 1998

James, N., 'British Cinema's US Surrender – A View from 2001' in Murphy, 2001

Jarvis, B., 'Monsters Inc.: Serial Killers and Consumer Culture', in Greer, 2010

Judt, T., *Post-war: A History of Europe Since 1945*, New York: Random House, 2010

Kimber, S., *Henry: Portrait of a Serial Killer*, London: Routledge, 2011

King, G., *New Hollywood Cinema: An Introduction*, London: I.B. Tauris, 2002

Kynaston, D., *Austerity Britain, 1945- 1951*, London: Bloomsbury Publishing, 2008

Kynaston, D., *Family Britain, 1951-57*, London: Bloomsbury, 2009

Landy, M., *British Genres: Cinema and Society, 1930 – 1960*, New Jersey: Princeton University Press, 1991

Lay, S., *British Social Realism: From Documentary to Brit Grit*, London: Wallflower, 2002

Leach, J., *British Film*, Cambridge: Cambridge University Press, 2004

Leitch, T., *Crime Films*, Cambridge: Cambridge University Press, 2002

Lumet, S., *Sidney Lumet: Interviews*, Oxford: University of Mississippi Press, 2006

MacArthur, C. *Underworld USA*, London: New York: Viking Adult, 1972

Maguire, M., R. Morgan and R. Reiner (eds), *The Oxford Handbook of Criminology*, Oxford: Oxford University Press, 2002

Maher, K., "The kids are all frights" in *The Times*, 26 June 2008

Marr, A., *A History of Modern Britain*, London: Pan, 2009

Marwick, A., *British Society Since 1945*, London: Penguin, 2003

Mason, F., *American Gangster Cinema: From Little Caesar to Pulp Fiction*, London; Palgrave Macmillan, 2003,

Mayhew, H., *London Labour and the London Poor*, Oxford: Oxford University Press, 2010

McCabe, C., *Performance*, London: BFI Publishing, 1998

McFarlane, B., 'The More Things Change…British Cinema in the '90s', in Murphy, 2001

McGilligan, P., *Alfred Hitchcock: A Life in Darkness and Light*, New York: John Wiley and Sons, 2004

McIlroy, B., 'The Repression of Communities: Visual Representations of Northern Ireland during the Thatcher Years', in Friedman, 2006

Miles, B., *The British Invasion: The Music, The Times, The Era*, London: Sterling Publishing, 2009

Monk, C., 'Monk in the '90s', in Murphy, R. (ed.), *British Cinema of the '90s*, London: BFI, 2001

Morton, J., *Gangland Omnibus, Vols. 1&2*, London: Time Warner Paperbacks, 2003

Morton, J., *Supergrasses and Informers and Bent Coppers: A Survey of Police Corruption*, London: Time Warner Paperbacks, 2002

Muncie, J., *The Trouble with Kids Today: Youth and Crime in Post-war Britain*, London: Hutchinson, 1984

Murphy, R., *Realism and Tinsel: Cinema and Society in Britain 1939 – 49*, London: Routledge, 1992

Murphy, R., *British Cinema of the '90s*, London: BFI Publishing, 2001

Napper, L. and M. Williams, 'The Curious Appeal of Ivor Novello', in Babington, B. (ed), *British Stars and Stardom From Alma Taylor to Sean Connery*, Manchester: Manchester University Press, 2001

Neale, S., 'Contemporary Crime and Detective Films', in C.A. Bernik (ed), *The Cinema Book*, London: BFI, 1999

Neville, C., *Classless: Recent Essays on British Film*, Winchester: Zero Books, 2010

Newburn, T., 'Young People, Crime and Youth Justice', in Maguire, Morgan and Reiner, 2002

Newton, M., *Gangsters Encyclopaedia*, London: Anova Books, 2007

O' Mahoney, B., *Essex Boys: A Terrifying Expose of the British Drugs Scene*, London: Mainstream Publishing, 2000

O' Regan, T., 'Cultural Exchange' in Miller, T. and R. Stam (eds), *A Companion to Film Theory*, London; Blackwell, 2004

Oldridge, D., 'Casting the Terror: The Press and the Early Whitechapel Murders', in Warwick, A. and M. Willis (eds), *Jack the Ripper: Media, Culture, History*, Manchester: Manchester University Press, 2007

Orwell, G., 'Decline of the English Murder', in *Essays*, London: Everyman, 1946/2002

Pearson, J., *Profession of Violence: The Rise and Fall of the Kray Twins*, London: Harper Collins, 1995

Phillips, A., *Rififi: French Film Guide*, London: I.B. Tauris, 2009

Pitts, J., *Reluctant Gangsters: The Changing Face of Youth Crime*, London: Willan, 2008

Powell, D., *Studying British Cinema: The 1960s*, Leighton Buzzard: Auteur, 2009.

Quart, L., 'The Religion of the Market: Thatcherite Politics and the British Film of the 1980s' in Friedman, L. (ed.), *Fires Were Started: British Cinema and Thatcherism*, London: Wallflower, 2007

Rafter, N., *Shots in the Mirror: Crime Films and Society*, Oxford: Oxford University Press, 2006

Reiner, R., 'The Dialectics of Dixon: The Changing Image of the TV Cop', in Greer, C (ed.), *Crime and Media: A Reader*, London; Routledge, 2010

Report of the Committee on Homosexual Offenses and Prostitution (The Wolfenden Report), London: HMSO, 1963

Ressler, R. and T. Shachtman, *Whoever Fights Monsters*, London: Simon and Schuster, 1992

Richards, J. and A. Aldgate, *Best of British: Cinema and Society from 1930 to the Present*, London: I.B. Tauris, 2009

Rockett, K., L. Gibbons and J. Hill, *Cinema and Ireland*, London: Taylor and Francis, 1987

Rollinson, D., *Alan Clarke*, Manchester: Manchester University Press, 2005

Rothman, W., *The Murderous Gaze*, Cambridge: Harvard University Press, 1982

Rutter, M. and H. Giller, *Juvenile Delinquency: Trends and Perspectives*, London: Penguin, 1984

Sandbrook, D., *State of Emergency: The Way We Were, Britain 1970-1974*, London: Penguin, 2011

Sandbrook, D., *Never Had it So Good, A History of Britain From Suez to the Beatles*, London: Abacus, 2005

Sargeant, A., *British Cinema: A Critical History*, London; BFI Publishing, 2005

Saunders. D., *Direct Cinema: Observational Documentary and the Politics of the Sixties*, London: Wallflower Press, 2007

Scala, M., *Diary of a Teddy Boy: A Memoir of the Long Sixties*, London: Mim Scala, 2009

Shadoian, J., *Dreams and Dead Ends: The American Gangster Film*, 2nd Edition, Oxford: Oxford University Press, 2003

Shail, R., 'Stanley Baker and British Lion: A Cautionary Tale', in Newland, P. (ed.), *Don't Look Now: British Cinema in the 1970s*, Bristol: Intellect, 2010

Shray, T., *Teen Movies: American Youth on Screen*, New York: Columbia University, 2006

Silver, A. and J. Ursini (eds), *Gangster Film Reader*, New Jersey: Limelight Editions, 2007

Spicer, A., *Film Noir*, London: Longman, 2002

Spicer, A., *Typical Men: The Representation of Masculinity in Popular British Cinema*, London: I.B. Tauris, 2001

Street, S., *British National Cinema, 2nd*, London: Routledge, 2009

Sydney Smith, S., *Beyond 'Dixon of Dock Green' Early British Police Series*, London: I.B. Tauris, 2002

Teays, W., *Seeing the Light: Exploring Ethics Through Movies*, London; Wiley Blackwell, 2012

The Brixton Disorders, 10-12 April 1981, Report of an Inquiry by the RT. Hon. The Lord Scarman, O.B.E, London: HSMO1981

Thompson, K., *Crime Films: Investigating the Scene*, London: Wallflower, 2007

Tougher Regimes in Detention Centres: Report of an Evaluation By the Young Offender Psychology Unit, London: HMSO, 1984

Turner, A., *Crisis? What Crisis?: Britain in the 1970s*, London: Aurum Press, 2009

Walker, A., *Hollywood England: The British Film Industry in the Sixties*, London: Orion, 1988

Walker, A., *National Heroes: British Cinema in the 70's and 80's*, London: Chambers, 1985

Walker, J., "A Wilderness of Horrors? British Horror Cinema in the New Millennium" in *Journal of British Cinema and Television*, Vol. 9, Number, 3, 2012

Walker, M., *Hitchcock's Motifs*, Amsterdam: University Amsterdam Press, 2005

Walkowitz, J., *Prostitution and Victorian Society: Women, Class and the State*, Cambridge: Cambridge University Press, 1982

Warshow, R., "The Gangster as Tragic Hero", in Silver, A. and James Ursini (eds), *Gangster Film Reader*, New Jersey: Limelight Editions, 2007

Willcock, H.D., *Report on Juvenile Delinquency*, London: Falcon Press, 1949

Wilson, D. and S. O' Sullivan, *Images of Incarceration: Representations of Prison in Film and Television*, London: Waterside Press, 2004

Wollen, P., 'Riff-Raff Realism' in *Paris Hollywood: Writing on Film*, London: Verso, 2002

Young, L., *Fear of the Dark: 'Race', Gender and Sexuality in the Cinema*, London: Routledge, 1996

INDEX